Louis Charles Willard
A Critical Study of the Euthalian Apparatus

Arbeiten zur
Neutestamentlichen Textforschung

Herausgegeben im Auftrag des
Instituts für Neutestamentliche Textforschung der Westfälischen
Wilhelms-Universität Münster/Westfalen

von David C. Parker und Holger Strutwolf

Band 41

Walter de Gruyter · Berlin · New York

Louis Charles Willard

A Critical Study of the Euthalian Apparatus

Walter de Gruyter · Berlin · New York

A Ph.D. dissertation originally submitted to Yale University in 1970

Prepared for publication by Simon Crisp

BS
2650.52
.W56
2009

∞ Printed on acid-free paper which falls within the guidelines
of the ANSI to ensure permanence and durability.

ISBN 978-3-11-021567-0
ISSN 0570-5509

Library of Congress Cataloging-in-Publication Data

A CIP catalogue record for this book is available from the Library of Congress.

Bibliographic information published by the Deutsche Nationalbibliothek

The Deutsche Nationalbibliothek lists this publication in the Deutsche Nationalbibliografie;
detailed bibliographic data are available in the Internet at http://dnb.d-nb.de.

Cover design: Christopher Schneider, Laufen

Printed in Germany

Foreword to A Critical Study of the Euthalian Apparatus (2009)

In a remarkable twist, a conversation with Kurt Aland in the early 1970s about the possibility of including this dissertation in the monograph series he edited, *Arbeiten zur neutestamentlichen Textforschung*, is coming to fruition almost forty years later. Thanks to the support of the publisher, Walter de Gruyter; David Parker of the University of Birmingham, who is currently co-editor of the series; and Simon Crisp of the United Bible Societies, who has overseen the scanning and editing of the original typescript, the dissertation that collected, collated, and summarized the bibliographic and manuscript witnesses to the scholarly study of the Euthalian apparatus up to 1970 is now much more widely available to the academic community.

Thanks also to the support of theological librarians at Trinity Western University in British Columbia (Bill Badke), Princeton Theological Seminary (Kate Skrebutenas and Don Vorp), Luther Seminary (Bruce Eldevik), and the Pontifical Institute of Medieval Studies in Toronto (James Farge), the bibliography in the present work expands the original bibliography in two ways. It now includes relevant bibliographic references to articles published since 1970 and, in addition, pre-1970 articles that might have appeared in the original bibliography but eluded the bibliographic net cast at the time by the author.

The second area of expansion is also a striking testimony both to the power of the Internet and digitized texts and indices, which were in their infancy in the late 1960s, and to the mastery of these new tools in the present by Bill Badke. It is a worthwhile story. Although I eagerly accepted the invitation for the inclusion of my dissertation in this series, *Arbeiten zur neutestamentlichen Textforschung*, I knew that I no longer had access to the extraordinary theological collections of Yale University and Princeton Theological Seminary, where the original research was done. I did, however, know Bill Badke, and his unique skills. He agreed to undertake the work of identifying relevant, post-1970 articles. At my request, he also sought relevant, pre-1970 articles that the original bibliography had not included. In two weeks, he produced a comprehensive list of new articles. In response to my additional request, he also found seventeen articles and reviews not in the original bibliography. His work stunningly demonstrates the power of digitally-supported research, compared to the inevitably labour intensive process of going through the limited, mostly post-1950 print indexes, going through the annual indexes and tables of contents of a select number of likely journals back to the late nineteenth century, and finally following the leads from the bibliographic notes and references in the first-found articles. For the most part, the articles that Bill found were in journals that, because some selectivity was required, were not included in that initial survey.

The bibliography appears in its original structure, except that the reference works and primary sources are now in a single sequence. The additions, both earlier and subsequent, are incorporated into the bibliography, tagged with an asterisk.

The research in the Euthalian apparatus summarized in the original work tended to focus on externals: Who was the author? When was it written? What were the original constitutive parts, and what parts were later additions? What light do the different versions shed on these questions? In the last thirty-five years, two significant developments occurred.

The first is the brilliant article by Nils A. Dahl, "The 'Euthalian Apparatus' and Affiliated 'Argumenta'" (2000). Having absorbed the studies of the external evidence, Dahl focuses on the content of the apparatus, in its constitutive parts, and reaches important conclusions with respect to authorship, provenance, dates, and the relationship among the various parts, e. g., prologues, chapter lists, *argumenta*, etc.

The second, reflected in the work of David Hellholm and Vemund Blomkvist, "Parainesis as an Ancient Genre-designation: The Case of the 'Euthalian Apparatus' and the 'Affiliated Argumenta,'" (2005) looks at the apparatus from the point of view of a literary form. Blomkvist identified the journal articles incorporating the new literary form approach to the Euthalian apparatus.

The brief note on the Georgian version of the Euthalian apparatus, in Chapter 11, should now be supplemented by the more detailed study of J. Neville Birdsall, "The Euthalian Material and Its Georgian Versions." Birdsall's work, in turn, was based on the critical edition of the Georgian version of the apparatus by Korneli Danelia (cited in Birdsall's article [172, fn. 8, "The Georgian Redaction of the Stichometry of Euthalius"]).

Finally, I want to acknowledge the work of Johannes G. van der Tak, who, in his monograph, *Euthalius the Deacon: Prologues and Abstracts in Greek and Church Slavic Translation* (2003), notes the existence of the Church Slavic version of the apparatus, which the 1970 dissertation did not know.

3 March 2009   Louis Charles Willard

Preface

Most introductory remarks of this sort, although preceding the subject matter at hand, are usually composed at the completion of the study; while it is, thus, fitting to review with thanks the variety of contributions that have made the work possible, I think it is also appropriate to give some consideration to the future. Although this has not been a labour of love, it has been one of a certain joy, and I am looking forward to continued study in the areas that this preliminary investigation has opened.

Materials to support the study of Euthalius have come from many places. I would like to express my appreciation for the book collections that have been gathered by Professor Raymond P. Morris of the Yale Divinity School and by my several predecessors at the Speer Library of Princeton Theological Seminary. I have used 680 with the permission of the Yale University Library, and I have appreciated the photographic facilities of the Harvard University Library, the Library of Congress, and the Biblioteca Apostolica Vaticana. Professor Harold H. Oliver granted me permission to quote from his unpublished Th.M. thesis, "'Helps for Readers' in Greek New Testament Manuscripts" (Princeton Theological Seminary, 1955), and I am grateful to Professor Bruce M. Metzger for the suggestion that I consult that thesis.

A special word is due the Institut für neutestamentliche Textforschung in Münster, West Germany. Professor Dr. Kurt Aland and Herr Klaus Junack provided me with exceedingly generous access to the substantial microfilm collection there. The comprehensive survey that I was able to make would, without the resources of this institute, not have been possible. Conclusions would have been restricted to the reports on a limited number of manuscripts used by scholars decades ago; the direction of further study would remain uncertain.

There has been other support as well. From my first year of study at Yale, the Danforth Foundation has provided both financial and intellectual support for graduate study. The Graduate School of Arts and Sciences of Yale University made a grant toward the translation of the major piece of secondary literature in Armenian, and I was fortunate in the linguistic skills of Miss Vartouhi Semerjian. The faculty of the

Yale University Divinity School made possible the travel to the Institut für neutestamentliche Textforschung through the award of a Two Brothers Fellowship.

I particularly appreciate the thoughtful attention of Professor Nils A. Dahl, in whose seminar this thesis germinated and who has provided consistently helpful advice and observations. Whatever useful advances may come from my translation of Euthalius' prologue to the Pauline letters have benefited from the unerring command of patristic Greek of Professor Rowan Greer.

Because wives frequently have a low priority in the process of a dissertation, it is no surprise that Nancy appears toward the end rather than the beginning of this part. Her understanding and positive support, however, have made an immeasurable contribution to the completion of this work. As a symbol of my recognition of that concern and support, I would like to dedicate this essay to her.

Princeton, Easter, 1970   Louis Charles Willard

Conventions

The monograph generally follows the citation, punctuation, and formatting rules outlined in *The SBL Handbook of Style for Ancient Near Eastern, Biblical, and Early Christian Studies* (ed. Patrick H. Alexander *et al.*; Peabody, Mass.: Hendrickson, 1999).

Abbreviations for the books of the Bible used in this dissertation are those used in *The Interpreter's Dictionary of the Bible*, edited by George Arthur Buttrick *et al.* (4 vols.; New York and Nashville, 1962). All other abbreviations or short titles for standard reference tools are those used in *Lexikon für Theologie und Kirche*, edited by Josef Höfer and Karl Rahner (2nd revised ed., 11 vols.; Freiburg: Herder, 1957–67) or have been based on that system.

The abbreviations and short titles for the standard reference tools in this publication come from Siegfried M. Schwertner, *Internationales Abkürzungsverzeichnis für Theologie und Grenzgebiete: Zeitschriften, Serien, Lexika, Quellenwerke mit bibliographischen Angaben = International Glossary of Abbreviations for Theology and Related Subjects: Periodicals, Series, Encyclopedias, Sources with Bibliographical Notes* (2nd, rev. and enlarged ed.; Berlin; New York: Walter de Gruyter: 1992).

Contents

Part Four

Excursus

Appendices

Introduction and Manuscript Tradition

This monograph deals with a body of material, ancillary to the Pauline and Catholic epistles and Acts, known as the Euthalian apparatus; this apparatus, in its most comprehensive form, includes prologues, chapter lists, *argumenta*, quotation lists, lection tables, and other literary notes. All or parts of it are found in numerous Greek as well as some Armenian and Syriac manuscripts of the New Testament; moreover, there may be traces in the Latin, Gothic, and Georgian versions. Some early printed editions of the Bible contained sections of the apparatus.[1] In 1698, Lorenzo Alessandro Zacagni published the first "critical" collection of this material,[2] and subsequently this text was reproduced by Gallandi[3] and Migne.[4]

---

1   The numbers identifying the following editions, where available, have been taken from Thomas Herbert Darlow and Horace Franklin Moule, comps., *Historical Catalogue of the Printed Editions of Holy Scripture in the Library of the British and Foreign Bible Society* (2 vols. in 4; London: The Bible House, 1903–11). Sources for these early editions were Lorenzo Alessandro Zacagni, *Collectanea monumentorum veterum ecclesiae graecae* (vol. 1; Rome: Typis Sacrae Congreg. de propag. fide, 1698), lxi, lxxxvi, and Albert Ehrhard, "Der Codex H ad epistulas Pauli und 'Euthalios diaconos,'" *ZfB* 8 (1891): 386.

     1. *Biblia sacra polyglotta*, studio et opera Cardinalis Francisci Ximenes de Cisneros (6 vols.; Academia Complutensi: A. G. de Brocario, 1514–17). 1412.

     2. *Nouum Instrumentū omne*, diligenter ab Erasmo Roterodamo recognitum & emendatum (Basel: In aedibus Ioannis Frobenii, 1516). 4591.

     3. Τῆς Καινῆς Διαθήκης ἅπαντα (Paris: Ex officina Roberti Stephani typographi Regii, Regiis typis, 1550). 4622.

     4. *Novum Testamentum*, accessit Prologus in Epistolas S. Apostolī Pauli, ex antiquissimo MSC (ed. by Johann Heinrich Boeckler; Strassburg: Mulbius, 1645). 4689. (2d ed.; Ex offic. I. Staedelii, 1660).

     5. *Expositiones antiquae* . . . ex diversis sanctorum patrum commentariis ab Oecumenio et Aretha collectae (ed. by B. Donato; Verona: Apud Stephanum & fratres Sabios, 1532).

2   Zacagni, *Collectanea*, 401–708. The author's name is sometimes spelled Zacagnius or Zaccagni.

3   Andreas Gallandi, ed., *Biblioteca veterum patrum antiquorumque scriptorum ecclesiasticorum* (vol. 10; Venice: Ex typographia Joannis Baptistae Albritii Hieron. fil., 1774), 197–320.

Our interest in this material was first aroused during a consideration of possible ways to trace what influence the library at Caesarea, as a center of learning and study of the text of the Bible, might have had on the text of the New Testament. In the course of this consideration we encountered the theory that associates the development of the Euthalian apparatus with the library at Caesarea. That encounter has not really been brought to an end, and this monograph represents a preliminary attempt to set out some of the results of our subsequent studies.

These studies have been shaped by three observations that seemed rather clear, following the initial examination of the secondary literature:

1. There is a disconnectedness about some of the arguments in this literature, a disconnectedness produced by an incomplete knowledge of or reference to the work of predecessors.
2. There is no English translation of any significant part of this apparatus. Although some critical points are rendered in the secondary literature and a translation of the chapter list of Acts, attributed to Pamphilus, is available,[5] there is nothing else.
3. There is little or no information on the distribution of the apparatus in many Greek manuscripts. There is even less evidence from the versions.

The purpose of this monograph is to deal with problems inherent in these observations, and we may formulate it as follows: To provide a critical summary and evaluation of the positions maintained in the secondary literature, supplemented by the results of an extensive survey of the manuscript tradition, and to offer an annotated translation of the prologue to the Pauline epistles.

Immediately following this introduction, we will take up in detail the manuscript sources for these investigations. Our own research was limited to the Greek tradition; most of it was carried out at the Institut für neutestamentliche Textforschung at Münster. We reviewed there, on microfilm, more than 400 manuscripts that we had identified as possibly containing all or parts of the apparatus. In these manuscripts, the

---

4   *PG* 85: 627–790. References to the text of Euthalius are noted both in Zacagni and in Migne, citing the page in Zacagni and the column and section in Migne, e.g., Z 528 f.; M 708A.
5   Pamphilus, "An Exposition of the Chapters of the Acts of the Apostles" (ANF 6; Buffalo: The Christian Literature Company, 1886), 166–68.

text of the New Testament itself does not stand alone but is accompanied by a quantity of supplementary material. In addition to numerous pages of prefatory material, such as the prologues, "lection" lists, and quotation lists that are the subject of our study, the texts of individual letters are sandwiched between chapter lists and *argumenta*. Frequently, there is surrounding commentary so that the actual text may occupy only the inside-middle quarter of two facing pages of a manuscript. Moreover, we discovered that parts of the apparatus, particularly the smaller pieces, have no fixed position in relation to other parts but tend to float. In this respect, the orderly presentation that follows should not deceive the reader.

The first major section is a review of the relationships and contents of the more prominent sections of the apparatus, including commentary from the secondary literature. There are a number of other pieces, associated in the manuscript tradition with, and fixed by Zacagni's edition to, the Euthalian apparatus; it is the function of the second major section to examine the probability of authenticity of these fringe elements.

The versional evidence represents an unusual sort of problem for us to handle. Apart from the difficulties surrounding the particular questions of this investigation, the several versions involved already manifest a complex array of unsolved riddles. Moreover, we are not equipped to handle these materials critically. We have, therefore, devoted the comprehensive discussion of the evidence that we have under review from these versions to a section following our review of the Greek tradition. There are, however, a number of instances in which the adducement of the facts from one or more of these versions was merited, e.g., where it is merely a question of the presence or absence of an entire piece from the tradition of a particular version or where the data are relatively straightforward and could usefully be taken into account in the general discussion, as in the case of the calendrical data in the *Martyrium*.

Following the comprehensive discussion of the versional evidence, we deal with the questions of dating, provenance, and authorship raised in the secondary literature. Finally, there is a summary restatement of the significant conclusions, together with an analysis of the important questions left unresolved with as much in the way of direction as may be appropriate.

The last part of the monograph is the annotated translation of the prologue to the Pauline epistles. The annotations include results of the manuscript survey together with notes on points that are significant

for an evaluation of the theological portrait of Paul implicit in the prologue.

For the purpose of an introductory orientation we will begin with
the prologues and the data they provide, looking briefly and rather un-
critically at what the author himself, whom we shall call Euthalius without prejudicing any final judgment of authorship, claims to have produced.

Even a very superficial examination turns up evidence that we are
here dealing with work that has taken shape in several stages. Remarks
appearing in the prologue to Acts distinguish between work at hand and
earlier work on the Pauline letters. Moreover, Euthalius indicates that
there are parts that are not original but were taken from an unnamed
predecessor. Thus, we already know that we are dealing with sources
and first and second editions; we may anticipate that there were probably "revised and enlarged" editions as well. These distinctions, however, we shall leave to later chapters.

There are three prologues. The Pauline is the longest and, according
to the internal testimony of the apparatus, the first to be written. It has
three major sections preceded by an elaborate apologia for the project.
The first and third sections deal with the life of Paul. The first is more
anecdotal, and the other, more narrowly chronological. The second section is a brief summary of the fourteen letters attributed to Paul. At the
end of the second section, Euthalius reviews what he has been about,
and this provides a minimal table of contents. He asserts

> καϑ' ἑκάστην δὲ συντόμως ἐπιστολὴν ἐν τοῖς ἑξῆς προτάξομεν τὴν τῶν κεφα-
> λαίων ἔκϑεσιν, ἑνὶ τῶν σοφωτάτων τινί, καὶ φιλοχρίστῳ πατέρων ἡμῶν
> πεπονημένην, οὐ μὴν ἀλλὰ καὶ τὴν τῶν ἀναγνώσεων ἀκριβεστάτην
> τομήν, τήν τε τῶν ϑείων μαρτυριῶν εὐαπόδεκτον εὕρεσιν ἡμεῖς τεχνολογή-
> σαντες ἀνεκεφαλαιωσάμεϑα, ἐπιπορευόμενοι τῇ τῆς ὑφῆς ἀναγνώσει.[6]

ἡ τῶν κεφαλαίων ἔκϑεσις represents an outline of the contents of
each letter, organized by chapters, some of which have subdivisions.

ἡ τῶν ἀναγνώσεων ἀκριβεστάτη τομή appears to be a table that
groups one or more chapters into ἀναγνώσεις of varying length.

ἡ τῶν ϑείων μαρτυριῶν εὐαπόδεκτος εὕρεσις is a list of quotations
found in the letters; these quotations are mostly from the Old Testament but also include some from the Gospels and a number of apocryphal books. In most manuscripts, there are two different types of lists,

---

6   Z 528 f.; M 708A.

and one of the purposes of the later, critical evaluation is to determine whether one of these preceded the other.

The other two prologues serve more the apologetic ends of the author than to introduce the material they preface. The prologue to the Catholic epistles repeats the announcement of the first and third items, "ἐγὼ δέ τοι στιχηδὸν τὰς καθολικὰς καθ' ἑξῆς ἐπιστολὰς ἀναγνώσομαι, τὴν τῶν κεφαλαίων ἔκθεσιν ἅμα, καὶ θείων μαρτυριῶν μετρίως ἐνθένδε ποιούμενος."[7] The prologue to Acts, while it does not specifically mention this material, remarks on other aspects of Euthalius' work, notably echoing part of the above, "πρῶτον δὴ οὖν ἔγωγε τὴν ἀποστολικὴν βίβλον στοιχιδὸν ἀναγνούς τε καὶ γράψας,"[8] and later, " . . . τήν τε τῶν πράξεων βίβλον ἅμα, καὶ καθολικῶν ἐπιστολῶν ἀναγνῶναί τε κατὰ προσῳδίαν, καὶ πῶς ἀνακεφαλαιώσασθαι, καὶ διειλεῖν τούτων ἑκάστης τὸν νοῦν λεπτομερῶς, . . . στοιχηδόν τε συνθεὶς τούτων τὸ ὕφος κατὰ τὴν ἐμαυτοῦ συμμετρίαν πρός εὔσημον ἀνάγνωσιν."[9] In this introduction, we have only sought a limited inventory of the evidence in the prologues for material contents; in the above passages, there are, above this, references to the *form* of the text, and it will be necessary to take up the question of Euthalian stichometry in an excursus.

In the pages that follow we will take up successively the prologues, the "lection" lists, the quotation lists, and the chapter lists. These four parts constitute those sections that are included in Zacagni's edition that also have some clear roots in Euthalius' own outline of his work. There are a considerable number of pieces that are also included in Zacagni's edition that have less *a priori* claim to inclusion. These we review following the discussion of the major pieces. Among these pieces are the following, which we here identify by title and briefly describe:

1. *Martyrium Pauli*:[10] This is a brief chronological note that states the martyrdom of Paul in Rome and dates it with several chronological co-ordinates. These chronological notices have supplied the primary data for most attempts to date the whole apparatus.
2. *Argumenta*: These are paragraph length summaries of each of the epistles and Acts.
3. Ἀποδημίαι:[11] A bare Pauline travelogue.

---

7 Z 477; M 668B.
8 Z 404; M 629A.
9 Z 409 f.; M 633Bf.
10 Z 535 ff.; M 713B-716A.
11 Z 425 ff.; M 649B-652A.

4. Τάδε ἔνεστιν Παύλου ἐπιστολαί:[12] This is a numbered listing of the Pauline epistles in order of appearance.
5. Διὰ τί Παύλου ἐπιστολαὶ δεκατέσσαρες λέγονται:[13] As we shall see later, the short paragraph that follows this title does not really answer the question set out for it.
6. Ἐπίγραμμα τοῦ ἐν Ἀθήναις Βωμοῦ:[14] Following this notice is the purported text of a short inscription.
7. Πλοῦς Παύλου τοῦ Ἀποστόλου ἐπὶ Ῥώμην:[15] This is another very short paragraph setting out some details of Paul's trip to Rome.
8. Πρὸς ἐμαυτόν: This is a prayer, about a paragraph in length. In the manuscripts that Zacagni used, the only evidence of the existence of this piece was the occurrence of the title in a subscription.[16] Since that time, both a Greek and an Armenian text have been located and identified.

We want to indicate below the primary resources that have been used in the discussions of the Greek, Syriac, and Armenian evidence.

Our survey of the Greek manuscript tradition was based on a preliminary checklist of manuscripts that we compiled. Our selection was based both on the lists of manuscripts that had been used by others in earlier research upon the Euthalian apparatus and upon our own review of general descriptive lists of manuscripts with attention to certain characteristics.

The edition of Zacagni was based upon nine Greek manuscripts in the Vatican library, namely, 133 181 436 450 451 623 625 1847 1914.[17] Von Dobschütz added a number of other manuscripts in the course of his discussion of these materials: 1 2 7 172 468.[18] Moreover, in a re-

---

12 Z 569; M 745C-748A.
13 Z 570; M 748A.
14 Z 514; M 692B.
15 Z 514; M 692B f.
16 Z 513; M 692A.
17 In addition to the notes in Zacagni, see also Ernst von Dobschütz, "Euthalius-studien," *ZKG* 19 (1898): 108, n. 1. Caspar René Gregory (*Textkritik des Neuen Testamentes* [3 vols.; Leipzig: J. C. Hinrichs, 1900–1909], 873, n. 1. There are three volumes in this set, but it is paged consecutively; hence, volume numbers will not be cited.) follows Zacagni (Z 515, n. 1; M 693, n. 1) in citing Vat. Reg. Gr. 32, but it must be Vat. Reg. Gr. 29, which is 450 (Cf. Gregory, *Textkritik*, 271; and Joseph Armitage Robinson, *Euthaliana* [TS 3.3; Cambridge: Cambridge University Press, 1895], 44.).
18 Ernst von Dobschütz, "Ein Beitrag zur Euthaliusfrage," *ZfB* 10 (1893): 67.

stricted study of the *Martyrium*, he included the following beyond the ones already noted: 88 257 432 603 1525.[19] Robinson broadened the discussion by bringing in the following manuscripts: 203 250 256 506 602 638.[20] In addition to a single new contribution to a list in a category he describes as non-Oecumenian manuscripts, 635, Turner provides the following list of "Oecumenian manuscripts with the Euthalian apparatus": 91 1162 1905 1906 1924 1933 1934 1970 1981.[21] Von Soden includes in his general discussion of the Euthalian apparatus, at one point or another, evidence from approximately sixty manuscripts.[22]

Our own list of more than 400 manuscripts was constructed by going through Gregory's descriptive list of manuscripts,[23] noting those that appeared to have some possibility of containing the Euthalian apparatus; we included not only those that were specifically designated as having the Euthalian apparatus,[24] but also those with designations that could fit the Euthalian apparatus without specifically naming it, e.g., prologues, chapter lists, *argumenta*, quotation lists, etc.

Von Dobschütz' work on Syriac manuscripts was limited to two: B.M. Add. 7157 and Oxford New College 333.[25] Zuntz included, as well, Cambridge Add. 1700.[26]

The first work with the Armenian tradition was produced by Conybeare using B.M. Add. 19,730; a codex at San Lazzaro; a codex belong-

---

19 *Ibid.*, 66 f.
20 Robinson, *Euthaliana*, 44.
21 Cuthbert Hamilton Turner, "Greek Patristic Commentaries on the Pauline Epistles," *DB(H)* 5: 529.
22 Hermann von Soden, *Die Schriften des Neuen Testaments in ihrer ältesten erreichbaren Textgestalt hergestellt auf Grund ihrer Textgeschichte* (vol. 1; Berlin: Alexander Dunker, 1902), 637–82.
23 Gregory, *Textkritik*.
24 The necessity for the comprehensiveness of this survey was underlined by the statement of Albert Ehrhard ("Codex H," 398, n. 1): "In einer freundlichen Zuschrift belehrt mich Hr. Prof. Gregory, dass die Sigel Euth. keinen abgrenzten Werth habe und nicht andeute, dass er genannt sei. Der Name komme vielleicht noch in einigen Codd. vor, wo das in seinem Cataloge nicht erwähnt sei."
25 Dobschütz, "Euthaliusstudien," 116.
26 Günther Zuntz, *The Ancestry of the Harklean New Testament* (BASP 7; London: Published for the British Academy by Humphrey Milford, Oxford University Press, 1945), 13.

ing to Lord Zouche; a fragment of a New Testament codex in the Ech-
miadzin library; and several other Armenian sources.[27]

Vardanian made use of a number of manuscripts in an important library in Venice, namely, the Biblioteca della Congregazione dei Mechi-
taristi.[28]

---

27 Frederick Cornwallis Conybeare, "On the Codex Pamphili and the Date of
    Euthalius," *JP* 23 (1895): 242, 245, 249, n. 1; and "The Date of Euthalius,"
    ZNW 5 (1904): 45 ff. Cf. Robinson, *Euthaliana*, 8, 44.
28 Vardanian collected his evidence in a series of articles appearing in the journal
    Handes Asorya between 1924 and 1927: "Euthaliana," *HA* 38 (1924): 385–408,
    481–98; 39 (1925): 1–26, 97–118, 203–26, 329–48, 423–34, 513–30; 40
    (1926): 1–15, 97–120, 193–208, 289–304, 417–36, 513–23; 41 (1927):
    1–11, 97–107, 225–35, 353–66, 481–92, 545–58. Pages in these articles
    are numbered as though they were divided into columns, although this is not
    the case. These articles were later collected into a single volume, which ap-
    peared in the series KASSU 3.1 (Vienna: Mechitharisten-Buchdr., 1930).

Part One: Major Pieces

1. Prologues

Each of the three sections of the apparatus is equipped with a prologue. All of the prologues give some attention to the enterprise in which Euthalius was engaged, and all present a certain amount of apologetic for this task. Aside from these similarities, there is a notable variation in the tenor and scope of the prologues. The prologue to the Catholic epistles, which is the shortest of the three, is about 240 words in length. The prologue to Acts is approximately 950 words in length, and the prologue to the Pauline epistles, about 2,450.

The prologue to the Pauline epistles opens with a long introductory paragraph, which is complex and discursive. Here, Euthalius enters a disclaimer, initiating a theme to which he returns in later prologues, of his own experience, appealing for the intercession of a "most honored father." Included in this paragraph are a quotation from Proverbs, an allusion to Moses, and a curious metaphor of a heavenly voyage.

The first major section is a summary of events in the life of Paul. Most of the information seems to have been derived from the account in Acts, although it is neither a paraphrase nor anything like a detailed presentation. It provides an unusual etymological explanation of the two names of Paul. It concludes with the information that Nero was responsible for the death of Paul and that the day of the annual celebration of this martyrdom is 29 June, indicated by two different calendars: three days before the calends of July and, as well, the fifth day of the month of Panemos.

The second section is a summary of each of the fourteen letters attributed to Paul. These summaries are mostly rather short, about a sentence, although 1 Thessalonians, 2 Timothy, and Philemon have summaries more nearly a brief paragraph in length. The order of the letters follows that of the present canon, except that Hebrews follows 2 Thessalonians. In this section, Euthalius gives several hints regarding the organizing principles behind his summaries and, indeed, the organizing principles of the letters as a whole. Leading off the paragraph, he remarks:

Πολλὰς δὲ καὶ πρὸ τούτου ἤδη παραινέσεις ὑπέρ τε βίου, καὶ ἀρετῆς ὁ
μακάριος ἐποιήσατο, καὶ πολλὰ περὶ τῶν πρακτέων τοῖς ἀνθρώποις εἰσηγή-
σατο Παῦλος ὁ ἀπόστολος. ἔτι δὲ καὶ ὅλως διὰ τῆς ὑφῆς τῶν δεκατεσσάρων
ἐπιστολῶν τούτων, τὴν ὅλην ἀνθρώποις διέγραψε πολιτείαν.[1]

Following the description of Hebrews, he notes, "ἐνταῦθα περικλείουσι
τὴν κατὰ τὸν λαὸν ἰδιωτικὴν αὔξησιν αἱ ἐπιστολαί."[2] Finally, he brings
these summaries to a close with the observation, "οὕτως ἡ πᾶσα βίβλος
περίεχει παντεῖον εἶδος πολιτειῶν κατὰ προσαύξησιν."[3]

The final section begins with the description of the apparatus Euthalius is going to provide, which we noted in the first part of this monograph. Following this general outline of his work, Euthalius presents a
more precise, chronological account of the ministry of Paul based, so
he says, on the work of Eusebius who, in contrast to other sources
only alluded to, is named. Included are some of the outrages of Nero
and a long direct quotation from 2 Timothy. This section concludes:
"The whole time of Paul's preaching is, therefore, twenty-one years
and another two years, which he spent in the prison in Caesarea, and
in addition to these, another two years in Rome and the last ten
years, so that all the years from his call to [his] consummation are thirty-five."[4] The last paragraph is a defense for having gone beyond the
evidence of Luke for information regarding the concluding part of
Paul's life.

As we have noted, the prologue to Acts is considerably shorter than
that to the Pauline epistles, but there are elements in common. Euthalius
again indicates a low estimate of his abilities, referring to himself as "οἷά
τις πῶλος ἀβαδής, ἢ νέος ἀμαθής."[5] There is much more rhetoric, as opposed to substance, in this prologue, including a long discourse on
μελέτη, which has occasioned a certain amount of speculation.[6] He
also refers to work on the Pauline letters as preceding that on Acts
and the Catholic epistles; it appears from these statements that he sent
the results of his labors on the Pauline material to someone other
than the recipient of the present prologue.[7] Relatively brief remarks

---

1   Z 523; M 701A.
2   Z 526; M 705A.
3   Z 528; M 708A.
4   Z 533 f.; M 712B.
5   Z 404; M 629A.
6   See James Rendel Harris, *Stichometry* (London: C. J. Clay & Sons, 1893), dis-
    cussed later in this monograph on pages 123–125.
7   Z 404; M 629A.

about the background of the author of Acts and its contents are reserved
for the conclusion of the prologue:

> [Luke] was an Antiochene by descent and a physician by skill; being in-
> structed by Paul, he wrote two books: the first, and earlier, was the Gospel,
> and the second was this [book] concerning the apostolic acts. Therefore,
> the whole story of this book is both about Christ's ascension to heaven
> after the resurrection and the manifestation of the Holy Spirit to the
> holy apostles and, thus, the great extent to which the disciples proclaimed
> devotion to Christ and what wonders they performed through prayer and
> faith in him; and [it is] about the heavenly, divine calling of Paul, his apos-
> tleship and flourishing preaching, and, to put it briefly, about the many and
> great dangers that the apostles endured for the sake of Christ.[8]

The prologue to the Catholic epistles is the shortest of the three. The
theme of unworthiness to undertake the task at hand, noted in the previous two prologues, is repeated here. The image of a small ship being
tossed about by an unruly sea, picked up from the Pauline prologue, is
offered in a reworked form.[9] The subject of the prologue, namely, an
introduction to the work on the Catholic epistles, is not mentioned
until the last sentence: "Accordingly, I shall read stichometrically, in
order, the Catholic epistles, doing the ἔκθεσις of the chapters while at
the same time, hence, the divine quotations as is befitting."[10]

The secondary literature has regularly taken the prologues as an important, initial stage in analysis of the Euthalian apparatus. Similarly, we
begin by going through these three pieces to find what internal evidence there is as to the announced intentions, circumstances, and intellectual environment of the writer.

In the descriptive section, we observed that the first paragraph of the
prologue to the Pauline epistles was a carefully wrought, complex literary device. J. Rendel Harris, incredibly, has located passages in the writings of two Armenian historians that bear such close resemblance to
some of the notes struck by Euthalius that there must be some connection.[11] Agathangelus, in the introductory remarks of *Histoire du règne de
Tiridate et de la prédication de Saint Grégoire l'Illuminateur*, makes a comparison between the literary artist and "the tempest-tossed voyager in a tiny

---

8   Z 410; M 633C-636A.
9   Z 475; M 665A.
10 Z 477; M 668B.
11 James Rendel Harris, "Euthalius and Eusebius," in *Hermas in Arcadia and Other
    Essays* (Cambridge: Cambridge University Press, 1896), 69 ff.

skiff." Included is a quotation from the Psalms.[12] Lazarus of Pharbi, who
wrote following Agathangelus, begins his history with the following remarks:

> Le présent ouvrage, œuvre de notre faiblesse, va former comme la troisième
> partie de ces annales. Nous sommes forcé d'[entreprendre] un semblable
> travail par ordre des princes et sur les exhortations des saints docteurs,
> n'osant pas nous opposer, en nous rappelant les menaces que la saint Écri-
> ture fait aux enfants désobéissants et de l'indulgence [qu'elle] montre vis-à-
> vis de ceux qui sont soumis et dociles.[13]

Harris does not believe that Euthalius based his work on that of these
two writers. In the instance of Lazarus of Pharbi, he is equally confident
that Lazarus has not imitated Euthalius, for he "was well acquainted
with Greek literature and was hardly likely to select for a model of
style so trifling a piece as Euthalius' prologue."[14] He believes rather
that "both writers are drawing upon some classic opening in which
the work of an historical writer is compared to the course of a ship na-
vigated in difficult and narrow seas."[15]

In the second section of the prologue, where the life of Paul is discussed, there are at least two items worthy of note. Following the conversion of Paul, the text of Euthalius in Zacagni is as follows:

> Τοσαύτην οὖν μεταβολὴν ὁ μακάριος Παῦλος ἐσχηκώς, ἔτι δὲ καὶ τοὔνομα
> μεταβαλών, καὶ καθ' ἑτέραν ἐπαληθεύσας αὐτοῦ προσηγορίαν· Σαῦλος
> γὰρ ἐσάλευε καθόλου τὸ πρὶν τὴν ἐκκλησίαν, Παῦλος δὲ τοι πέπαυται τοῦ
> διώκειν λοιπόν, καὶ λοιμαίνεσθαι τοῖς Χριστοῦ μαθηταῖς.[16]

This is the word play on the names of Paul that we have previously
mentioned. Zacagni notes that the operative words, καὶ καθ' . . . μαθη-
ταῖς, are missing from two of his manuscripts, 450 and 1914.[17]

---

12 Victor Langlois, *Collection des historiens anciens et moderns de l'Arménie* (vol. 1;
    Paris: Firmin Didot, 1867), 105, 109, cited by Harris, "Euthalius and Euse-
    bius," 71.
13 Langlois, *Collection des historiens,* 2:259, cited by Harris, "Euthalius and Euse-
    bius," 70.
14 Harris, "Euthalius and Eusebius," 70.
15 *Ibid.*, 71.
16 Z 519 f.; M 697B.
17 Z 519, n. 8; M 697 f., n. 41. Harris, who argues that Euthalius is a great pla-
    giarist of Eusebius, refuses to credit this particularly bad pun to this source (Har-
    ris, "Euthalius and Eusebius," 75, n. 1). Vardanian is relieved that the Armenian
    text does not support this reading ("Euthaliana," 39 [1925]: 5 f.).

Toward the conclusion of this section, the celebration of Paul's martyrdom in Rome is described. Zacagni has noted considerable variation in the dates reported, and additional evidence for these variations has been collected by Robinson.[18]

In the descriptive section we briefly noted the comments that Euthalius makes regarding the purpose of the letters of Paul; we also noted that the order of these fourteen epistles mirrors that of the present canon except that Hebrews follows 2 Thessalonians. It is clear that Euthalius felt that there was an intimate connection between the purposes behind the epistles and the order in which he has presented them. Perhaps Euthalius' own peculiar word προσαύξησις best expresses this principle. The epistles, at least those directed to churches contrasted with individuals, are ordered according to the growth of the communities involved, "ein Bild des Fortschrittes in religiösem Erkennen und Handeln."[19] It is noteworthy that, of the summaries themselves, we encounter the ones for Romans and Galatians, with some modifications, in some manuscripts as a sort of prologue or introduction to the two letters.[20] The disproportionate comments made by Euthalius on some of the letters, compared to the length of the texts, as in Philippians, 2 Timothy, and Philemon, caused von Soden to remark that Euthalius had no sense for architechtonic balance;[21] we will have occasion later to note Zuntz' unfavorable comparison between the craft of summary in the prologue as opposed to that represented by the chapter lists.[22]

We may further observe that the summary for Ephesians represents Paul as not having set eyes upon the Ephesians before sending the letter; he only knew of them by report.[23] The remarks about Philemon carry the non-scriptural tradition that Onesimus was martyred in Rome under Tertullus, his legs being broken.[24]

By the end of this chapter, we will have reviewed from several perspectives the announcements that Euthalius makes in the next section of

---

18 Z 523; M 701A; and Robinson, *Euthaliana*, 44 f.
19 Michael Islinger, *Die Verdienste des Euthalius um den neutestamentlichen Bibeltext* (Stadtamhof: Joseph Mayr, 1867), 12. Cf. Nathaniel Lardner, *The Credibility of the Gospel History* (vol. 2.11; London: Printed for J. Chandler, 1754), 213.
20 51 234 425 457 644 1405 1456 1573 1863 1891 2085 2279 2511. Cf. Soden, *Schriften des Neuen Testaments*, 656.
21 *Ibid.*
22 Zuntz, *Ancestry*, 83, cited on page 56 of this monograph.
23 Z 524; M 704A.
24 Z 528; M 705C.

this prologue in regard to the structure and contents of his work. There is a certain disagreement about precisely what he might have meant at certain points, both in terms of form and in terms of claims of originality. Insofar as *what* is concerned, it is clear that Euthalius speaks of chapter lists and quotation lists. There is no doubt that we have these lists in many manuscripts, although there is some question as to which of two types of quotation lists, or possibly some simpler form of one or both, appeared in the original edition. It has been argued that the third item mentioned in this summary, "τὴν τῶν ἀναγνώσεων ἀκριβεστάτην τομήν," is not an announcement of the tables of readings that turn up in the manuscripts. Others, who do not credit Euthalius with much originality in the construction of "lection" tables, propose variously that he has merely summarized, in a table-form, a system already extant in manuscripts that he used, or that the tables that we find have been interpolated at a later time, having had some independent existence or having been developed *ad hoc* in response to a misunderstanding of the vocabulary of the prologue.

The remainder of the prologue to the Pauline epistles is a chronological account of the life of Paul, in which Euthalius refers to Eusebius as a primary source; although Euthalius makes explicit reference to the *Chronicles* and to the *Ecclesiastical History*,[25] it becomes apparent that other work of Eusebius has also been used heavily, both here and other places. J. Rendel Harris has presented the most thorough documentation of this dependence. This demonstration of dependence by Harris is associated with a secondary attempt to support his contentions regarding the date and authorship of the Euthalian apparatus. We shall have occasion to review the further end to which his investigations are directed later in this monograph. His conclusions regarding the indebtedness to Eusebius stand on their own merits.

Harris found instances of direct dependence and many parallels between the prologues to both the Pauline letters and Acts and several works of Eusebius still extant; this dependence was not limited to factual, narrative data, but also included thematic and rhetorical elements. The evidence that he gathered is found in his detailed essay, "Euthalius and Eusebius,"[26] and we do not here propose an extensive rehearsal of that evidence. One sample, however, may serve to indicate both the level of dependence and the quality of Euthalius as a literary artisan.

---

25 Z 529; M 708B and Z 531; M 709B, respectively.
26 Pages 60−83, especially 64−69.

In the section of the prologue that we are now discussing, Euthalius describes the appointment of Stephen and the other deacons as follows: "καὶ μεθ᾽ ἡμέρας τινὰς ὀλίγας εἶδον ἐκεῖ προχειριζομένους τοὺς Ἀποστόλους εἰς διακονίαν τὸν αὐτοφερώνυμον (vl. πανυφερώνυμον 625; αὐτῷ φερώνυμον 450, so Zacagni, n. 8; M, n. 42) Στέφανον, καὶ τοὺς ἀμφ᾽ αὐτόν."[27] Harris observed that this was clearly dependent upon the account in *Hist. eccl.* 2.1.1:[28] "πρῶτος τὸν αὐτῷ φερώνυμον τῶν ἀξιονίκων τοῦ Χριστοῦ μαρτύρων ἀποφέρεται στέφανον," in regard to the martyrdom of Stephen.[29] Here, it is appropriate to let Harris speak for himself:

> Here a curious fact comes to light, viz, that Euthalius has failed to understand Eusebius' language. Eusebius speaks of Stephen as bearing away the martyr's crown, which is appropriately named (στέφανος) for him. Here the play upon the words has taken Euthalius' fancy, but he has blunderingly carried off αὐτῷ φερώνυμον and applied it to Stephen, without mentioning the crown to complete the parallel. He might have contented himself with calling Stephen φερώνυμος and leaving his readers to see the obvious play upon the name; but he was appropriating from Eusebius, . . . and so we have the impossible reading that appears in [450] as αὐτῷ φερώνυμον, in other MSS as a single impossible word αὐτοφερώνυμον, and in [625], by emendation, as πάνυ φερώνυμον.[30]

We have previously noted that Eusebius is the only source, other than the Bible, to which Euthalius makes explicit reference. There are two other observations that have some important implications for the distance of Euthalius from the time of Eusebius as well as the stature of his works in the time of Euthalius. Eusebius is referred to as Εὐσέβιος ὁ Χρονόγραφος toward the end of the prologue.[31] Harris claims that such a title is not likely to have been attributed to him until some time following his death.[32] This estimate is supported by the argument pursued immediately prior to this in the prologue. Euthalius anticipates that some objection will be registered to his having ventured beyond the testimony of Luke in describing the final years of Paul. "The manner of making the reply in which such deference is paid to the opinion of Eu-

---

27 Z 529; M 708B.
28 Harris, "Euthalius and Eusebius," 66.
29 The text is in that translated by Kirsopp Lake (LCL; London: William Heinemann, [1926]).
30 Harris, "Euthalius and Eusebius," 66.
31 Z 534; M 713A.
32 Harris, "Euthalius and Eusebius," 83.

sebius . . . shows that Euthalius is writing after the death of Eusebius, and probably some time after."[33]

This chronological description of the life of Paul is in some tension with the other discussion of the life of Paul. The first discussion of Paul's life makes no mention of any preliminary release from Roman captivity nor any second defense.[34] Precisely the reverse is indicated, for once Paul has been brought to Rome, μικρὸν γὰρ ὕστερον he is martyred. The chronological account, however, describes a ten year period of ministry between a first and a second defense before Nero.[35] In the second interpretation, Euthalius follows Eusebius, including the exegesis of parts of 2 Timothy (4: 6, 11, 16−18),[36] although Eusebius' own concern in this discussion was to demonstrate that the Lucan narrative in Acts did not cover the period in which Paul was martyred. Both Eusebius and Euthalius take no sides on the question of where Paul was during the interval. Euthalius covers the period with vague phrases such as, "Paul was sent ἐπὶ τὴν τοῦ κηρύγματος διακονίαν so the story goes" or later merely, "τὰ τελευταῖα . . . ἔτη δέκα."[37]

We have already noted the different impression of the content and tone of the prologue to the Acts as over against the prologue for the Pauline letters, although the style appears consistent.[38] Von Soden has also noticed this "schriftstellerischen" tone,[39] which extends to the prologue of the Catholic epistles as well, and he has an elaborate, speculative reconstruction of Euthalius' life to account for it;[40] this reconstruction we will deal with later. We have also noted above some of the literary imagery, e.g., the comparison of the author's task to that of a storm-tossed vessel, which is picked up in this prologue. We have observed the depreciatory phrases with which Euthalius characterizes himself. We may here take note of two other comments that he makes about the sequence of his labors: "πρώην," he says, "I sent [the Pauline epistles] to one of our fathers in Christ."[41] A little further on he says, ἔναγχος τοίνυν ... having read the book of Paul, αὐτίκα δῆτα, and hav-

---

33 *Ibid.*
34 Z 522; M 700C.
35 Z 531 f; M709C.
36 *Hist.eccl.* 2.22.
37 Z 531 f.; M 709C and Z 534; M 712B, respectively.
38 Ehrhard, "Codex H," 400.
39 Soden, *Schriften des Neuen Testaments*, 645, 670.
40 *Ibid.*, 645−49.
41 Z 404; M 629A.

ing labored over the [book] of the apostolic Acts together with the seven Catholic epistles, I sent [them] immediately to you."[42] There has been considerable discussion in the secondary literature as to the interpretation of these temporal phrases. Since the concern of those who wish to read them in other than a literal sense is at least influenced by a larger concern to have more than a brief interval between the work on the Pauline letters and the other parts of the apparatus in order to qualify certain dates and personalities, we will take up their remarks in detail in the discussion of dating, authorship, and provenance.

We saw in the Pauline prologue that Euthalius gives some evidence of an interest in the etymology of names. There is nothing explicit in the prologues to Acts and the Catholic epistles, although the attention of some critics has been drawn to several interesting possibilities. A few manuscripts carry a heading for the prologue to Acts that bears a dedication to one Athanasius, Bishop of Alexandria.[43] Zahn finds in addition to the name itself, without the title, possible plays on this name in the prologue to Acts.[44] He also uncovers veiled references to the elusive Euthalius at two points in the prologue to the Acts and once in the Pauline prologue.[45]

Harris has advanced a comprehensive theory of the authorship of these prologues that is predicated upon an interpretation he gives to a long discourse on μελέτη, which occurs in the middle of the prologue to Acts.[46] Harris believes that this digression is an elaborate literary device to honor the addressee who, Harris believes, was Meletius. Support for this interpretation comes in the description of μελέτη as τὴν πάνυ φερώνυμον.[47] Harris notes that this remark is in the style of the earlier discussion of the name of Stephen in the prologue to the Pauline material; he argues that it, together with a comment that μελέτη is a namesake, would hardly be apt here if the recipient, to whom this discourse is clearly directed, were named Athanasius, as it would now appear from the text of the prologue as well as in the heading in some manuscripts.

---

42 Z 405; M 629B.
43 See Soden, *Schriften des Neuen Testaments*, 667.
44 Z 409; M 633C; Z 403; M 628A; and Z 404; M 629A, respectively, cited by Theodor von Zahn, "Neues und Altes über den Isagogiker Euthalius," *NKZ* 15 (1904): 314, n. 1.
45 Z 406; M 632A; Z 410; M 636A; and Z 518; M 696B, respectively, cited by Zahn, "Neues und Altes," 314, n. 1.
46 Harris, *Stichometry*, 80–85; and Harris, "Euthalius and Eusebius," 63 f.
47 Z 406; M 632A, cited and discussed by Harris in *Stichometry*, 80 ff.

Harris then ventures to suggest that the prologue was, in fact, originally addressed to a Meletius; the name was later erased, for "there never was a Meletius, worth mentioning, who was not a schismatic."[48] No one has been particularly happy with this suggestion, although the arguments against it have either been somewhat subjective[49] or indirect.[50] No one denies that there is a word game here, although Zuntz brings evidence to support his contention that Euthalius "was following an established usage when prefacing his edition of Acts by that long diatribe on the τῶν θείων Λογίων μελέτη."[51] None of this, of course, touches the principal argument in Harris' thesis, and Euthalius is no less clever if he is able to turn what may be a common rhetorical device into a personal compliment.

For ourselves, this long passage appears rather suspicious. We believe that it begins somewhat abruptly in the context of the whole, or what is left, of the prologue and that a close examination of several aspects of style and word usage in this section compared with the remainder of the prologue might provide some significant differences.[52]

Von Soden, who finds the very abbreviated summary of Acts at the conclusion of this prologue widespread in the manuscript tradition as an isolated piece, believes that it must remain an open question as to whether Euthalius is the author of what became an extract or whether he has taken it up from the tradition, in a manner analogous to the way von Soden believes he has used other materials.[53]

Although we have noted some divergence in tone between the first prologue and the other two, as well as some tensions that could be further explored within one or more of the prologues, we are not prepared to argue that the form in which they originally circulated with the apparatus was substantially different from the present text. It is likely that a critical edition would make some alterations in the conflated text provided by Zacagni, particularly at the points of the notations of date; moreover, it is probable that close scrutiny will develop some hitherto unnoted links with the patristic tradition that may provide some easing

---

48 Harris, *Stichometry*, 83.
49 "Unwarranted inferences" is Zuntz' remark (*Ancestry*, 171).
50 Robinson (*Euthaliana*, 7 f. and later) believes that his evidence for a pre-396 date invalidates Harris' conclusions.
51 Zuntz, *Ancestry*, 17.
52 The passage begins ἀλλ᾽ ἐν ἀδελφοῖς (Z 406; M 629C) and continues through ἐξασκοῦσά τε, καὶ ἀναβιβάζουσα (Z 409; M 633B).
53 Soden, *Schriften des Neuen Testaments*, 670.

of the tensions we have described. At this point, however, our primary concern has been the development of a critical description of the prologues with particular attention paid to the evidence bearing on the form and content of the other parts of the apparatus.

2. "Lection" Lists

In the prologue to the Pauline epistles, we previously observed that Euthalius, in describing his work, noted, "τὴν τῶν ἀναγνώσεων ἀκριβεστάτην τομήν, τήν τε τῶν θείων μαρτυριῶν εὐαπόδεκτον εὕρεσιν ἡμεῖς τεχνολογήσαντες ἀνεκεφαλαιωσάμεθα, ἐπιπορευόμενοι τῇ τῆς ὑφῆς ἀναγνώσει."[1] There is no analogous reference in the prologue to the Catholic epistles.[2] Data in the prologue to Acts appear to be only tenuously related to these references in the Pauline material: "τήν τε τῶν πράξεων βίβλον ἅμα, καὶ καθολικῶν ἐπιστολῶν ἀναγνῶναί τε κατὰ προσῳδίαν, καὶ πῶς ἀνακεφαλαιώσασθαι, . . . στοιχηδόν τε συνθεὶς τούτων τὸ ὕφος κατὰ τὴν ἐμαυτοῦ συμμετρίαν πρὸς εὔσημον ἀνάγνωσιν."[3]

In some of the manuscripts containing the Euthalian apparatus, including the one in the Vatican library that formed the primary basis for Zacagni's edition, there are tables that appear to correspond roughly to what Euthalius describes as "the most accurate division of the 'lections.'"[4] The table generally follows the prologue, and there is a table for each of the three parts of the apparatus.

The table for the Pauline epistles has the following heading: "Ἀνακεφαλαίωσις τῶν ἀναγνώσεων καὶ ὧν ἔχουσι κεφαλαίων, καί μαρτυριῶν καθ' ἑκάστην ἐπιστολὴν τοῦ Ἀποστόλου καὶ ὅσων ἑκάστη τούτων στίχων τυγχάνει."[5]

After the general title, there is a tabulation of statistics for each of the letters in this general pattern: "Ἐν τῇ πρὸς Ῥωμαίους ἐπιστολῇ ἀνα-

---

1 Z 529; M 708A.
2 This "omission" is referred by von Soden (*Schriften des Neuen Testaments*, 673) to a scribe, for "Euthalius selbst hier das, was deutlich der Hauptzweck seiner Ausgabe ist, kaum übersprungen haben kann." The genitive θείων μαρτυριῶν with ἅμα may support von Soden's thesis as it rarely occurs with a genitive instead of an accusative.
3 Z 409 f.; M 633Bf.
4 Zuntz (*Ancestry*, 105) notes, "Although the normal term for lesson is ἀνάγνωσμα, the word ἀνάγνωσις, too, can bear this sense." The manuscripts containing one or more of these lists are as follows: 5 81 88 181 466 619 621 623 637 915 917 919 1162 1244 1836 1845 1846 1874 1875.
5 Z 537; M 716Af.

γνώσεις ε΄. Κεφάλαια ιθ΄. μαρτυρίαι μη΄. στίχοι λκ΄. Ἀνάγνωσις πρώτη κεφαλαίων δ΄. α΄, β΄, γ΄, δ΄. μαρτυριῶν θ΄. α΄, β΄, γ΄, δ΄, ε΄, ς΄, ζ΄, η΄, θ΄. στίχων σμβ΄." The second "lection" follows and so on through the entire letter, in the case of Romans for five "lections," then taking up with 1 Corinthians and continuing through the corpus of fourteen letters. The table for the Catholic epistles follows the pattern found in the Paulines,[6] with the following exception: before the listing of the individual "lections," there is no general summary statement of the numbers of "lections," chapters, and quotations, as in the Pauline material;[7] after the identification of the letter, the apparatus moves directly to the first "lection." The form of the table for Acts[8] is also slightly different, inasmuch as the notation for each "lection" includes, in addition to the itemized information about the number of chapters and quotations, the first words of the Biblical text beginning the "lection," e.g., "Ἀνάγνωσις πρώτη, οὕτως, Τὸν μὲν πρῶτον λόγον. Κεφαλαίου ἑνός, α΄. μαρτυρίας μιᾶς, α΄. στίχων μ΄."[9] We may note at this point the similarity between this unique feature of Acts in the "lection" list and another point where the pattern in Acts diverges from that of the other two sections, namely, in a second list of chapters, numbering thirty-six, which has been constructed to include a citation of the first words of each chapter. The actual listing of the chapters, however, divided among the sixteen "lections," corresponds to the forty chapter list.

There are a few discrepancies between the figures in the "lections" and evidence from the parts that are summarized; there are also a number of minor variations in the internal patterns. Some of these variants, of course, may be merely textual; no control was attempted, in the survey of the manuscripts, in these areas. The concluding summary at the end of the Pauline "lection" list gives the total number of chapters as 147. This agrees with the number of chapters described in this list, but the total of those listed in the ἐκθέσεις is 148. The difference lies in 2 Corinthians: In the list of chapters, the tenth begins with 10:1 and has two subdivisions; the eleventh begins with 11:21b and has one subdivision. The "lection" list for this epistle gives a total of ten

---

6   Z 478 f.; M 668B–669B.
7   In the Pauline letters that have only one ἀνάγνωσις, i .e., 1 Thessalonians, 2 Thessalonians, 1 Timothy, 2 Timothy, Titus, and Philemon, there is no summary.
8   Z 411–13; M 636B–637C.
9   Z 411; M 636B. Zacagni notes (n. 3; M, n. 72), "Numerum versuum a librario omissum, nos ex Actuum textu supplevimus."

chapters, in which the tenth, constituting the only chapter of the final "lection," begins with 10:1.[10]

Similar discrepancies occur in the Catholic epistles, where the "lection" list shows only a single chapter for each of the last two letters of John; the count in the chapter lists shows 2 John with two and 3 John with three.[11]

One final note may be made of the omission, in the "lection" lists of the letters to Timothy, Titus, and Philemon, of the itemization of the chapters contained in the "lection" of each of these epistles; that is, all we are given here is the total number of chapters in each "lection."

The "lection" list for each of the two collections of letters concludes with a recapitulation of the totals, e.g., in the Pauline section "Ὁμοῦ τῶν δεκατεσσάρων ἐπιστολῶν ἀναγνώσεις λα´, κεφάλαια ρμζ´, μαρτυρίαι ρκζ´, στίχοι ͵δ᾽λϛ´."[12] There is next, in all three cases, a short paragraph, which we have set out in parallel columns below:

Paul: Διεῖλον τὰς ἀναγνώσεις καὶ ἐστίχισα πᾶσαν   τὴν ἀποστολικὴν
Acts: Διεῖλον τὰς ἀναγνώσεις   τῆς
Cath.:   Διεῖλον τὰς ἀναγνώσεις   τῶν

         βίβλον   ἀκριβῶς κατὰ πεντήκοντα
         βίβλου τῶν πράξεων τῶν Ἀποστόλων,
         καθολικῶν,

         στίχους, καὶ τὰ κεφάλαια ἑκάστης ἀναγνώσεως παρέθηκα, καὶ
                  καὶ τὰ κεφάλαια ἑκάστης ἀναγνώσεως παρέθηκα, καὶ
                  καὶ τὰ κεφάλαια ἑκάστης ἀναγνώσεως παρέθηκα,

     τὰς ἐν αὐτῇ φερομένας μαρτυρίας,   ἔτι δὲ καὶ ὅσων
     τὰς ἐν αὐτῇ φερομένας μαρτυρίας,   ἔτι δὲ καὶ ὅσων ἑκάστη
                                ἔτι δὲ καὶ ὅσων ἑκάστη

       στίχων   ἡ ἀνάγνωσις   τυγχάνει. στίχοι ξ´.
       στίχων   τυγχάνει.
ἐπιστολή,   καὶ ἀνάγνωσις στίχων   τυγχάνει.[13]

---

10   Cf. Z 541; M 720B. There is considerable manuscript evidence on both sides at the conclusion of the chapter list for 2 Corinthians. See also Vardanian, "Euthaliana," 39 (1925): 105 f., for the Armenian data.

11   Cf. the remarks in the preceding footnote, which also apply here.

12   Zuntz (*Ancestry*, 13, 16 f.) has emended the Syriac to translate στίχοι τετρακισχίλιοι ᾽λϛ´ instead of the sequence 4,000 plus 80 plus 30 plus 6, arguing that the sampi (᾽) was misread for a pi.

13   Z 541; M 720B (Paul); Z 413; M 637C (Acts); and Z 479; M 669B (Catholic epistles).

We may note here the unique reference, in the Pauline material, to "ἐστίχισα πᾶσαν τὴν ἀποστολικὴν βίβλον ἀκριβῶς κατὰ πεντήκοντα στίχους," which apparently refers to marginal notations in the text cumulating the stichometry by fifties. In the manuscripts used by Zacagni, the paragraph for the Catholic epistles has omitted reference to the quotations.

The critical secondary literature has focussed on two sorts of problems in discussing the "lections." The first question deals with the actual function of these lists; the second question concerns the role played by Euthalius, if any, in the formulation of these lists.

There are a total of fifty-seven "lections": thirty-one, sixteen, and ten in the Pauline letters, Acts, and the Catholic letters respectively. Given the title that these lists carry, it is no surprise that attempts have been made to fit the "lections" into a lectionary system for the church year. It has been noted that the Jews divided the Law into fifty-three *Parashim*, according to the number of Sabbaths, taking into account leap year.[14] Moreover, Clement of Alexandria is found to have mentioned a μεγίστη περικοπή,[15] which may be external evidence for lections of great length.[16] The most logical suggestion seems to give fifty-three of these lections to the Sundays of a year and the remaining four to great feast days.[17]

One problem in defending this interpretation is that there is no evidence that a lectionary system with such lengthy excerpts was ever used

---

14 John Leonhard Hug, *An Introduction to the Writings of the New Testament* (trans. Daniel Guildford Wait; vol. 1; London: Printed for C. & J. Rivington by R. Gilbert, 1827), 254; and Gregory, *Textkritik*, 1213.

15 *Strom.*, 7.14.84, cited by Otto Schmid, *Über verschiedene Eintheilungen der Heiligen Schrift: Inbesondere über die Capital-eintheilung Stephan Langtons im XIII. Jahrhunderte* (Graz: Leuschner & Lubensky, 1892), 15.

16 The longest is Acts 11:27–14:28. Among the short ones are Acts 1:15–26; 2 John; 3 John, all cited by Georg Rietschel, *Lehrbuch der Liturgik* (rev. Paul Graff; 2d ed.; 2 vols. in 1; Göttingen: Vandenhoeck & Ruprecht, 1951-52), 189.

17 Zacagni, *Collectanea*, lxxiv; Schmid, *Verschiedene Eintheilungen*, 15; Gregory, *Textkritik*, 1214; Adolf Jülicher, *An Introduction to the New Testament* (trans. Janet Penrose Ward, with a prefatory note by Mrs. Humphrey Ward; London: Smith, Elder, 1904), 586; Adolf Jülicher, *Einleitung in das Neue Testament* (rev. with Erich Fascher; 7th ed.; Tübingen: Mohr [Siebeck], 1931), 575; and Rietschel, *Lehrbuch der Liturgik*, 189. The days are Christmas, Easter, Ascension, and Pentecost. Zacagni (so Gregory, *Textkritik*, 1214) suggests Epiphany instead of Pentecost (*Collectanea*, lxxxii). Hug (*Writings*, 254) errs in referring only fifty-six lections to this system, naming the three feast days Christmas, Easter, and Whitsuntide.

in the church.[18] Zuntz compared the divisions offered by these lists to those of a number of lectionary systems, including two sets of *lectio continua* of the Jerusalem lectionary.[19] Although he noted a number of co-incidences in the beginnings of these different lists, which is no surprise, he concludes, "These analogies are hardly sufficient to support the suggestions proposed."[20] It has been argued that the system proposed in these lists is simply too unwieldy to be of use in public worship services.[21] Some have suggested other purposes to which these lists may have been put, e.g., "divisions of a commentator,"[22] "sections of the sacred text set for study at the catechetical school in Caesarea,"[23] or some monastic use.[24]

The other area to which critical thought has been given is the relationship of Euthalius to this material, i.e., did some or all of this material precede him, did he construct the entire set of lists himself, or are the lists later interpolations with which Euthalius himself had nothing to do?

Robinson opposes attribution of any part in the construction of these lists to Euthalius. He argues that the title for the piece in Acts is the full one that he has brought evidence to show in other places is not Euthalian.[25] He also notes that the lists contain stichometrical data, which he has denied to Euthalius; moreover, he observes that the attestation for this section in the Euthalian manuscripts is not strong. In order to support this interpretation, Robinson must provide a credible explanation for the language of the prologues that appears to speak of these "lections." He first declares that the phrase, "τὴν τῶν ἀναγνώσεων ἀκριβεστάτην τομήν,"[26] is not clear; it may be that it is to be interpreted by the expression in the prologue to Acts, "μετρίαις ταῖς τῆς ὀλιγομαθοῦς ἡμῶν ἀναγνώσεως τομαῖς."[27] Since Robinson is

---

18 Gregory, *Textkritik*, 1214.
19 Zuntz, *Ancestry*, 106 ff.
20 *Ibid.*, 109.
21 Jülicher, *Einleitung*, 575. Cf. Zuntz (*Ancestry*, 105), "On the whole, however, they are too irregular in length, and some of them far too long, for this purpose."
22 Robinson, *Euthaliana*, 15.
23 Zuntz, *Ancestry*, 105.
24 Rietschel, *Lehrbuch der Liturgik*, 190.
25 Robinson, *Euthaliana*, 6. Refer to page 41 of this monograph.
26 Z 529; M 708A.
27 Z 405; M 629B. These arguments are advanced in Robinson, *Euthaliana*, 12.

unclear about the meaning of these phrases, he suspects that others may also have been, and accordingly, these tables were later inserted in what appeared to be a gap.[28]

This sort of argument has not been so persuasive to others; von Soden, at least, asserts that the construction of these lists was the primary contribution of Euthalius.[29] Others have not been quite so extravagant. Gregory believes that although it is clear that Euthalius was claiming an important part in the production of this material, he can hardly have been suggesting that he had originated these divisions, since they long predated him; rather, he must have intended to provide the *authoritative* division.[30] Zahn has observed a distinction between the use of ἀναγνώσεις in these lists, referring to "lections" composed of one or more chapters, and the Euthalian use of ἀνάγνωσις, referring to a reading of the text in which Euthalius delimited sense lines.[31]

To argue that this material is not from Euthalius is not, of course, to settle the question of priority. We may observe at this point that the line of reasoning that finds in the existence of fifty-seven divisions an ecclesiastical significance is almost certainly predicated upon a conception of a scheme embracing the entire corpus. Given the probable sequence in the development of the two parts of the work, we believe that it is unlikely that Euthalius would himself have conceived such a framework. Furthermore, as Zuntz suggests, if these lists were Euthalius' own product, he would not have alluded to "τῆς ὀλιγομαθοῦς ἡμῶν ἀναγνώσεως τομαῖς" in a sense that invites misapprehension.[32]

Zuntz goes on to argue that Euthalius found these materials together with the short paragraphs that follow them in the exemplar that he used to fashion his edition. In a manner alike to his adoption of the chapter lists, including the general heading, he has merely copied this material into his edition. Zuntz interprets the language in the prologue to the Pauline epistles as follows: "I have devised a skillful scheme for sundering accurately the ἀναγνώσεις and ascertaining comfortably the quotations: in going through the text, I have compiled tables of them."[33] This Zuntz takes to mean that Euthalius does not claim to have selected

---

28   Robinson, *Euthaliana*, 16.
29   Soden, *Schriften des Neuen Testments*, 659.
30   Gregory, *Textkritik*, 1212.
31   Theodor von Zahn, "Euthaliana," *ThLBl* 16 (1895): 601.
32   Zuntz, *Ancestry*, 104 f.
33   *Ibid.*, 84.

either the quotations or the "lections" but has merely collected them in convenient tables. A full assessment of this theory will come later in this monograph, for an important factor is the degree to which Euthalius may be demonstrated to be dependent upon the work of others in a rather direct fashion.

In general, we are inclined to accept the hypothesis offered by Zuntz, which, it seems to us, accounts for several pieces of data that are not comfortably resolved by other interpretations. It accounts for Euthalius' use of the same language in somewhat different ways, and it makes credible the presence, in a work produced in stages, of a scheme of division predicated on a larger whole. That is to say, if one of the theories positing an ecclesiastical significance to the fifty-seven divisions is correct, then Zuntz' suggestion of origin explains how such a framework could have appeared already in the construction of the apparatus to the Pauline epistles with no thought having been given by the author to the later construction of a similar apparatus for Acts and the Catholic epistles.

3. Quotation Lists

Examination of the manuscripts turns up two different sorts of lists of quotations. One type is a brief summary of citations only by number; the other is a longer, ordered listing of the citations quoted in full. There are also introductory paragraphs explaining the numeration systems purportedly used in the lists as well as several supplementary annotations; however, we want to leave consideration of all the ancillary material until we have covered thoroughly the primary pieces. There are six of these, three of each type, which are paired, one group each for the Pauline epistles, Acts, and the Catholic epistles; there are, as one might expect, manuscripts lacking one or more of these pairs or containing incomplete pairs. In this section, we will describe in detail the structure of these six lists, beginning with the long lists, and then analyze the relationships and discrepancies as closely as possible. First, however, let us briefly examine the introductory paragraphs.

Five of the six lists of quotations are preceded by short paragraphs explaining the numeration system that each uses; the five are three for the short lists and one each for the long lists of the Pauline and Catholic epistles.[1] These paragraphs are called προγράμματα.

The προγράμματα for the short lists state that Euthalius has indicated the total number of times each source is cited by a black number and that he has also listed the quotations, in order according to source, using red numbers. These red numbers are repeated in the text next to the citation involved, and they begin again with each epistle. The language of the προγράμματα for the epistolary lists is virtually identical, varying only where it is necessary to distinguish between the letters of Paul and the Catholic epistles. The πρόγραμμα for Acts is shorter, and the language is different, but the message is the same.

The paragraphs preceding the long lists, like those of the corresponding sections of the short lists, have the same text except for the ob-

---

1   The short lists appear on the following pages: Acts: Z 414; M 637D; Catholic epistles: Z 479 f.; M 669B; and Pauline epistles: Z 542 ff.; M 720Bf. The long lists appear on the following pages: Catholic epistles: Z 481 ff.; M 672Af. and Pauline epistles: Z 549 ff.; M 725Bf.

vious changes. These paragraphs explain that a double numeration system is employed in the table following and that the numbers are distinguished by the colors that are used. They state that a red number denotes the order of the quotations consecutively as they appear within each epistle and that this numbering begins again with each epistle.

This is the same function, of course, as the red numbers in the short lists. The other set of numbers is black, but in this list, a black number designates how many times a particular source has been cited, up to and including the particular quotation, and it continues to cumulate through an entire corpus of letters. Moreover, the paragraphs conclude, the red number is repeated in the margin of the text of the letter at the point that the quotation is made.

All three long lists have the same general purpose, namely, to provide a catalog of quotations in order of appearance in the text. A superficial examination of the lists indicates that the lists have been compiled by copying out the appropriate New Testament text of Acts or the letters rather than the text of the source cited.[2] The Psalms are cited according to their division in the LXX rather than the Hebrew text.

The quotation list for the Pauline epistles, titled Ἀνακεφαλαίωσις θείων μαρτυριῶν,[3] is printed by Zacagni with three sets of numbers, e.g., in 1 Corinthians, "I. μθ΄. Ἡσαΐου Προφήτου ιε΄."[4] The first number, I, represents a consecutive counting of the quotations, which begins anew with each epistle. The second, μθ΄, is a consecutive numbering of all the quotations in the fourteen epistles; this set is Zacagni's own invention[5] and has no support in the manuscript tradition examined. The third number, following the source citation, ιε΄, cumulates by source and continues through the whole corpus of fourteen letters. Although the Psalms are cited by individual number, they are treated as forming a single source in the cumulative totals.

Occasionally, two sources are indicated for the same quotation:

2 A clear example of this is in 2 Cor. 4:6a, which Euthalius cites as ἐκ σκότους φῶς λάμψαι, attributing it to Isaiah (Z 558; M 736B). The nearest verse in Isaiah is 9:1 (LXX), "ὁ λαὸς ὁ πορευόμενος ἐν σκότει, ἴδετε φῶς μέγα· οἱ κατοικοῦντες ἐν χώρᾳ καὶ σκιᾷ θανάτου, φῶς λάμψει ἐφ' ὑμᾶς."
3 Z 549–67; M 725D-745A.
4 Z 556; M 733A.
5 Z 549, n. 3; M 727, n. 34. Zacagni believed he was conforming the tables to the instructions of the introductory paragraphs, a belief in which he was mistaken, as noted by Robinson (*Euthaliana*, 19). Von Dobschütz observed that an ancient Syriac scribe has made the same error ("Euthaliusstudien," 151).

1. Romans IV at 3:10−14 is referred to Psalm 13 (13:1) and 52 (52:2−4), i. e., IV. Ψαλμοῦ ιγ'. καὶ νβ'. αὐτὴ β'.[6] As far as the quotation includes the two Psalms, it duplicates them.

2. Romans XXI at 10:5, which is also Galatians V at 3:12; both are referred to Ezekiel (20:11) and Deuteronomy. The two New Testament texts are parallel to the Ezekiel passage, but, as Zacagni observes,[7] it is Lev. 18:5 and not anything in Deuteronomy that provides another parallel.

3. Romans XXV at 10:15 is referred to Nahum (2:1) and Isaiah (52:7). In this instance, there is only verbal similarity among all three.

4. Romans XLIV at 15:9 is referred to 2 Kings and Psalm 17. So far as they are quoted, the passages are virtually identical.

5. 1 Corinthians II at 1:31, which is also 2 Corinthians X at 10:17; both are referred to 1 Kings and Jeremiah, and there is verbal similarity among the four.

6. Hebrews XII at 3:7b-11, cited as Δευτερονομίου καὶ Ψαλμοῦ ϙδ' ἡ αὐτὴ ιγ',[8] the quotation is virtually identical with the Psalm passage, but there is only a bare link to Deuteronomy at 33:8 (cf. Exod. 17:7; Num 20:1−13).

The list also cites as sources Matthew (twice) and six non-canonical writings:

1. 1 Corinthians III at 2:9 is referred to Ἠλία ἀποκρύφου.

2. 1 Corinthians XIV at 15:32 is referred to Λακωνικὴ παροιμία.[9]

3. 1 Corinthians XV at 15:33 is referred to Μενάνδρου κωμῳδιογράφου γνώμη.[10]

4. Galatians XI at 6:15 is referred to Μωϋσέως ἀποκρύφου.

5. Ephesians IV at 5:14 is referred to Ἐν ἀποκρύφῳ Ἰερεμίου τοῦ Προφήτου.

---

6 The Roman numeral indicates the number of the quotation. We use this system rather than Zacagni's form of numeration. We have omitted Zacagni's unsupported elaboration of the system and use only two numbers.

7 Z 552, n. 1; M 729 f., n. 38.

8 Zacagni (Z 564; M 742A) mistranslates this last phrase, "decima tertia vice ex Psalterio." It is the thirteenth citation from Deuteronomy.

9 In the short list, cited as Δημάδου λακωνικὴ παροιμία. In Supplement 1 (Z 546; M 724B), cited as Λακωνική, καὶ ἀρχαία παροιμία.

10 In the short list, cited as Μενάνδρου γνώμη, and in Supplement 1 as well (*ibid.*).

6. Titus I at 1:12 is referred to Ἐπιμενίδου Κρητὸς μάντεως χρησμός.[11]

The quotation list for Acts is, in all printed editions of the apparatus, furnished only with a single system, consecutively numbering all the quotations in order of appearance, corresponding to the first number set in the Pauline list.[12] There is, however, manuscript evidence for a second set of numbers corresponding to a similar system in the Pauline list. (See Appendix Two for full documentation.) In this list, the sources are not specified in further detail than the particular book, the Psalms being identified by number according to the LXX although, as in the corresponding system for the Pauline letters, treated as a single group in the source cumulation. There is a single double citation in the list for Acts, which is II at 1:20, Ψαλμοῦ ξη΄ καὶ ρη΄. Here the text of the quotation is two excerpts from the respective Psalms connected, in both Acts and the citation, by καί; by way of contrast, it may be noted that similar situations in the Pauline list, e.g., Romans XXXVIII and XXXIX at 12:19b-20 and Hebrews XX and XXI at 10:30,[13] are treated by separating the quotations into two distinct citations. There are instances in Acts of attribution to a Gospel (Matthew, Acts I at 1:5) and to non-canonical sources (Aratus the astronomer and Homer the poet, Acts XXVIII at 17:28, and the *Apostolic Constitutions*, Acts XXIX at 20:35).

Zacagni notes that numbers were missing from his manuscripts of the long quotation list for the Catholic epistles[14] but that he has supplemented this deficiency "juxta ordinem in epistolis D. Pauli observatum."[15] As the Pauline list, this one has three numbers, only two of which are supported by any manuscript evidence. Since an examination of a microfilm copy of the manuscript (181) in which Zacagni found this piece turned up no clear numeration system at this point other than identification of particular Psalms, it would appear that the entire numeration of the longer list in the Catholic epistles was the contribution of Zacagni. Moreover, although the first numeration, which cites

---

11 In the short list, cited as Ἐπιμενίδου Κρητὸς, καὶ μάντεως χρησμὸς, καὶ Καλλιμάχου Κυρηναίου ποιητοῦ ἡ αὐτή. In Supplement 1 (Z 546; M 724B), it is cited as Ἐπιμενίδου μάντεως χρησμός.
12 Z 415 ff.; M 640B-645A.
13 There is something more in the way of distinction in the text between the two parts in each set in the Pauline material so that this difference should not be pressed.
14 Z 482 ff.; M 672C-676B.
15 Z 482, n. 1; M 671 f., n. 30.

the quotations in order of appearance and begins anew with each epistle, is analogous to the Pauline model, the second system, which provides a running total of the citations from a particular source, *also* begins anew with each epistle rather than cumulating through the seven epistles. Thus, 1 Peter I and VII are Lev. α′ and Exod. α′, respectively, although each of these sources was cited previously in James (I and II). However, a close examination of the manuscripts suggests that Zacagni has departed not only from the Pauline model he professes to follow and the προ-γράμματα but also from any manuscript evidence.[16] Thus, in 1 Peter, I is Lev. β′; VII is Exod. β′; XIII and XIV are Prov. β′ and γ′, following James IV, which is Prov. α′; 2 Peter III is Prov. δ′, instead of Prov. α′ as in Zacagni's representation.

In the Catholic epistles, there are no instances of double citations; however, Matthew and John are each cited (Matthew twice: 2 Peter I at 1:18 and II at 2:20; and John, 1 John I, at 1:5). There are also citations of apocryphal sources, namely the Apocryphon of Moses (Jude I at 9) and the Apocryphon of Enoch (Jude II at 14).

The shorter type of list appears to complement the longer one. In all three lists of this type, the general pattern is to list the source, then to give the total times the source is cited, followed by the numbers of the citations corresponding to their order of appearance. The list for the Pauline epistles is initially broken down into the fourteen letters.[17] For example, Romans appears as follows:

Ἐν τῇ πρὸς Ῥωμαίους ἐπιστολῇ μη′. Γενέσεως ϛ′: ϛ′, η′, ϑ′, ια′, ιβ′, ιγ′. Ἐξόδου γ′: ιε′, ιϛ′, μ′. Λευιτικοῦ α′: μα′. Δευτερονομίου ε′: κβ′, κγ′, κη′, λη′, με′. Βασιλειῶν δευτέρας, καὶ Ψαλμοῦ ιζ′, ἡ αὐτὴ α′: μδ′. Βασιλειῶν τρίτης β′: λα′, λβ′. Ψαλμοῦ ιγ′ καὶ νβ′, ἡ αὐτὴ α′: δ′. Ψαλμοῦ ιη′ α′: κζ′. Ψαλμοῦ λα′ α′: ζ′. Ψαλμοῦ μγ′ α′: ι′. Ψαλμοῦ ν′ α′: γ′. Ψαλμοῦ ξη′ β′: λδ′, μγ′. Ψαλμοῦ ριϛ′ α′: μϛ′. Παροιμιῶν Σολομῶντος β′: λζ′, λϑ′. Ὡσηὲ Προφήτου α′: ιζ′. Ἰωὴλ Προφήτου α′; κδ′. Ναοὺμ Προφήτου, καὶ Ἡσαΐου α′; κε′. Ἀμβακοὺμ Προφήτου α′: α′. Μαλαχίου Προφήτου α′: ιδ′. Ἡσαΐου Προφήτου ιδ′: β′, ε′, ιη′, ιϑ′, κ′, κϛ′, κϑ′, λ′, λγ′, λε′, λϛ′, μβ′, μζ′, μη′. Ἰεζεκιὴλ Προφήτου, καὶ Δευτερονομίου ἡ αὐτὴ μία: κα′.[18]

For each letter, the sources are listed according to the order in the LXX. The Psalms are individually considered as separate sources. The double citations in this list are apparently considered as separate items, for the

16 Our major witness for this is 1845 (Vat. Gr. 1971) supported, with some lacunae, by 1846 (Vat. Gr. 2099).

17 Z 542 ff.; M 720C-724A.

18 Z 542 f.; M 720C-721A.

section on Hebrews omits XII from the general citations from Deuteronomy and enters it as a separate item at the end of the list. The evidence for the other four double citations is ambiguous, inasmuch as in
no other letter is the first named of the two sources cited separately, i.e.,
in Romans, II Kings, Psalm 13, Nahum, and Ezekiel only occur once
each, although there are other citations of Deuteronomy and Isaiah.
The citations from Matthew and the non-canonical sources come at
the end of the letters in which they occur.

In the shorter list for Acts,[19] the characteristics of the form are the
same except that the Psalms are considered as a single unit, a pattern
that we have noted in the longer list for both the Pauline epistles and
Acts. The citation from Matthew comes at the end of the list, followed
by the non-canonical citations. The double quotations are apparently
taken together in the listing of Psalms, although since they are both
Psalms, this is not conclusive.

In the shorter list for the Catholic epistles, the pattern we found in
the shorter Pauline list is repeated, except that, as in the case of Acts, the
Psalms are considered as a single body, rather than individually. It will be
recalled that there were no double citations in the Catholic epistles.

What we have here presented is an idealized picture of the forms in
which these six lists, three pairs of two types, appear. In succeeding
paragraphs we are going to discuss a number of discrepancies in this idealized form, but for the moment, let us note the contrasts that, even in
conception, these various lists present. Now, it must be observed that it
is a presumption that the lists ought to be co-ordinate, either the short
and the long lists for the same section, e.g., the Pauline epistles, or between the long lists for analogous sections, e.g., the Pauline and Catholic epistles. We think that this is a warranted presumption, resting on
the initial premise that the same person is responsible for all of them
and the observation that the paragraphs describing the numbering systems used are virtually identical for the same type and that there are parallels in the language of both types.[20]

---

19 Z 414 f.; M 640Af.

20 The προγράμματα for the short tables of the Pauline and Catholic epistles are
identical except for obvious changes. e.g., τοῦ τεύχους τῶν καθολικῶν instead
of τοῦ ἀποστολικοῦ τεύχους. The short πρόγραμμα for Acts is very similar to
those of the other two, omitting material appropriate to collections of letters
and some more significant revisions. The προγράμματα for the long Pauline
and Catholic epistle lists are identical with the same sorts of exceptions noted
above. There is none for Acts.

We first ask whether the Pauline lists, taken separately, are internally consistent. In the case of the long list, the answer is affirmative; in the case of the short list, there is a small discrepancy, which becomes a little larger upon comparison with the long list. The citation Hebrews XII[21] at 3:7b-11 is a double one, which we have examined earlier,[22] attributed to Deuteronomy and Psalm 94. This citation appears at the end of the list of sources of quotations in Hebrews; in all the other instances of double-shared quotations, the citation is listed in the normal order of sources, according to the first of the two sources in the particular citation. When we examine more closely the citation as it appears in the long list, we find that the source is followed by the number ιγ΄, which in this instance means that it is taken, in the long list, to be the thirteenth citation of Deuteronomy. This is the way that the other double citations are treated in the long list of the Pauline material, i. e., as forming part of the count of citations from the first listed of the two sources. This discrepancy holds between the lists, as we noted earlier, in that the short list shows six citations in Hebrews for Deuteronomy, excluding the one under consideration; the total number of citations for Deuteronomy in the short list is eighteen, while the last citation of Deuteronomy in the Pauline letters is 1 Timothy I at 5:18, which is, in the cumulative numbering of source citations, nineteen.[23]

We have, then, two points at which the pattern of the short list in the Pauline material diverges from the complementary long list in the Pauline material and, for that matter, from all of the other lists, so far as a control is available: The Psalms are treated individually as separate

---

21 Z 545; M 721D and Z 564; M 741A.
22 Page 31 of this monograph.
23 Z 567; M 744C. There is another problem in Hebrews, involving the citation of quotation XIV (Z 564; M 741A). According to the entry in the long quotation list, the citation is the twenty-second from Psalms, being Psalm 109. The citation is quoted as follows: "Ὤμοσε Κύριος, καὶ οὐ μεταμεληθήσεται, σὺ ἱερεὺς εἰς τὸν αἰῶνα κατὰ τὴν τάξιν Μελχισεδέκ." This citation is located by Zacagni, although not by Euthalius, who did not, of course, provide contemporary locations, at 5:6. Zacagni was doubtless pressed to this location because XIII is located at 4:4 and XV at 6:14. A close examination of the text shows that the more appropriate location of the full citation is 7:21, reading the longer of the two variants shown in the Nestle text (cf. 7:17). This quandary is not so likely to show up to one framing the quotation tables; hence it is no surprise that there were no significant variants in this respect in the tables themselves. In the text, in those manuscripts in which the citations are noted in the margin, confusion is more probable, and there are several different patterns.

sources for quotations, and those instances where two sources are cited for the same quotation are not counted as part of the cumulative totals for either of the sources involved.

Once the numeration system provided by Zacagni has been rectified, the quotation lists for the Catholic epistles do not have any internal contradictions, and both sets are compatible with the idealized forms of the other lists, except as noted earlier.

The sections on Acts are more problematic, both in terms of printing or transcription errors and in terms of contradictions that occur in the manuscript tradition. We have divided the discussion of these problems between simple errors of attribution and more complex disagreements between and within the two lists.

The errors of attribution are at least easier to describe. VII at 3:22 f. is ascribed by Euthalius to Exodus.[24] An apparently more nearly accurate source, as noted by Zacagni,[25] is Deut. 18:15; the marginal notations in the Nestle edition indicate material is also taken from other parts of Deuteronomy as well as Leviticus. Shortly, we will consider additional evidence related to this ascription and the implications for more serious problems in the quotation lists. The next is XVIII at 7:49 f. Euthalius locates this in Haggai, whereas the more appropriate citation is Isa. 66:1 f.[26] In both places, Zacagni observes that the mis-citation of source is repeated in the margin of the text of the manuscript witnesses. Moreover, both the short and the long quotation lists are in agreement on the incorrect sources. XX at 13:22 is attributed to 1 Kings (1 Samuel in the MT). Zacagni prefers Ps. 88:21 (not 87:21) as a more nearly accurate location of the text.[27]

The relationship between the internal and mutual discrepancies in the two lists is very confused. There seem to have been several variables in the tradition, and the present manuscript witness is not at all clear. First of all, the heading for the short list, together with the concluding summary statements of both lists, states that there are thirty-one quota-

---

24 Z 417; M 641A.

25 Z 417, n. 1; M 641, n. 78.

26 Z 419, n. 1; M 643 f., n. 85. N.A.Dahl has suggested a possible explanation for the otherwise unintelligible attribution to Haggai. The original work was done from a marginally annotated text. The accurate ascription to ΗΣΑΙΟΥ had become worn to the point that only ΑΙΟΥ was legible, which the scribe mistook for the final letters of ΑΓΓΑΙΟΥ.

27 Z 419, n. 2; M 643 f., n. 86. Misprints in Zacagni's edition read 13:23 and Ps. 87:21.

tions in Acts; the manuscript tradition that we have been able to examine is strong in supporting this. A cursory glance at the lists in Zacagni's edition gives no evidence of any inconsistency, inasmuch as the last quotation in the long list, from Isaiah, is XXXI, and the fourth and last citation from Isaiah in the short list is XXXI. A closer examination, however, discloses that there is no XXIV in either list. Zacagni observes this and adds that where XXIV would be expected in the text of 181, the following notation is made: "Ψαλμοῦ ιε′ ββ′."[28] He explains that this quotation, at 13:3, falling between XXIII at 13:34 and XXV at 13:40 f., is part of Psalm 15. Inasmuch as this Psalm has been already cited at IV (2:25 ff.), he suggests that this notation may be taken to mean that this is the second time that the quotation comes from Psalm 15. Unfortunately, the same manuscript also offers in the margin of the text of Acts, at 2:31, this notation: "Ψαλμοῦ ιε′ β′." This is a duplicate of the notation appearing in the margin beside 2:25 ff., except that the latter has an additional number indicating that it is the fourth quotation in consecutive order in Acts. The β′ indicates that this is the second time that a quotation has come from the Psalms, not that this is the second time this particular Psalm is cited.

The problem is not clarified in the short list. Zacagni notes that there were some scribal errors and omissions in the manuscript, which he has corrected by emendation and addition.[29] Unfortunately, this has not helped very much. In the brief list as it stands in Zacagni's edition, there are two XVs and two XXVs. There is, of course, no XXIV. The two XXVs are probably due to a misprint, for there is no XXVI, and one of the XXVs, Isaiah, is XXVI in the long list.

In the short list, citation XV appears with both Exodus and Deuteronomy. In the long list, there was no citation from Deuteronomy, although we noted that Euthalius had attributed what appears likely to be a quotation from that book to Exodus. These are not, however, the same citations; the latter attribution occurs in citation VII at 3:22. XV is 7:40, where the quotation involved is correctly attributed to Exodus.[30] On the other hand, it may be observed that the first part of the apparently Deuteronomic quotation at 3:22 appears again at Acts 7:37, which would be the appropriate place for a citation numbered

---

28 Z 420, n. 1; M 644, n. 88. Migne has "corrected" the difficulty by providing consecutive numbering, concluding with XXX).
29 Z 414, n. 2; M 639, n. 75.
30 Exod. 32:1, not 30:1, as Z 418, which is corrected in M 642D.

XV, correctly attributed to Deuteronomy, were it not for the fact that XV is correctly attributed to Exodus at 7:40. Zacagni felt that possibly Euthalius had seen Deuteronomy listed in a register of the books cited in Acts.[31]

There are a number of facts and probabilities with which we need to deal. First, the tradition of thirty-one quotations in Acts seems rather firm. Many manuscripts that do not follow 181 in omitting XXIV, but rather adjust the consequent figures to conclude with a correct number of thirty to match the actual number of quotations, nevertheless claim thirty-one at the head or conclusion of the lists. At least two manuscripts resolve the problem in a different fashion. 917 and 1874 divide what Zacagni cites as XXV (13:40 f.) into two parts: 13:40 is numbered XXIV and 13:41, XXV. At least 1874 attributes both quotations to Habakkuk, although 13:40 is at best an echo of Matt. 13:14. In both cases this adjustment is made in the long list; in the short list, both show only XXIV for Habakkuk.

Second, no manuscript that we have examined attributes citation VII to Deuteronomy rather than Exodus. Third, there is a group of manuscripts that omit Deuteronomy from the short list, have thirty correctly numbered citations, and claim only thirty quotations in the headings or conclusions.[32]

This intriguing enigma would doubtless have remained had not Nils A. Dahl made the remarkable observation that there is some evidence that 3:22 f. did, in fact, appear in Exodus.[33] This is witnessed by the Samaritan text[34] and, indirectly, by 4Q *Testimonies* following Exod. 20:21b.[35] Dahl proposes a tentative reconstruction of the circumstances

---

31 Z 414, n. 3; M 639 f., n. 76.
32 (88) 919 1244 1845.
33 Private discussion, 31 October 1969. The process of collection and integration of the data necessary for this conclusion defies description.
34 Frederick Field, ed., *Prolegomena. Genesis-Esther* (vol. 1 of *Origenis Hexaplorum quae supersunt: Sive, veterum interpretum graecorum in totum Vetus Testamentum fragmenta;* 2 vols; Oxford: Clarendon Press, 1875), 116; and Alan England Brooke and Norman McLean, eds., *The Octateuch* (vol. 1 of *The Old Testament in Greek according to the Text of Codex Vaticanus;* 2 vols; Cambridge: Cambridge University Press, 1917), 221.
35 The text and translation are provided by John Marco Allegro ("Further Messianic References in Qumran Literature," *JBL* 75 [1956]: 182 f.). The observation that this citation is not, in the Qumran document, a collection of texts drawn from Deuteronomy but a single text from Exodus in the Samaritan re-

rendered intelligible by his observation. His hypothesis begins with the assumption that the pre-Euthalian identification of the quotations was a system of providing marginal notations of the source, possibly consecutively numbered. In this form, 3:22 f. was VII, "correctly" attributed to Exodus; XV was at 7:37, attributed to Deuteronomy; and XVI was at 7:40, attributed to Exodus. So far, this explains several difficulties, including the presence of Deuteronomy in source lists, the attribution of XV to it, and the total of thirty-one quotations.

Dahl then theorizes that the editor of the Euthalian archetype noticed the partial identity of VII and XV and proceeded to delete XV (cf. the treatment of Psalm 15 at 2:31 and 13:35, following a citation at 2:25). Leaving VII ascribed to Exodus, he re-numbered citations following the old XV so that Exod. 32:1 at 7:40 becomes XV; then Amos 5:25 ff. at 7:42b-43 becomes XVI and so forth. Dahl suggests that some of the remaining difficulties may be explained on the supposition that the revision was not completely carried out. The editor left off the re-numbering after changing XXIV to XXIII, leaving the remainder to a scribe. The scribe carelessly and mechanically based his work on the incomplete revision, hence the omission of XXIV. An alternative, which has the greater weight of manuscript evidence, is that the tradition that includes Zacagni's 181 is representative of a secondary attempt to reconcile a list of thirty quotations with a tradition of thirty-one quotations, an attempt similar to the splitting of XXV in 917 and 1874 into two quotations. It may have been that the appearance of the citation of Psalm 15 for the third (and second unnumbered) time following XXIII (at 13:35, following 13:34) provided some grounds for the break at that particular point. There is no evidence that a quotation is repeated in a single letter or book, although we know that several times the same quotation, or part of one, is cited again when it appears in another letter in the Pauline corpus.

We have noted numerous discrepancies among the several lists, and it is time to ask what significance these discrepancies may have. It ought to be noted that before the work of Robinson,[36] there was no critical discussion of these lists beyond the suggestions of Zacagni. Robinson observes, first of all, that there is a discrepancy, and he then argues, partly on the basis of this observation, that there is a matter of chronological

---

cension of the Pentateuch was first made by Patrick W. Skehan ("The Period of the Biblical Texts from Khirbet Qumran," *CBQ* 19 [1957]: 435).

36 Robinson, *Euthaliana*.

priority involved. Robinson feels that the problem of the missing XXIV in Acts suggests a priority for the longer of the two lists;[37] we shall consider this more fully below.

The fixity of most of these discrepancies in the manuscript tradition means that the ascription to errors in transmission is not a long range solution. Moreover, the problems that we have just reviewed, namely, the omission of XXIV from the long list in Acts, the appearance of Deuteronomy as a source in the short list of Acts, and the manner in which the Psalms are listed in the short list in the Pauline letters, suggest to us that it is difficult to understand these lists as the creation of a single individual, or as the product of a consistent framework. Some have argued that, even in their idealized form and free of inconsistency, one type of list is self-evidently intended as a substitute for the other.[38]

The existence of manuscripts showing a quotation system in the long list and in the margin of the text of Acts, unknown to Zacagni and others, bringing this list into conformity with the other two, together with the fact that no πρόγραμμα for this system in Acts has turned up, is positive evidence of a tendency to elaborate; no one would argue that this hitherto unknown system was part of an earlier tradition that faded. Thus the question of strata within the form of lists is a legitimate one to raise.

An initial question may be addressed to the text of the prologues, whether statements in them can be interpreted as describing one or the other of the lists exclusively. The answer is negative or at best equivocal, evidenced by the fact that at one time or another critics have claimed with equal vigor that the witness of the prologues vindicates the claim of priority of each type of list.[39]

The manuscript evidence is also unhelpful. There is no clear evidence, in the manuscripts that we were able to examine, that points to the priority of one or the other of the two types. No manuscript contains positive evidence of the longer Pauline list without the shorter, except in a few instances where the quotation list is distributed among the individual letters; no manuscript contains positive evidence, i. e., with-

---

37 *Ibid.*, 17 f.
38 Turner, "Patristic Commentaries," 526. Cf. Robinson (*Euthaliana*, 17) who uses this argument to declare the short list secondary and von Soden (*Schriften des Neuen Testaments*, 662) who argues the opposite.
39 Robinson (*Euthaliana*, 18) for the long list and Zuntz (*Ancestry*, 85, n.1) for the short list.

out lacunae, of the short list without the longer in the Pauline letters. Only three manuscripts in the Catholic epistles, 82 915 2484, offer any evidence of one list and not the other, and in these manuscripts, the quotations are distributed among the individual letters. For Acts, there is a group of manuscripts that share some characteristics, including the presentation of the long quotation list without the short one: 82 378 (436) 462 603 635 1828 1891 2484. Most of these manuscripts give the quotations only in an abbreviated form, and it is not clear that they represent an early form as opposed to a later deterioration.

Robinson's first move is to eliminate, on the basis of the longer list in Acts, the double numeration system in the two epistolary sets and the προγράμματα that go with them.[40] He supports this move by reference to the system of identifying the quotations in the margin of Codex H[Paul] (015), which consists only of the consecutive numbering within epistles and the source. Robinson feels that it is more reasonable to suppose that the double numeration system is a later elaboration of the type found in 015 than that 015 gives an incomplete form. In speaking of the quotations in the long list, Robinson states, "To each is prefixed a number, which will be found later on in the margin of the text itself."[41] He does not explain how, without a πρόγραμμα, anyone is to know this, nor does he consider how to reconcile the fact that 015 is both incomplete in its marginal citations and, at the same time, possessed of marginal source citations, an elaboration not promised even by the πρόγραμμα.[42]

Robinson also notes that the heading for the short list for Acts contains the phrase, πράξεις τῶν ἀποστόλων.[43] He has previously[44] shown that the phrase is not one that Euthalius uses in the prologue to Acts. Von Dobschütz notes further that the only two occasions when this particular phrase is used in the prologue to the Pauline epistles are both dependent upon Eusebius.[45] In this same line, Robinson argues that the

---

40   Robinson, *Euthaliana*, 18 ff.
41   *Ibid.*, 18.
42   015 also has stichometrical notations that Robinson considers secondary additions (*ibid.*, 17).
43   *Ibid.*
44   *Ibid.*, 16.
45   Ernst von Dobschütz, "A Hitherto Unpublished Prologue to the Acts of the Apostles (probably by Theodore of Mopsuestia)," *AJT* 2 (1898): 385, n. 35, referring to *Hist. eccl.* 2.22.1 and 6. Von Dobschütz further observes that in Alex-

subscription to the short list in Acts runs, "Ὁμοῦ μαρτυρίαι λα΄." He contrasts this with what he takes to be the Euthalian cast of the subscription of the long list, "Ἅπᾶσαι αἱ μαρτυρίαι τῶν Πράξεων λα΄."[46]

Finally, in addition to the subjective claims that are made by both sides, Robinson urges that the inconsistencies between the two lists in Acts favor the priority of the longer list.[47] The result of his critical labors is a long list for all three sections, with a single numeration scheme, no προγράμματα, and no short lists. These latter aspects of the present apparatus are later elaborations, together with the supplementary paragraphs at the conclusion of some of the lists. There is, however, evidence that suggests the priority of the short list. Von Soden thinks that the long list has no worth beside the first, inasmuch as it merely cites the New Testament text rather than that of the source.[48] Although he feels that this is an argument against the priority of the long list, one is almost inclined, by accepting the the force of this argument, to see just the opposite demonstrated. Von Soden also thinks that the προγράμματα of the longer lists are clearly predicated upon those of the first, although they do not make reference to them.[49] Zuntz, on the other hand, while he favors von Soden's general evaluation of the two lists, feels that the short προγράμματα may be rather an extract of the long, which he takes to be in the Euthalian vein and stylistically superior to the short.[50] Another argument of von Soden, "Dazu kommt, dass das Buch der kleinen Propheten in ersten Verzeichnis vor, in diesem zweiten nach der grossen Propheten aufgezählt wird,"[51] does not appear to us to reflect accurately the facts; the long quotation list is not set out in such a fashion as to show the order of the prophets or to permit an inference thereto.[52]

---

andria both πράξεις and πράξεις τῶν ἀποστόλων were both known, but in Antioch, only the latter.

46 Robinson, *Euthaliana*, 17. Note, however, that Zacagni (Z 568, n. 1; M 745, n. 2) reports that one of his manuscripts reads the "non-Euthalian" phraseology at this point in the Pauline list.

47 Robinson, *Euthaliana*, 18.

48 Soden, *Schriften des Neuen Testaments*, 662.

49 *Ibid.*, 661 f.

50 Zuntz, *Ancestry*, 85, n. 1.

51 Soden, *Schriften des Neuen Testaments*, 662.

52 We find only in the short quotation list of Acts (Z 415; M 640Af.) is there any variation from the order we have described; the exception to which von Soden refers must be in the supplementary list attached to the long quotation list (Z

The observation least susceptible to subjective interpretation was made by H. H. Oliver,[53] who notes that in the long quotation list for the Catholic epistles, at the point that the list deals with 2 and 3 John, the text states that there are no citations in these letters, "ὡς ἤδη εἴρηται."[54] Unfortunately, this reading was not controlled in the survey of the manuscripts, so there is no way of knowing whether there might be evidence that this is no more than a late scribal interpolation. In its present form, it is the clearest evidence we have for the priority of the short lists.

Another observation of von Soden, also of uncertain strength, is that the manuscripts with the long quotation lists are regularly associated with a variant in the *Martyrium*, another part of the apparatus, which von Soden, with more justification, argues is later.[55] We have seen, however, that there is a close connection between both types of lists in the manuscript tradition so that one can scarcely speak of a localized variation that does not include both lists.

We have already noted a number of instances that suggest that there was a certain amount of fluidity in the tradition, e. g., the appearance of Deuteronomy in the short list of Acts, the variation in the designation of XIV in Hebrews in the text, and the activity of 917 and 1874 in dealing with the missing XXIV in the long list of Acts. We feel that this activity is partly the result of attempts to reconcile points at which materials supposedly complementary diverge.

There is another piece of evidence whose existence is more or less of a problem depending upon the date claimed for the original formulation of these lists.[56] We have purposely excluded consideration of this subject from these chapters, inasmuch as in the secondary literature, it appeared that notions of dating often predetermined considerations of authenticity. We have previously noted that the prologues and headings of the quotations refer to these citations as θεῖαι μαρτυρίαι; we have also

---

568 f.; M 745A-C), but no evidence is advanced that necessarily connects this supplement to the long list.

53   Oliver, "'Helps for Readers' in Greek New Testament Manuscripts" (unpublished Th.M. thesis, Princeton Theological Seminary, 1955), 140, cited by permission of the author.

54   Z 485; M 676A.

55   Soden, *Schriften des Neuen Testaments*, 663. See the discussion of the "Egyptian" elaboration on page 66 of this monograph.

56   Rendel Harris (*Stichometry*, 83) says that the difficulty Zahn takes up below arises only from a wrong chronological idea about Euthalius.

noted that included among these citations are ones from several apocryphal books as well as some pagan writings. Zahn and Oliver have both
observed that the inclusion of such materials in a listing so titled is puz-
zling. Oliver feels, "From such a diverse listing it can be inferred that the
term, 'Divine Citations,' had come to have simply a conventionalized
meaning."[57] Zahn, on the other hand, would doubt that this phrase
could have had such a "conventionalized meaning" to Euthalius and
suggests that such citations must have come into the apparatus later.[58]
There is a little more than a difference of opinion on Zahn's side.
Zahn notes that citation XXVIII in Acts is attributed to the *Apostolic
Constitutions*.[59] Zacagni supposed that this citation was to be referred
to 4.3.[60] This line of the *Apostolic Constitutions* does not occur in the *Didascalia,* which, according to critical consensus,[61] means that the *Constitutions* could not have been cited as the source of this part of Acts before
the last quarter of the fourth century. Moreover, Zahn continues, the
very short abbreviation used by the Euthalian apparatus, "ἐκ τῶν δια-
τάξεων," presupposes a distribution and fame not possible before the
fifth century.[62]

To these observations and inferences, we may only add that there is
no positive evidence in the manuscripts that we were able to examine
that any of the lists or marginal citations was ever transmitted omitting
the citation from the *Apostolic Constitutions* or from any of the non-canonical sources.

Is there any theory of development that is able to render intelligible
the variations in these lists? There is, it seems to us, evidence of different
strata in these lists, but the development is more complex than merely
first the short lists and then the long lists. What follows is a preliminary
lining out of some of the possibilities.

---

57   Oliver, "Helps," 134.
58   Zahn, "Neues und Altes," 388, n. 1. Cf. *Didascalia et Constitutiones Apostolorum,*
     ed. by Franz Xaver von Funk (2 vols. in 1; Paderborn: F. Schoeningh, 1905):
     16.
59   Zahn, "Euthaliana," 601; "Neues und Altes," 388, n. 1; and "Der Exeget Am-
     monius und andere Ammonii," *ZKG* 38 (1920): 320.
60   Z 420. n. 2; M 644, n. 89.
61   Berthold Altaner, *Patrology* (trans. from the 5th German ed. by Hilda C. Graef;
     New York: Herder and Herder, 1960), 59; and E. Schwartz, "Unzeitgemässe
     Beobachtungen zu den Clementinen," *ZNW* 31 (1932): 178.
62   Zahn, "Euthaliana," 601.

First of all, we believe that it is clear that the long lists must have been supplied with the source cumulations secondarily. The fact that we have evidence of the list of Acts still in the earlier pattern and the fact that the source cumulations for the Pauline letters contradict the short list source cumulations are sufficient indications of this. Second, we think that it is not likely that either list was constructed directly on the basis of the other, particularly the short upon the long. Third, we think that the tradition of thirty-one quotations in Acts is early and firm. Fourth, we think that the balance of probability is that the short list in some form preceded the long list in any form.

The following order of development is one way of accounting for the divergencies. The first list constructed was a short list showing only the sources and the total number of quotations for each source; this would have been like a supplementary list that follows the short list in the Pauline letters.[63] This list would have shown Deuteronomy as one of the sources, with a single quotation. This list would not have counted the second and third (2:31; 13:35) instances of Psalm 15. The total of quotations thus cited would have been thirty-one. We can offer no logical explanation for the divergence between the treatment of Psalms in the Pauline letters and the other two parts; it may be suggested that the other two followed, together, the work on the Pauline material, and that the compiler might have found the Pauline system more elaborate than necessary or desirable for analysis of Acts and the Catholic epistles.

The long lists were constructed independently of any short list. We presume that there never was a citation in the long list of Acts for the vacant XXIV of Zacagni's list, as though a citation had dropped out, the line taken by Zacagni. Either the "omission" was the result of an incomplete scribal editing from the beginning or it was the result of a later attempt at a reconciliation. This first list may have had consecutive numbers.

We believe that the discrepancies in the present lists may be the result of attempts to reconcile the two forms of lists. The uniform fashion of considering Psalms as a single corpus in the source cumulations of all three sections of the long lists points to a single concept; the unique form of the Pauline short list, which we know preceded the other two, suggests that this form was prior to the one used in the long lists. We suspect that confrontation with a well established tradition of

---

63   Z 545 f.; M 724Af.

thirty-one quotations in Acts may have produced the different expansions to accommodate this number to the long list. The confusion with Deuteronomy in the short list for Acts would result when the integrator attempted to locate this citation in the long list. There are manuscripts that retain the claim of thirty-one quotations and include Deuteronomy but only show a consecutive numbering through XXX, giving both Deuteronomy and Isaiah XV (181 917 1162 1874 1875). There is another group that claims, in the super- or subscriptions, only thirty quotations. This group revises the last numbers shown in the list by Zacagni so that there is a uniform progression from XXIV to XXX; this group also omits any mention of Deuteronomy (919 1845). 88 and 1244 fall in this pattern except that they omit consecutive numbers. Unfortunately, the numbers shown in these lists, particularly the short list, are generally even more confused in the manuscripts than they are in Zacagni's emended list.

4. Chapter Lists

Each of the Pauline and Catholic letters, as well as Acts, comes equipped with a systematic summary of the contents in the form of chapter headings. In the prologues, there is no elaboration of the purpose of these expositions, although in the prologue to the Pauline epistles, Euthalius refers to a predecessor as the source of at least those summaries: "τὴν τῶν κεφαλαίων ἔκθεσιν, ἑνὶ τῶν σοφωτάτων τινί, καὶ φιλοχρίστῳ πατέρων ἡμῶν πεπονημένην."[1] In the prologue to the Catholic epistles, the chapters are mentioned only briefly, and there is no such note at all in the prologue to Acts. In a prefatory note to the actual list of Acts, a different relationship to the past is indicated: "Ἐκ Πατέρων ἡμεῖς καὶ διδασκάλων τὸν τρόπον, καὶ τὸν τύπον ὠφελήμενοι, ἐγχειροῦμεν μετρίως τῇδε τῶν κεφαλαίων ἐκθέσει."[2] Although it appears that Euthalius wishes to credit a predecessor with the substantive work on the Pauline chapter list and to suggest that he himself has done this work for at least the chapters of Acts, merely following the pattern that he found for the Pauline material, there is evidence that will be reviewed later that suggests that the same person was responsible for all three lists.

The ἔκθεσις of the third chapter of Romans, for example, is as follows: "Περὶ ὑπεροχῆς Ἰσραὴλ τοῦ τυγχάνοντος τῆς ἐπαγγελίας."[3] This pattern is characteristic of most of these headings, that is, brief phrases beginning with περί or mere fragments.

The chapters that are thus described are not those of modern Bibles but follow a different system. These lists occur most frequently, in the manuscripts, at the beginning of each letter; there are, however, a number of variations, in which the lists are collected all together at, the beginning of the corpus – Pauline, Catholic, Acts – or spread throughout a manuscript, in the upper and/or lower margins of the text.

Sometimes, these chapter lists are supplied with a further breakdown of the contents of particular chapters in the form of ὑποδιαιρέσεις. For example, the first chapter of 1 Corinthians, which has the general state-

---

1   Z 528; M 708A.
2   Z 428; M 652B.
3   Z 574; M 749D.

ment, "Μετὰ τὸ προοίμιον, Περὶ τοῦ μὴ διχονοεῖν πρὸς ἀλλήλους ἐκ φιλοδοξίας τῆς ἐπὶ σοφίᾳ ἀνθρωπίνῃ,"[4] has the following sub-statements:

1. Ἐν ᾧ περὶ θείας σοφίας.
2. Περὶ λειτουργιῶν.
3. Περὶ τοῦ μὴ κρίνειν διδασκάλους.
4. Περὶ τοῦ μὴ ἐπαίρεσθαι.

There is evidence that these subdivisions were sometimes transmitted as a part of the chapter summary instead of being separated.

Each chapter list is ordinarily preceded by a brief title or heading. The heading for Romans is as follows: "Ἔκθεσις κεφαλαίων καθολικῶν καθ᾽ ἑκάστην ἐπιστολὴν τοῦ Ἀποστόλου, ἐχόντων τινῶν καὶ μερικὰς ὑποδιαιρέσεις τὰς διὰ τοῦ κινναβάρεως. κεφαλαία τῆς πρὸς Ῥωμαίους ἐπιστολῆς Παύλου ιθ᾽."[5] By way of contrast, here are the headings for 1 Corinthians and Ephesians:

> Ἔκθεσις κεφαλαίων καθολικῶν τῆς πρὸς Κορινθίους α᾽ ἐπιστολῆς τοῦ Ἀποστόλου, ἐχόντων τίνων καὶ μερικὰς ὑποδιαιρέσεις, τὰς διὰ τοῦ κινναβάρεως. κεφαλαία τῆς πρὸς Κορινθίους α᾽ ἐπιστολῆς Παύλου θ᾽.[6]

> Ἔκθεσις κεφαλαίων τῆς πρὸς Ἐφεσίους ἐπιστολῆς Παύλου. οὔκ ἔχει ἡ πρὸς Ἐφεσίους ἐπιστολὴ ὑποδιαίρεσιν κεφαλαίων, διὰ τοῦτο οὐδὲ ἔχει διὰ κινναβάρεως ἀριθμὸν γεγραμμένον.[7]

There are a number of items in these headings to which we may call attention. First, there is a peculiar redundancy in the phraseology of the headings. Commentators have noted this before, and their observations will be reviewed in detail later. Here we may note that while the heading for Romans holds together logically, the one for 1 Corinthians appears to be an attempt to maintain the form of the heading for Romans, modifying it only so far as necessary to make it fit the context, hence the insertion of τῆς πρὸς Κορινθίους for καθ᾽ ἑκάστην ἐπιστολήν. This particular form of the heading continues only through Galatians, and it is not picked up in the Catholic epistles or in Acts.

---

4   Z 591 f.; M 753D.
5   Z 573; M 749C.
6   Z 591; M 753C.
7   Z 635; M 764A.

Next, the headings carry the information that the subdivisions, in those lists having them, are marked in red. Those without have an appropriate, corresponding note, as for example in Ephesians.[8] There has been some discussion concerning the origin of the method of marking the subdivisions, and this literature will be reviewed later.

For Acts, many manuscripts, in addition to the list that we have described, contain another, having thirty-six chapters. Zacagni's manuscripts made the following transition: "Καὶ οὗτοι οἱ ἀριθμοί, οὓς εὑρήσεις κειμένους ἐν τῷ τεύχει κατὰ τὸ ὕφος τῆς ἀναγνώσεως μετὰ μ΄ κεφάλαια, καὶ λ΄ μαρτυρίας· εἰσὶν δὲ οἱ πάντες λς΄."[9] The first of these, "Τὸν μὲν πρῶτον λόγον ἐποιησάμην περὶ πάντων, ὦ Θεόφιλε," which is the pattern followed by the others, indicates that this list does not provide summaries; rather, we are given the first words at the beginning of each chapter in the list. This is a pattern that is reflected in another part of the Euthalian apparatus for Acts, the "lection" list, but in no other section either in Acts or in the other parts of the New Testament covered by this material. There has been some critical discussion of the relationship of the thirty-six chapter list to the longer list as well as the possible relationship of both lists, including those for the letters, to other lists of chapters that are known to have been developed for the New Testament. This discussion is reviewed following the descriptive section.

The chapter lists of Acts are preceded by an introductory paragraph, which is more substantial than the headings of the lists of the letters:

---

8   The following table shows the number of chapters and subdivisions accorded each letter or book:

Romans	19 / 6	Hebrews	22 / 8	James	6 / 9
1 Corinthians	9 / 16	1 Timothy	18 / 2	1 Peter	8 / 5
2 Corinthians	11 / 4*	2 Timothy	9	2 Peter	4 / 1
Galatians	12	Titus	6	1 John	7 / 8
Ephesians	10	Philemon	2	2 John	2 / 1*
Philippians	7		———	3 John	3 / 1*
Colossians	10 / 1		148 / 40	Jude	4 / 1
1 Thessalonians	7				———
2 Thessalonians	6 / 3	Acts	40 / 47		34 / 26

*See the discussion of these numbers on pages 23 f. of this monograph.

9   Z 438; M 661C. 181 reads εὑρησειμένους, which Zacagni conjectured (n. 1; M 661 f., n. 61) to be εὑρήσεις κειμένους, which is supported by manuscript evidence: 619 917 1103 1244 1845. Three other manuscripts, which have the thirty-six chapter list besides 181, are either fragmentary or not legible at this point: 1162 1874 1875.

Ἐκ Πατέρων ἡμεῖς καὶ διδασκάλων τὸν τρόπον, καὶ τὸν τύπον ὠφελήμενοι,
ἐγχειροῦμεν μετρίως τῇδε τῶν κεφαλαίων ἐκθέσει, αἰτοῦντες συγνώμην προπετείας, οἱ νέοι χρόνων τε, καὶ μαθημάτων παρ' ὑμῶν ἑκάστου τῶν ἀναγι-
νωσκόντων, εὐχῇ, τῇ ὑπὲρ ἡμῶν, τὴν συμπεριφορὰν κομιζόμενοι. ἐκτιθέμεθα
γοῦν αὐτὴν καθ' ἱστορίαν Λουκᾶ τοῦ Εὐαγγελιστοῦ, καὶ συγγραφέως, τοι-
γαροῦν διὰ μὲν τοῦ μέλανος αὐτοτελῆ τὰ κεφάλαια· διὰ δὲ τοῦ κινναβάρεως
τὰς ἐν μέρει τούτων ἐχομένας ὑποδιαιρέσεις ἐσημειωσάμεθα.[10]

So far as we have reviewed the literature, Robinson is the first to call
attention to the peculiar redundancy in the headings connected to the
chapter lists of the first few letters of the Pauline corpus.[11] He suggests
that the second and briefer of the two is probably the original. This sort
of reasoning is in keeping with a general principle that Robinson uses
often, namely, when there is a choice, always credit Euthalius with
the less elaborate form. Von Soden also recognizes that the general
form of the first of the two headings is unlikely to have been formulated
at the point that the chapter lists were fixed in their present form, that is,
before each of the letters.[12] He believes that the predecessor, to whom
Euthalius gave credit for the construction of the lists in the Pauline materials, was probably responsible. Almost half a century later, Zuntz has
been able to provide a general theory for the development of the Euthalian apparatus that, among other things, accounts for the double headings in a more precise fashion than the general suggestion of von
Soden. Zuntz holds that virtually all of the analytic pieces of the apparatus, including the chapter lists, were merely taken over by Euthalius
from an exemplar in the library at Caesarea;[13] Euthalius' contribution
at this point was only the distribution of the lists among the different
letters. Zuntz produces an array of evidence from ancient sources to
demonstrate that a common literary device was the construction of a
proemium, προέκθεσις. This gradually developed, he notes, into a
more formal table of contents, containing lists of chapters constructed
in a fashion exactly analogous to those in the Euthalian apparatus.
Such a table of contents prefaced the exemplar that Euthalius used,
and he has taken it over, including phraseology that is no longer
quite appropriate. Thus, continues Zuntz, the phrase in the introductory

10 Z 428; M 652B.
11 Robinson, *Euthaliana*, 20. He notes that the longer heading is missing from a
    printed edition of the Armenian version.
12 Soden, *Schriften des Neuen Testaments*, 664. Cf. also Turner, "Patristic Commen-
    taries," 527.
13 Zuntz, *Ancestry*, particularly 78–88.

lines before the Roman chapter, "καθ' ἑκάστην ἐπιστολήν," means "with reference to" not "prefixed to."[14]

We observed earlier in the discussion of the chapter lists that the first list in Acts, containing forty chapters and forty-eight subdivisions, is followed by a second list that has only thirty-six chapters and no subdivisions. A number of critics have observed that this second list of chapters is strikingly like the older of a double set of chapter numbers in Vaticanus.[15] Moreover, the later of these two sets in Vaticanus is repeated in Sinaiticus through Acts 15. Now no one is inclined to argue for an original connection between the thirty-six chapter list and the Euthalian apparatus. The note introducing it (cited on page 49 of this monograph) suggests that it was found in the margin of the text. Robinson observes that Zacagni found this list in only one of his manuscripts, and subsequent researches have not increased this number substantially.[16] Von Soden claims that the two systems of forty and thirty-six are not independent of each other, given the exact agreement of twenty-one of the chapter beginnings and the difference of only one or two verses in another six.[17] Although he is not willing to make a final decision regarding the priority of one or the other, he does feel that it is easier to understand the modification of the shorter to produce the longer.[18]

Robinson was, of course, more interested in analyzing the possible relationships between the list that he was willing to credit to Euthalius and the longer, although secondary, lists in Vaticanus and Sinaiticus. To follow the force of his arguments, it is necessary first to examine another thesis that he developed in regard to the way that the subdivisions were marked in the lists and in the text. We observed that included in the prefatory remarks at the head of some lists of chapters, there was a note as to the presence of subdivisions in the chapters that followed, including the remark that such subdivisions were marked in red. Those in

---

14 *Ibid.*, 82, citing (n. 2) von Dobschütz as having observed this earlier ("Euthaliusstudien," 149).
15 Gregory, *Textkritik*, 875 f.; Schmid, *Verschiedene Eintheilungen*, 19; Harris, *Stichometry*, 74; and Robinson, *Euthaliana*, 24 ff.
16 181 619 917 1103 1162 (1175?) 1244 (1248? von Soden) 1845 1874 (1875). In addition to these, the forty chapter list appears in almost seventy other manuscripts that we examined.
17 Soden, *Schriften des Neuen Testaments*, 442.
18 *Ibid.*, 443 f.

015 that are marked follow this pattern.[19] Robinson observes that there
are several variations on this system, and he believes that there is an earlier form discernable among them, which will also account for some of
the variations in the numeration of the chapters. There is one variation
in which all of the chapters, including those that Zacagni found described as subdivisions in his manuscripts, are consecutively numbered.[20]
There are four variations on a system, which has subdivisions, in which
the main chapters are numbered consecutively. In one of these, the subdivisions are marked by asterisks.[21] In a second, the subdivisions are
numbered with red and begin again with each letter, but the main chapter, in each case, is also numbered with the subdivisions.[22] The third is
like the second, except that the main chapter is not counted with the
subdivisions.[23] The fourth is like the third, except that the subdivisions
are numbered consecutively throughout the whole corpus rather than
beginning anew with each epistle.[24]

Robinson summarizes his conclusions as follows: "So remarkable a
variety in methods of numeration is perhaps most easily explained if we
regard the asterisks as the original marks of the subdivisions, and this
view is supported by the frequent dropping of subdivisions altogeth-
er."[25] Von Soden supplements this argument by claiming that Euthalius
was not, himself, likely to have been the innovator of the subdivisions;
otherwise, von Soden continues, he would not have been so objective
about their presence or absence in any particular letter, but would have
written something like, "I found no occasion in this letter to divide
some chapters into subdivisions."[26] Von Soden feels that Euthalius him-

---

19 Ehrhard, "Codex H," 393. The chapter list, however, for 1 Timothy does not
    subdivide chapters six and seven. Cf. Robinson, *Euthaliana*, 22.
20 Paris, B. N. Arm. 9 in Romans, cited by Robinson, *Euthaliana*, 24.
21 Described in Coisl. XXV, but not carried out; cited by Robinson, *ibid.*, 23.
    Cf., so Robinson, Cambridge Univ. Lib. Kk vi 4 and Ff i 30.
22 015, cited by Robinson, *Euthaliana*, 24.
23 That of Zacagni and, according to Robinson (*ibid.*) "in many Greek and Arme-
    nian MSS."
24 Cited by Robinson (*ibid.*): B.M. Add. 28,816 and Wake 12, except that in the
    latter, the color of the numerals is reversed.
25 *Ibid.* Cf. James Hardy Ropes, *The Text of Acts* (vol. 3 of *The Beginnings of Chris-
    tianity. Pt. 1. The Acts of the Apostles*, ed. Frederick John Foakes-Jackson and
    Kirsopp Lake; London: Macmillan, 1926), xlii.
26 Soden, *Schriften des Neuen Testaments*, 665.

self was responsible for the introduction of the red coloring into the system.[27]

In pulling together his reflections on the development of the different number systems, Robinson is attracted to the probability that the system of sixty-nine chapters came from a basic system like that represented in the chapter divisions of Euthalius. With a total of eighty-eight different "Euthalian" divisions from which to choose, it is clear that some may have been considered not sufficiently distinctive as to designate a separate chapter. Robinson constructed a chart that demonstrates the relationship between the forty chapters and the forty-eight subdivisions of Euthalius and the systems found in Vaticanus and Sinaiticus.[28] From this chart, he concludes that, of the main Euthalian chapters, twenty-eight are "exactly represented" in Sinaiticus or Vaticanus, five are "represented within a verse," and five are there "with further displacement."[29] Among the subdivisions, there are twenty represented in one or both of the two codices, three within a verse, and eight with further displacements.[30] Of the seventeen that were dropped, Robinson notes that six are cases where Zacagni's chapters had only one subdivision and six more were "dropped by carelessness in B.M. Add. 28,816, or were never intended to be given."[31] Robinson recognizes that a certain amount of coincidence must be attributed to natural breaks in the narrative of Acts.[32] He counters this by noting that another chapter system of Acts with fifty-three chapters has at least twenty-five that do not correspond within a verse of the Euthalian divisions. Moreover, he continues, there are a number of unlikely divisions that are shared by the Euthalian system and that of Vaticanus and Sinaiticus.[33] This view is supported by von Dobschütz who also argues that the subdivisions are not really secondary divisions of a chapter but are used to indicate a part of the main chapter that is of particular worth.[34]

Robinson urges, then, that the system found in the Euthalian chapter list of Acts is at the base of the system found in Vaticanus and Sinai-

---

27   *Ibid.*; cf. Zuntz, *Ancestry*, 83.
28   Robinson, *Euthaliana*, 39 f.
29   *Ibid.*, 41.
30   *Ibid.*
31   *Ibid.*
32   *Ibid.*, 42.
33   *Ibid.*, 7:11; 10:30; 12:18; 15:23; 22:12; 23:22. Cf. Ropes, *Text of Acts*, lii, citing von Soden (*Schriften des Neuen Testaments*, 444 ff.).
34   Dobschütz, "Euthaliusfrage," 55, n. 1.

ticus."[35] He further observes that fundamentally the same system occurs in Amiatinus and Fuldensis, which supply three divisions agreeing with Euthalius but lacking in Sinaiticus and Vaticanus.[36] He concludes, citing Hort,[37] that the differences in detail between Vaticanus and Sinaiticus are sufficient to show that the scribes followed different originals,[38] that the differences of both from the existing Latin arrangement are still greater, but that the differences are not so great in any case to allow doubt as to the identity of the ultimate origin. The divisions themselves, of course, are more ancient than the summaries, which, at least in the case of the Pauline letters, Euthalius clearly attributes to a predecessor.[39]

The identity of this predecessor, of course, has been a question that has exercised a great many minds. As we noted in the descriptive section, the surface implication of statements in the prologue to the Pauline letters and the prefatory paragraph to the chapter list for Acts is that Euthalius took over directly from his mentor the chapter listings for the Pauline material and that following this pattern, he constructed the lists for Acts and the Catholic epistles himself.[40] A closer examination of the texts before us, however, has convinced many that the real circumstances of these lists are not quite so self-evident.

First of all, Robinson observes that there are clear parallels in the vocabulary of all three lists.[41] Robinson thinks that the parallels are sufficiently clear to surmise, "Either . . . Euthalius must have based his later work most carefully upon the Pauline summaries, which he had previously borrowed, or . . . his indebtedness to his unnamed predecessor cannot have been so great as his modesty would lead us to suppose."[42] There is other evidence, however, which suggests that although the same person wrote these chapter lists, he was not Euthalius. Part of the force of this argument depends upon an estimate of the literary ability of Euthalius himself; there is some disagreement about this in the

---

35 So also Ropes, *Text of Acts*, xliii.
36 Robinson, *Euthaliana*, 43.
37 *Ibid.*, 42, giving the reference for Hort as *Introduction*, 266.
38 Cf. Ropes, *Text of Acts*, xliii.
39 Eugène Jacquier, *Le Texte du Nouveau Testament* (vol. 2 of *Le Nouveau Testament dans l'Eglise Chrétienne;* Paris: Victor Lecoffre, 1913), 52.
40 So Lardner, *Credibility*, 206 f.; Hug, *Writings*, 253 ff.; and Islinger, *Verdienste*, 10.
41 Robinson, *Euthaliana*, 25 f.
42 *Ibid.*, 26.

secondary literature, which we will review in a later chapter. Robinson, for example, is convinced of the literary excellence of Euthalius, and this influences his estimate of the alternatives.

One of the things that critics have noted is a superscription to the list of the forty chapters of Acts in some manuscripts[43] that attributes the list to Pamphilus. There are several ways in which this information has been reconciled with the apparent thrust of statements made by Euthalius. One option is that the phrase designating Pamphilus as the author of this material is a conjecture,[44] possibly based upon the colophon that connects the manuscript to the library at Caesarea. The other option is to deny this list or all of the chapter lists to Euthalius. Tregelles denies that Euthalius was responsible for any of the lists; others simply observe that he must have copied at least the material in Acts from Pamphilus.[45] Bousset suggests that with the list ascribed to Pamphilus, we may now interpret the statements by Euthalius in the prologue to Acts, "στοιχη-δόν τε συνθεὶς . . . ἀνακεφαλαίωσιν,"[46] in a manner that limits the claims of Euthalius merely to stichometric division of Acts.[47] Of the two alternatives that von Soden sees, he prefers the one that has Euthalius copying not only the list itself but also the introductory paragraph and the superscription.[48]

Zuntz is convinced that Euthalius borrowed all three lists. He notes, however, that there are literary parallels between the introductory paragraph and the prologue to Acts that compel the conclusion that the same

43 Zuntz (*Ancestry*, 87, n. 1) cites 307 453 610 1678, referring to von Soden (*Schriften des Neuen Testaments*, 683).
44 Robinson, *Euthaliana*, 22; cf. Gregory, *Textkritik*, 877.
45 Samuel Prideaux Tregelles, *An Introduction to the Textual Criticism of the New Testament* (vol. 4 of *An Introduction to the Critical Study and Knowledge of the Holy Scripture*; rev., corrected, and brought down to the present time by Thomas Hartwell Horne, Samuel Davidson, and Samuel Prideaux Tregelles; 10th ed.; London: Longman, Brown, Green, Longmans, & Roberts, 1856), 32. Also see Brooke Foss Westcott, *A General Survey of the History of the Canon in the New Testament during the First Four Centuries* (Cambridge: Macmillan, 1855), 451; and Jean Pierre Paulin Martin, *Introduction à la Critique textuelle du Nouveau Testament. Partie théorique* (Paris: Au Secrétariat de l'Institut Catholique, [n.d.]), 631.
46 Z 409 f.; M 633C.
47 Wilhelm Bousset, *Textkritische Studien zum Neuen Testament* (TUGAL 11.4; Leipzig: J. C. Hinrichs, 1894), 50.
48 Soden, *Schriften des Neuen Testaments*, 671.

author was responsible for both.[49] Later he notes that Euthalius' own abilities in the construction of summaries of letters, which we find demonstrated in the prologue to the Pauline epistles, "contrast poorly with the very adroit and pertinent summaries that he owed to the 'Christ-loving father.'"[50]

The evidence, in sum, argues that the same hand is responsible for all three sets of chapter lists. The clear attribution of the set in the Pauline letters, taken together with the demonstrated dependence of Euthalius upon predecessors in other areas as well, suggests that this hand was probably not that of Euthalius.

---

49 Zuntz, *Ancestry*, 79, n. 3.
50 *Ibid.*, 83.

Part Two: Minor Pieces

5. Martyrium Pauli

Immediately following the prologue to the Pauline epistles is a short piece titled Μαρτύριον Παύλου τοῦ Ἀποστόλου.[1] Because of chronological data that this piece contains, it has played an extremely significant role in the dating of the Euthalian material. We cite this piece with parallels to the prologue that were uncovered by Robinson.[2]

Prologue to Pauline Epistles	Μαρτύριον Παύλου τοῦ Ἀποστόλου
Z 522; M 700C–710A. Αὐτόθι οὖν ὁ μακάριος Παῦλος τὸν καλὸν ἀγῶνα ἀγωνισάμενος, ὡς φησὶν αὐτός, τῷ τῶν ἱερονίκων Χριστοῦ μαρτύρων στεφάνῳ κατεκοσμήθη. Ῥωμαῖοι δὲ περικαλλέσιν οἴκοις, καὶ βασιλείοις τούτου λείψανα καθείρξαντες ἐπέτειον αὐτῷ. μνήμης ἡμέραν πανηγυρίζουσι, τῇ πρὸ τριῶν καλανδῶν Ἰουλίων, πέμπτῃ Πανέμου μηνός, τούτου τὸ μαρτύριον ἑορτάζοντες.	Ἐπὶ Νέρωνος τοῦ Καίσαρος Ῥωμαίων ἐμαρτύρησεν αὐτόθι Παῦλος ὁ ἀπόστολος, ξίφει τὴν κεφαλὴν ἀποτμηθεὶς ἐν τῷ τριακοστῷ καὶ ἕκτῳ ἔτει τοῦ σωτηρίου πάθους, τὸν καλὸν ἀγῶνα ἀγωνισάμενος ἐν Ῥώμῃ, πέμπτῃ ἡμέρᾳ Πανέμου μηνός, ἥτις λέγοιτο ἂν παρὰ Ῥωμαίοις ἡ πρὸ τριῶν καλανδῶν Ἰουλίων, καθ' ἣν ἐτελειώθη ὁ ἅγιος ἀπόστολος τῷ κατ' αὐτὸν μαρτυρίῳ, ἐξηκοστῷ καὶ ἐννάτῳ ἔτει τῆς τοῦ σωτῆρος ἡμῶν Ἰησοῦ Χριστοῦ παρουσίας.
Z 532; M 709D–712A. Ἔνθα δὴ συνέβη τὸν Παῦλον τριακοστῷ ἕκτῳ ἔτει τοῦ σωτηρίου πάθους τρισκαιδεκάτῳ δὲ Νέρωνος μαρτυρῆσαι, ξίφει τὴν κεφαλὴν ἀποτμηθέντα.	Ἔστιν οὖν ὁ πᾶς χρόνος ἐξ οὗ ἐμαρτύρησε τριακόσια τριάκοντα ἔτη μέχρι τῆς παρούσης ταύτης ὑπατείας, τετάρτης μὲν Ἀρκαδίου τρίτης δὲ Ὀνωρίου τῶν δύο ἀδελφῶν αὐτοκρατόρων Αὐγούστων, ἐννάτης ἰνδικτιῶνος τῆς πεντεκαιδεκαετηρικῆς περιόδου, μηνὸς Ἰουνίου εἰκοστῇ ἐννάτῃ ἡμέρᾳ.
Z 533; M 712B. Περὶ δὲ τῆς δευτέρας (ἀπολογίας), ἐν ᾗ καὶ τελειοῦται τῷ κατ' αὐτὸν μαρτυρίῳ, φησίν· κ. τ. λ. Ἔστιν οὖν ὁ πᾶς χρόνος τοῦ κηρύγματος Παύλου κ. τ. λ.	Ἐσημειωσάμην ἀκριβῶς τὸν χρόνον τοῦ μαρτυρίου Παύλου ἀποστόλου.

---

1 Z 535–37; M 713B–716A.
2 Robinson, *Euthaliana*, 29, 47.

Z 529; M 708B. Ἀναγκαῖον δὲ
ἡγησάμην ἐν βραχεῖ καὶ τὸν χρόνον
ἐπισημειώσασθαι τοῦ κηρύγματος
Παύλου, ἐκ τῶν χρονικῶν κανόνων
Εὐσεβίου τοῦ Παμφίλου τὴν
ἀνακεφαλαιώσιν ποιούμενος.

Καὶ ἀπὸ τῆς ὑπατίας τετάρτης μὲν
Ἀρκαδίου, τρίτης δὲ Ὁνωρίου, μέχρι
τῆς παρούσης ταύτης ὑπατίας,
πρώτης Λέοντος Αὐγούστου,
ἰνδικτιῶνος δωδεκάτης, Ἐπιφὶ ε΄,
Διοκλετιανοῦ ροδ΄, ἔτη ξγ΄. ὡς εἶναι τὰ
πάντα ἀπὸ τῆς τοῦ Σωτῆρος ἡμῶν
παρουσίας μέχρι τοῦ προκειμένου
ἔτους ἔτη τετρακόσια ἑξήκοντα δύο.

Zacagni's text has been emended by Robinson by the omission of the
phrase κατὰ Συρομακεδόνας following πέμπτῃ ἡμέρᾳ, by the omission
of the phrase παρ᾿ Αἰγυπτίοις Ἐπιφὶ ε΄ between ἥτις λέγοιτο ἂν and
παρά, and by the omission of δέ following παρά.

As a preliminary note of manuscript evidence, there are manuscripts
that omit the last, the last two, or the last three paragraphs.

We may observe that the *Martyrium* contains several different methods of reckoning time. Paul's death is accounted both from the birth of
Jesus, sixty-nine years, and from the passion of Jesus, thirty-six years.
The actual date is given both in a Syro-Macedonian calendar and in
the Roman calendar. It may be recalled that in the Pauline prologue,
the same dates are given in reverse order. Zahn argues that this reversal
indicates the dependence of the compiler of the *Martyrium* on the prologue.[3] Since the prologue speaks of the celebration of the Romans, it is
natural that the calendar in use there would be the one cited. Since no
such need exists in the *Martyrium*, the fact that the Roman dating is inserted anyway suggests dependence. In the second paragraph, the two
Roman emperors are named in an order that demonstrated to von
Soden[4] that the location of the writer was the Byzantine East, the do-
main of Arcadius, the first named.

Before Robinson, it was maintained (a) that Euthalius himself found
the *Martyrium* in the form without the final paragraph and added the last
paragraph to contemporize the piece,[5] or (b) that Euthalius composed
the *Martyrium* himself, except for the final paragraph, which was the
work of a later editor.[6] Robinson argues, however, that neither date
may be appropriately assigned to Euthalius; rather, there is a literary de-

---

3   Zahn, "Neues und Altes," 389, n. 1.
4   Soden, *Schriften des Neuen Testaments*, 658.
5   Zacagni, so Gustave Bardy, "Euthalius," *DBSup* 2:1217.
6   Conybeare, so Bardy, *ibid.*

pendence of the *Martyrium* on the prologue, and, moreover, it is also unlikely that Euthalius himself was responsible for this extract.[7]

This literary relationship is suggested by the parallel arrangement of the *Martyrium* and, *ex hypothesi*, the sections of the prologue from which it was derived. Robinson's argument has both subjective and objective aspects. Representative of the former is his claim, "It is almost inconceivable that a writer who has so great a wealth of expression as the author of the prologue should repeat his own language in this slavish manner."[8] He also rejects the notion that it is the prologue that is dependent upon the *Martyrium*: the degree of separation of the parts of the prologue in which the phrases appear is sufficiently great to discourage this possibility, although not the work of an abbreviator producing the *Martyrium*.

Moreover, he continues, there is additional evidence that demonstrates the direction of the relationship:

1. The phrase, τῷ κατ' αὐτὸν μαρτυρίῳ, is one signal. Robinson feels that the prepositional phrase κατ' αὐτὸν is an awkward construction, whether the αὐτὸν refers to Nero or to Paul; however, the ambiguity, which is unresolved in the *Martyrium*, is not present in the prologue, where the pronoun clearly refers to Nero: "'so I was rescued from the lion's mouth.' By ['the lion'] he means Nero. And it is in reference to the second [defense], in which he is perfected through martyrdom before him, that he says, 'Fulfill your noble ministry.'"[9]

2. The *Martyrium* contains at least two different ways of expressing the date 29 June, namely, "ἡ πρὸ τριῶν καλανδῶν Ἰουλίων" and "μηνὸς Ἰουνίου, εἰκοστῇ ἐννάτῃ ἡμέρᾳ." According to the hypothesis, the former falls in the paragraph that is most heavily indebted to the prologue and copies the way in which the prologue expresses the date, while the latter is the more natural mode of expression of the author of the *Martyrium*.

3. The author of the *Martyrium* places the date of the martyrdom of Paul on 29 June. This, however, was a later deduction from the fact that the Roman church kept the festivals of Saints Peter and Paul on that day. Robinson observes that, as the Liberian Catalog (354 A.D.) shows, this was simply the day of the Deposition, which occurred in 258 A.D. "The mistake," he says, "was common,

---

7   Robinson, *Euthaliana*, 28 ff.
8   *Ibid.*, 29.
9   Z 533; M 712B.

if not universal, in later times, but it is not made by the writer of the Prologue."[10]

This demonstration has appropriately been accorded wide acceptance in the secondary literature dealing with Euthalius;[11] nevertheless, several temporizing observations are in order:

1. What we have termed subjective evaluations of the two pieces are greatly dependent upon *a priori* considerations of the ability of Euthalius, particularly his literary skills. Thus, whether Euthalius would repeat material in a "slavish manner" is already determined by the estimate that he possesses "so great a wealth of expression." We have previously noted that Harris found that much material in the prologues was taken by Euthalius from Eusebius, a great deal more than was acknowledged; Harris thinks that Euthalius was dependent as well on other literary pieces. Zuntz refers to Euthalius' "uninspired pen" and makes other depreciatory remarks about his creative talent.[12] Zuntz, we have noted, regards Euthalius' chief contribution to have been (a) the collection of materials available in another form and (b) the construction of the prologues.

2. The latter part of Harris' essay, "Euthalius and Eusebius," is an attack upon the three internal arguments that Robinson uses to demonstrate that the *Martyrium* is dependent upon the prologue. The first of these attacks we established independently of that essay.

The force of the argument centering on the use of the phrase κατ' αὐτὸν is somewhat diminished by a closer consideration of the larger context of the section. At this point in the prologue, Euthalius is admittedly dependent upon Eusebius' *Ecclesiastical History*, in particular, Book 2. It turns out that the phraseology of the prologue here is a fairly literal paraphrase from 2.22.2, "Tradition has it that after defending himself, the Apostle was again sent on the ministry of preaching, and coming a second time to the same city τῷ κατ' αὐτὸν τελειοθῆναι μαρτυρίῳ." The translator of the Loeb volume offers, "suffered martyrdom under Nero," but this is, at first examination, no more self-evident than Rob-

---

10 Robinson, *Euthaliana*, 30.
11 E.g., Zuntz (*Ancestry*, 79, n. 2) states, "The demonstration of the spuriousness of the *Martyrium* is . . . the most brilliant achievement of Robinson's justly famous *Euthaliana*." Conybeare ("Date of Euthalius," 41) asserts that the argument from τῷ κατ' αὐτὸν μαρτυρίῳ is conclusive in itself.
12 Zuntz, *Ancestry*, 85, n. 1.

inson's assertion that "in the Prologue . . . αὐτὸν . . . clearly refers to Nero."[13]

Harsh as the expression κατ᾽ αὐτὸν may appear to Robinson in the prologue and the *Martyrium*, there are a number of analogous constructions turned up by a superficial survey of Book 2 of the *Ecclesiastical History* (cf. 4.3; 8.1; 9.4; 13.2,6). These instances suggest that the pronoun could easily refer to Paul and that the phrase is equivalent to a simple possessive, as in Acts 17:28; 18:15; Rom. 1:15; Eph. 1:15. The decisive evidence, however, is provided by an earlier passage in 2.22.1: "Τοῦτο δὲ Φῆστος ὑπὸ Νέρωνος διάδοχος πέμπεται, καθ᾽ ὃν δικαιολογησάμενος ὁ Παῦλος," that is, "Festus, before whom Paul was tried, was sent as his successor by Nero." The immediate context indicates that the antecedent of this pronoun is Festus; the later κατ᾽ αὐτόν, which has been taken up in to the prologue and (indirectly?) the *Martyrium*, is simply another example of this mode of expression. Thus, it is in Eusebius that clarification is provided, not the prologue. Robinson, hence, may at best argue for parallel paraphrasing, but not for priority or dependence.

Harris, in the course of his discussion, is able to show that many, although not all, of the phrases that Robinson uses to demonstrate dependence upon the prologue may be found in Eusebius.[14] In view of Harris' previous evidence of the dependence of the author of the prologue upon Eusebius, there is merit to his suggestion that these phrases may as well have been taken directly from Eusebius as from the prologue.

Robinson's second argument rests upon an assumption that the language in the prologue has been consciously framed to maintain the distinction between the date of the *celebration* of the martyrdom and the martyrdom itself. Robinson believes that the compiler of the *Martyrium* was not aware of such a distinction. Harris, basing his argument on the heavy dependence that he has shown the prologue to have on the works of Eusebius, thinks that he may weaken Robinson's second argument by demonstrating that confusion between the date of the martyrdom and the date of the Deposition existed already in Eusebius. He would

---

13 Robinson, *Euthaliana*, 30.
14 Harris, "Euthalius and Eusebius," 79 f. He is able to find, however, in the *Martyrium* only one "Eusebian" phrase that does not also occur in the prologue, i.e., ἥτις λέγοιτο ἄν.

then suggest that the distinction in the prologue was imagined or accidental.

Harris refers first to *Hist. eccl.* 3.31.1,[15] "The time and manner of the
death of Paul and of Peter, and the place where their corpses were laid
after their departure from this life, have been already described by us."
Harris argues that a review of the text of this previous description
(2.25.7) demonstrates that the "place" is in fact the places in the Vatican
and the Ostian way. He concludes

> We say, therefore, that not only is the language of the Prologue at the point
> in question Eusebian language but that it certainly does not refer to the
> Catacombs, for the resting places of the Martyrs are splendid churches,
> in the plural; this must mean the Vatican and the church on the Ostian
> Way. It appears therefore that the confusion between the Martyrdom
> and the Depositio exists equally in the Prologue and the *Martyrium*.[16]

Harris' discussion of the third argument of Robinson is, like the second,
based on inference. He is not able to show that the dates in the prologue
are dependent upon Eusebius. He argues that in any case the method of
dating that is found in the prologue must antedate Eusebius' dating of
the martyrdoms in his account of the Palestine Martyrs, that "the
months . . . are the Roman months with Syro-Macedonian names;
the Syro-Macedonian calendar has, therefore, been displaced." On
the other hand, the Panemos date in the prologue is the old calendar intact and, therefore, must predate Eusebius.[17] He concludes

> The document from which our information comes must have contained
> more than the allusion to the fifth day of Panemos. But even with the at-
> tached Roman date there is still some ambiguity; for Panemos itself has be-
> come ambiguous; and we may regard it as certain that the calendar, which
> in Eusebius' time had been changed from Syro-Macedonian arrangement
> to Roman arrangement, while retaining the names, would in the end
> take up Roman names as well as the Roman arrangement of the months;
> and these names amongst a Greek speaking people will appear as Greek
> names. It is therefore quite natural that we should find in the *Martyrium*
> in the passage in which the writer brings the dates down to his day, the
> statement that the Martyrdom is commemorated on the [twenty-ninth]
> of June.[18]

---

15 *Ibid.*, 81. The translation and text are those of Kirsopp Lake.
16 Harris, "Euthalius and Eusebius," 81 f.
17 *Ibid.*, 82.
18 *Ibid.*

The textual history of this piece has many variations, and we may usefully note two important types of variations at this point in the discussion: the pattern in which major parts are omitted or added in the tradition and the development of the dating.

Robinson's rendering of the piece in the beginning of this section
shows the simplest of the variants in the Greek tradition, which dates
the martyrdom πέμπτῃ ἡμέρᾳ Πανέμου μηνός· ἥτις λέγοιτο ἂν παρὰ
Ῥωμαίοις ἡ πρὸ τριῶν καλανδῶν Ἰουλίων. He believes that this reading
is probably the original one,[19] and Conybeare supports this conclusion
on the basis of the evidence in the Armenian.[20]

The first corruption of the original text probably, according to
Robinson, was the insertion of κατ' Αἰγυπτίους Ἐπιφὶ ε′ following
Ῥωμαίοις, resulting from an unintelligent insertion of a marginal gloss
in to the text.[21] The third reading, πέμπτῃ ἡμέρᾳ κατὰ Συρομακέδονας
Πανέμου μηνός· ἥτις λέγοιτο ἂν παρ' Αἰγυπτίους Ἐπιφί, παρὰ δὲ Ῥωμαίοις ἡ πρὸ τριῶν καλανδῶν Ἰουλίων, came from a more skillful revision of
such a situation.[22]

The Syriac texts offer some alternative reconstructions of this part of
the Greek text, and we review here the work of von Dobschütz and
Hemmerdinger.

The texts of the two Syriac manuscripts used by von Dobschütz, at
the point under consideration, are translated by him as follows: " . . .
am 5. Wochentag im Monat Tamuz, am 29. in ihm."[23] Von Dobschütz
believes that a variant in the Greek tradition, which he found in Mill,
was also part of the original edition, namely, reading "καλανδῶν Ἰουλίων μηνὶ Ἰουνίῳ κθ′."[24] He is uncertain that the old Roman and the
Egyptian forms were present, but he is confident of the Syro-Macedonian, for it has led to the mistaken interpretation that the day was further
specified as Thursday. Hemmerdinger places a different interpretation

---

19 Robinson, *Euthaliana*, 46.
20 Conybeare, "Codex Pamphili," 249, n. 1.
21 Robinson, *Euthaliana*, 46. He is supported here by Bertrand Hemmerdinger
    ("Euthaliana," *JTS* New Series 11 [1960]: 351).
22 Robinson, *Euthaliana*, 46. According to Hemmerdinger ("Euthaliana," 351) the
    second text "évidemment fautif" is corrected with a certain elegance, as in 436.
    Zahn ("Neues und Altes," 389) suggests that a later writer added the Syro-Mac-
    edonian note and the Egyptian dating inasmuch as the original writer lived in
    Syria and it was not necessary to designate whence Panemos came.
23 Dobschütz, "Euthaliusstudien," 134.
24 *Ibid.*, 136, n. 1.

on the Syriac witness. Hemmerdinger believes that he has already established that the author of the Euthalian material was Evagrius of Antioch.[25] From that he argues that Evagrius used only the Roman months,
and all the different chronological co-ordinates, Πανέμου εʹ, Ἐπιφὶ εʹ,
Λώου ςʹ, have been added by an Alexandrian scholiast.[26] He believes
that the original version ran Πέμπτῃ ἡμέρᾳ πρὸ τριῶν καλανδῶν Ἰουλίων. The Syriac translator has only erred in giving the month intended
as July instead of June. The fact that 29 June, 66 A.D. (*sic*), fell on Sun-
day and not Thursday is of little importance since Evagrius would not
have had such accurate chronological manuals as we.

A coincidence between the πέμπτη in the text and the εʹ of Πανέμου
εʹ in the marginal scholium produced the following reading, found in
the Greek column of Paris B. N. arm. 27, *olim* 9: πέμπτη ἡμέρᾳ
Πανέμου μῆνος, ἥτις λέγοιτʼ ἂν παρὰ Ῥωμαίοις ἡ πρὸ τριῶν καλανδῶν
Ἰουλίων.[27]

The longest recension, containing a final paragraph that updates the
Martyrium, is found in a relatively small number of manuscripts and is
probably the latest.[28] It may be suggested that the presence of the Egyptian dating in this paragraph indicates that it originated in Egypt.[29] A
supplementary suggestion, made by one who supported the view that
Athanasius in the headings and the body of the prologue to Acts was
a later insertion, is that the last paragraph was added by someone who
wanted to place the construction of the material at a plausible time.[30]

The evidence suggests that the authenticating sentence was originally part of the first two paragraphs and was dropped in some later copies,
but without the stichometric note, which was added later.[31]

There is manuscript evidence for texts ending with παρουσίας and
for texts ending with ἡμέρα. These forms led naturally to speculation
that there are at least four different recensions of the *Martyrium*, ending
respectively with the first, second, third, and fourth paragraphs.[32] Von

---

25 Hemmerdinger, "Euthaliana," 349.
26 *Ibid.*, 350.
27 *Ibid.*, 351.
28 See a full discussion of this in von Soden, *Schriften des Neuen Testaments*, 369–
    74. Cf. Dobschütz, "Euthaliusfrage," 66 ff.; Zahn, "Neues und Altes," 325 f.;
    Robinson, *Euthaliana*, 46 f.; and Conybeare, "Codex Pamphili," 249 f.
29 Robinson, *Euthaliana*, 47. See also von Dobschütz, "Euthaliusfrage," 67 f.
30 Conybeare, "Codex Pamphili," 250.
31 Soden, *Schriften des Neuen Testaments*, 374, 658.
32 Dobschütz, "Euthaliusfrage," 66.

Soden has discerned a still more primitive form imbedded in the first paragraph:[33] the material καθ' ἥν . . . παρουσίας is a later addition. This is suggested to him, in spite of the fact that there is no manuscript evidence for this variant,[34] by the recalculation of the death of Paul, from the birth of Jesus. Other signals are the "Nachhinken" of the sentence, the "ungeschickte Anknüpfung" of the relative connective, the solemn phraseology, and the way Paul is characterized.

Finally, there has been some discussion of the function that the *Martyrium* was expected to perform, in whatever shape and time it came into the tradition of the apparatus. Zahn, while agreeing with Robinson that it is a later fabrication from the prologue, thinks that it is an appropriate concluding addition to an historical work, which has certain literary analogies.[35] Others have noted that the *Martyrium* tends to float about in the tradition. Oecumenius placed it before his commentary on Acts and did not include the final paragraph.[36] It is frequently associated with the ἀποδημίαι;[37] there are manuscripts that have it without parts of the prologue to the Pauline epistles, as well as manuscripts that contain it in more than one form. Manuscripts with the *Martyrium* but no part of the prologue to the Pauline letters include the following: 93 216 (367) 421 429 451 459 547 605 614 621 665 (1610) 1643 1719 1751 1828 1830 1849 1895 1906 2189 2243. Manuscripts with duplicate texts of the *Martyrium* include the following: (42) 451 619 1162 1894.

We believe, in conclusion, that it is clear that the dependence is that of the *Martyrium* on the prologue. We believe that the massive dependence of Euthalius upon the narrative and vocabulary of the work of Eusebius has been shown. In view of the particular vocabulary involved, the argument that the author of the *Martyrium* is dependent directly upon the work of Eusebius is conceivable, but unlikely. It is, we think, an open question as to whether the author of the *Martyrium*

---

33 Soden, *Schriften des Neuen Testaments*, 373.

34 Von Soden (*ibid.*, 374) feels it was added before the *Martyrium* was introduced into any New Testament manuscript. A suspicion that the *Martyrium* could have had no independent circulation before it was connected with the prologues is supported by Zahn ("Neues und Altes," 325), although Zahn believes Robinson's theory about its origin.

35 Zahn, "Neues und Altes," 325.

36 Lardner, *Credibility*, 208; and Robinson, *Euthaliana*, 5 f.

37 2 42 90 93 94 102 216 367 3984 459 614 665 1102 1247 1270 1297 1597 1643 1751 1847 1849 1894 1896 1952 2183 2189.

was merely dependent upon the prologue or was identical with the author of the prologue.

The secondary nature of the final paragraph of the longest recension
has been rather clearly demonstrated. We have no firm opinion regarding the third paragraph, attesting the accuracy of the codicil. We think
that the variation in the manuscripts between the appearance of one or
both of the first two paragraphs may be a useful device in associating
related manuscripts, but we do not believe that the variation arose
until after the original publication of the apparatus as a whole. Von Soden's suggestion of an even more primitive form imbedded in the first
paragraph must, until other evidence is available, remain speculative.

6. Argumenta

In virtually every manuscript that has been examined in this survey, there have appeared, closely associated with the chapter lists, ὑποθέσεις. These were also found by Zacagni in his manuscripts, and he has provided the texts of these pieces for all the letters and Acts. An ὑπόθεσις is basically a summary of the letter or book under consideration; it is much longer than the brief, sentence summary of the prologue and generally somewhat longer than the chapter list. In most manuscripts where they occur, they immediately precede the chapter list for each letter.

As in the case of the chapter lists, the headings for the first three letters of Paul are somewhat more elaborate than those for the letters that follow; as examples, we cite the headings for Romans, 2 Corinthians, and Galatians:[1]

Romans: Ὑπόθεσις πρώτης πρὸς Ῥωμαίους ἐπιστολῆς.
2 Corinthians: Ὑπόθεσις τρίτης μὲν ἐπιστολῆς τοῦ Ἀποστόλου δευτέρας δὲ πρὸς Κορινθίους.
Galatians: Ὑπόθεσις τῆς πρὸς Γαλάτας ἐπιστολῆς.

The heading for the Catholic epistles generally follows this pattern: Ὑπόθεσις Πέτρου β′ ἐπιστολῆς.[2]

In the Pauline epistles, the *argumenta* begin in the same fashion, i. e., Ταύτην ἐπιστέλλει ἀπό (place), and continue with some variation on the notice in Romans, "μήπω ἑωρακὼς Ῥωμαίους."[3] Moreover, with the notable exceptions of Colossians and Hebrews, they all conclude with the words τελειοῖ τὴν ἐπιστολήν.[4]

---

1   Z 570; M 748A; Z 611; M 756C; and Z 624; M 760B, respectively.
2   Z 497; M 781B.
3   Z 570; M 748A.
4   This standard phrase, in Colossians (Z 649 f.; M768Af.), continues with "παραγγέλλει μέντοι αὐτοῖς ἵνα ὅταν ἀναγνωσθῇ παρ᾽ αὐτοῖς ἡ ἐπιστολή, ποιήσωσι καὶ τὴν ἐν Λαοδικείαν ἐκκλησίᾳ αὐτὴν ἀναγνωσθῆναι, καὶ τὴν ἐκ Λαοδικείας καὶ αὐτοὺς ἀναγνῶναι." The appendage in Hebrews, which appears in some texts separated from the *argumentum*, is a discussion of the Pauline authorship of this epistle. It begins, following the regular "conclusion," "Ἡ δὲ πρὸς Ἑβραίους ἐπιστολὴ δοκεῖ μὲν οὐκ εἶναι Παύλου διά τε τὸν χαρακτῆρα, καὶ τὸ μὴ προγράφειν, ὡς ἐν ἁπάσαις ταῖς ἐπιστολαῖς" (Z 669; M 776A) and con-

A preliminary comparison of the *argumentum* of Ephesians with its
chapter list suggests that the former, although longer, is less thorough
in its description of the entire letter. Whether or not this observation
can be sustained by a close analysis of all of the relevant materials is
not a question that we attempted to resolve. The *argumentum* of Acts
is something of a special case. A casual examination of the critical
notes made by Zacagni indicates something of the uneven textual history of this piece.[5] Von Soden has made three divisions of the text,
namely, a preliminary part, a list of the names of the apostles and deacons, and a list of wonders that were performed.[6]

That there was any connection, originally, between these *argumenta*
and the primary body of the Euthalian apparatus has been denied from
Zacagni onwards.

The arguments against the inclusion of the *argumenta* in the original
edition of the Euthalian materials are basically three: they are not forecast by Euthalius in any of the prologues; data in them concerning the
places from which some of the Pauline letters were written are contradicted by the subscriptions to the letters as well as a note appended to
one of the quotation lists; and there is a discernable variance in some
letters between the chief point, or points, noted in the *argumenta* and
that in the summaries of the letters in the Pauline prologue. It is also
a fact that these *argumenta*, including the whole of the one to Acts, appear, together with *argumenta* for the other books in the Bible, in the
Synopsis scripturae sacrae, inaccurately attributed to Athanasius.[7]

The earliest critics of the Euthalian apparatus focussed upon the discrepancies between the information in some *argumenta* and that furnished by the corresponding subscriptions.[8] Three or four letters are noteworthy in this respect. The *argumentum* of 1 Corinthians claims that

---

cludes "πολλὰ δὲ καὶ ἄλλα γνωρίζουσιν ἡμῖν αὐτοῦ τυγχάνειν τὴν ἐπιστολήν,
ὡς καὶ ἡ ἀνάγνωσις αὐτὴ προϊοῦσα διδάξει." (Z 761; M 776Cf.)

5   See the following places: Z 421, n. 7; M 645, n. 96; Z 422, nn. 2, 7; M 646,
    nn. 1, 6; Z 422, n. 9; M 647, n. 8; Z 423, n. 3; M 647, n. 11; and Z 423, nn. 4,
    5; M 648, nn. 12, 13.
6   Soden, *Schriften des Neuen Testaments*, 671.
7   PG 28:283–438. The text here does contain the extension of the *argumentum*
    to Colossians, but it does not have the second half of the *argumentum* to He-
    brews.
8   Zacagni, *Collectanea*, lx; *Novum Testamentum graecum* (John Mill, ed.; Rotter-
    dam: Caspar Fritsch & Michael Böhm, 1710), 95; Johann Jakob Wettstein,
    Ē kainē diathēkē: Novum Testamentum graecum (vol. 1; Amsterdam: Ex officina
    Dommeriana, 1751), 75; Hug, *Writings*, 251; and Ehrhard, "Codex H," 391 f.

the letter was written in Ephesus of Asia; the corresponding subscription and the source list following the short quotation list show Philippi.[9] For 2 Corinthians, the *argumentum* shows Macedonia; the other two agree again on Philippi.[10] For 2 Thessalonians, the *argumentum* shows Rome; the other two, Athens.[11] Finally, manuscripts frequently show Macedonia as the place of origin of 1 Timothy in the *argumentum*; the subscription and the appended note, together with a regular variant in the text of the *argumentum*, show Laodicea.[12] Our own feeling is that this is, of itself, not a strong argument, inasmuch as it presupposes the authenticity of the subscriptions and the addendum, which has not been demonstrated any more than that of the *argumenta*.

The Synopsis in which these pieces are located, together with the Διὰ τί,[13] is dated by Zahn in the sixth century or later.[14] Von Dobschütz claims that there are, in fact, several recensions of this material, one of which is that which appears in the Euthalian manuscripts.[15]

The last argument is advanced by Ehrhard.[16] We have previously noted the contrast between the *argumentum* and the chapter list for Ephesians. Ehrhard asserts that the differences between the prologue to the Pauline epistles and the *argumenta* in regard to vocabulary and selection of the main point of the letters make it impossible that Euthalius could have been the author of the *argumenta*. He specifies this contention by noting that there is no mention in the *argumenta* of the relationship between Romans and Ephesians described in the summaries in the prologue; he observes, further, that there are perceptibly different interpretations in the two of Philippians, Colossians, and particularly 2 Timothy, where the two pieces are almost equal in extent.

The data that the versions provide about the *argumenta* are very interesting. In the manuscript designated O by von Dobschütz, the *argumenta* are entirely lacking with the exception of the long paragraph at the end of the *argumentum* for Hebrews, which appears at the head of

---

9   Z 589; M 752D; Z 611; and Z 547; M 624C, respectively.

10   Z 611; M 756C; Z 624; and Z 547; M 724C, respectively.

11   Z 663; M 772B; Z 668; and Z 547; M 724D, respectively.

12   Z 686; M 780C; Z 695; and Z 547; M 725A, respectively.

13   Turner, "Patristic Commentaries," 527.

14   Theodor von Zahn, *Geschichte des Neutestamentlichen Kanons* (vol. 2; Erlangen; Leipzig: A. Deichert, 1892), 315.

15   Dobschütz, "Euthaliusfrage," 70.

16   Ehrhard, "Codex H," 391f.

the chapter list for that letter.[17] Vardanian, reviewing the evidence in the Armenian tradition, found that although the manuscripts with which he was working did contain the *argumenta*, they are not of a piece, linguistically, with what he describes as the authentic Euthalian materials; the exception to this discontinuity is, again, the final paragraph to the *argumentum* of Hebrews as printed by Zacagni, which he finds composed of the appropriately characteristic language.[18]

There is one remarkable fact that should be brought into the discussion at this point. Very few of the manuscripts that we have examined do not include the *argumenta*. In addition to 015, only 81 330 1243 1720 lack the *argumenta* but have some other part of the apparatus. Only 81 includes some part of the apparatus other than material from the chapter lists.[19] Since we are inclined to accept the arguments for the existence of all of the chapter lists prior to the work of Euthalius, the implication of this evidence is that the entire Greek tradition, with few exceptions, stems from a recension subsequent to the development and introduction of the *argumenta*. Turner was confident that his calculations using the quire numbers appearing on the leaves of 015 demonstrated that there must have been enough space at the beginning of the codex for "some prefatory matter," which he does not specify further.[20] We have not been convinced by our own attempts to verify these calculations. Since there is no reason other scribes could not have used the same exemplar that Euthalius did, we are left with the possibility that 81 is the only Greek manuscript of a clearly Euthalian character bearing a tradition not derived from the *argumenta* expansion stage.

---

17 Dobschütz, "Euthaliusstudien," 130.
18 Vardanian, "Euthaliana," 40 (1926): 107 f.
19 81 is also remarkable in that, aside from 1828, it is the only manuscript we surveyed that contained the so-called Egyptian addition to the *Martyrium* but none of the elaborations of dating in the first paragraph.
20 Turner, "Patristic Commentaries," 527 f.

7. Miscellaneous Pieces

Ἀποδημίαι

In numerous manuscripts containing the prologues and other parts of the Euthalian corpus that we have reviewed earlier, there is also a piece titled, Ἀποδημίαι Παύλου τοῦ Ἀποστόλου.[1] This is a rather short text, covering less than three pages in Zacagni's text, which occurs in his edition following the *argumentum* to Acts.[2] It is a lackluster recitation of the itinerary of Paul, drawn largely from the narrative in Acts. It takes up, "Ἀπὸ Δαμασκοῦ ἤρξατο, καὶ ἀνῆλθεν εἰς Ἰερουσαλήμ," and concludes, "Καὶ λοιπὸν εἰσελθὼν εἰς Ῥώμην· καὶ διδάξας ἐκεῖ χρόνον ἱκανόν, ὕστερον ἐν αὐτῇ τῇ Ῥώμῃ ἐμαρτύρησεν."

The textual history of this piece is rather checkered. In the manuscripts that we have examined, it occurs as an independent item not only in the position represented by Zacagni's text,[3] but also associated with other parts of the Euthalian apparatus.[4] Moreover, it sometimes incorporates parts of the prologue to the Pauline epistles or is itself absorbed into this prologue and becomes, in many instances, an integral part of it. When it is incorporated into the prologue, it is ordinarily inserted toward the conclusion of the first of the two sections dealing with the life of Paul.[5]

---

1   Z 425–27; M 649B-652A. Misprinted in Zacagni ΑΠΟΛΗΜΙΑΙ.
2   This is not the only place where it turns up, as we shall have occasion to note in the critical discussion that follows.
3   See the appendix containing the manuscript survey for a complete list of manuscripts in which the ἀποδημίαι occurs.
4   E.g., 2 3 51 205 209 223 234 463 479 621 912 1103 1161 1240 1248 1405 1573 1594 1598 1599 1626 1753 1847 1863 1877 1886 1892 1894 1932 1952 2131 2189 2279.
5   The following expansion is described, although not necessarily following the conclusions we have drawn, by von Soden (*Schriften des Neuen Testaments*, 694 f.); it occurs in the prologue at Z 522; M 700C through M 701A, beginning, καὶ καθιστᾷ οὐρανοῦ κληρονόμον, ὃν τῆς γῆς ἀπεστέρης, εἶσιν οὖν αἱ πολιτεῖαι, ἃς τῷ κηρύγματι περίηλθεν ὁ πανεύφημος τοῦ Χριστοῦ ἀπόστολος Παῦλος, ὡς ἐν συντόμῳ εἰπεῖν αὐταί, then inserting the ἀποδημίαι, which, following its regular conclusion, continues αὐτόθι τὸν καλὸν ἀγῶνα ἠγωνισαμένος, Ῥωμαῖοι περικαλλέσιν . . . ἑορτάζοντες.

There are other modifications of this pattern, which we believe are most likely to be explained as variations on the preceding form. It appears as an independent piece, beginning as usual but carrying on through the continuation of the prologue to the point that the summaries of the letters begin, i. e., through πολιτείαν.[6] Another variation is composed of the previous one with the addition of an extract from the last section of the Pauline prologue.[7] This same extract also occurs as a distinct paragraph, titled, but immediately followed or preceded by the ἀποδημίαι.[8] There are also modifications of these forms.[9]

From Zacagni onwards, the critical literature has consistently denied that this piece was originally associated with Euthalius.[10] Robinson notes that in Oecumenius, "the same piece goes on further to speak of the Festival of S. Paul at Rome. . . . No one will, I think, be disposed to claim this piece for Euthalius."[11]

Τάδε Ἔνεστιν Παύλου Ἐπιστολαί

A short paragraph with the heading Τάδε Ἔνεστιν Παύλου Ἐπιστολαί[12] appears in about fifteen manuscripts that we examined;[13] in Zacagni's manuscripts, it follows the list citing the quotations in full and is succeeded by a short paragraph that we will describe below, the *argumentum*, and the chapter list of Romans. It is noteworthy, in this respect, that the quotation lists occur in almost every manuscript containing this paragraph and that, with a few insignificant exceptions, no manuscript containing the tables of quotations is without this paragraph. The table is simply a list of the letters of Paul, as it indicates, beginning with Ἡ πρὸς Ῥωμαίους and concluding with Ἡ πρὸς Φιλήμονα.

---

6 3 205 209.
7 1894. The extract is the section beginning Ἀναγκαῖον (Z 529; M 708B) through πέντε (Z 534; M 712B). This manuscript also contains the ἀποδημίαι in the prologue itself.
8 Following: 1594. Preceding: 1573 1753 1863 2279.
9 2 51 479 1103 1599 2131.
10 Zacagni, *Collectanea*, lxvi; Ehrhard, "Codex H," 398; and Robinson, *Euthaliana*, 26.
11 Robinson, *Euthaliana*, 26.
12 Z 569; M 745C-748A.
13 88 181 619 (621) 623 915 917 1162 (1244) 1828 1836 1845 1846 1874 1875 1981 2242.

This piece has received little attention in the secondary literature. Robinson dismissed it with a casual, "It is somewhat belated where it occurs, and is probably a subsequent addition."[14] Von Soden notes that associated with this piece in all manuscripts, with the exception of 88, is the Διὰ τί, which is also found in the Pseudo-Athanasian *Synopsis*.[15] Von Soden thinks that this material, as well as other that he discusses, was merely incorporated by Euthalius into his apparatus. He also thinks that the more appropriate place for these two pieces is either before or after the short piece following the shorter quotation list. If his theory about the priority of the shorter list be correct, he notes, then these lists have simply been displaced from their original location by the interpolation of the longer list of quotations. He does not, however, venture a final opinion in the matter.

Zuntz is the only critic whom we have reviewed who provides a persuasive explanation for the piece as a part of a comprehensive theory of origin. His hypothesis describes the chapter lists as originally coming at the beginning of the codex containing the text of the letters. This piece, then, would have been the table of contents prefatory to the longer chapter lists. He concludes, "[It] was likewise devotedly copied out by 'Euthalius.' It has its apposite place at the very beginning of the book. 'Euthalius' left it where he found it, that is, before the ἔκθεσις. But he prefixed to it his prologue and compiled tables. Hence, its present, absurd, position."[16]

Διὰ Τί

Immediately following the "contents" of the Pauline corpus, which we have just reviewed, there appears in Zacagni's main manuscript witness, another paragraph titled Διὰ τί Παύλου ἐπιστολαὶ δεκατέσυαρες λέγονται.[17] This is the text:

Ἐπειδὴ ταύτας αὐτὸς ὁ Ἀπόστολος ἰδίᾳ ἐπιστέλλει, καὶ διὰ τούτων, οὓς μὲν ἤδη ἑώρακεν, καὶ ἐδίδαξεν, ὑπομιμνήσκει, καὶ διορθοῦται· οὓς δὲ μὴ ἑώρακεν σπουδάζει κατηχεῖν, καὶ διδάσκειν, ὡς ἔστιν ἀπ᾽ αὐτῶν τὸν ἐντυγχάνοντα καταμαθεῖν.

---

14 Robinson, *Euthaliana*, 20.
15 Soden, *Schriften des Neuen Testaments*, 663. Our survey of the manuscripts has added others to 88.
16 Zuntz, *Ancestry*, 86.
17 Z 570; M748A.

It has been noted that the paragraph does not clearly answer the question that is set out in the title. This convinced Robinson that this piece is not authentic.[18] Moreover, the paragraph tends to float about in the manuscript tradition and has no forecast in the descriptions by Euthalius of his work. It may be observed that the author of this paragraph categorizes the letters according to whether they were written to those whom Paul had seen or otherwise. In the prologue to the Pauline letters, Euthalius notes in his brief summaries that Paul had seen neither the Romans nor the Ephesians, but he does not divide or discuss them further in those terms.

This piece occurs, with the *argumenta*, in the Pseudo-Athanasian *Synopsis*.[19] Von Soden suggests, as we have noted, that it, together with several other pieces, was simply taken up by Euthalius into his work. He further suggests that the original position of this piece, together with the τάδε ἔνεστιν, has, perhaps, been altered by the interpolation of the longer quotation list.[20] This piece is missing from Syriac texts,[21] and Vardanian is doubtful of its authenticity in the Armenian.[22]

Ἐπίγραμμα and Πλοῦς

Following the text of Jude in Zacagni's edition,[23] there are two short pieces that occur in some manuscripts.[24] As was the case with the Διὰ τί, these have a tendency to float around in the tradition.[25] The first of these is merely a notice of an inscription titled Ἐπίγραμμα τοῦ ἐν Ἀθήναις βωμοῦ with the following text: "Θεοῖς Ἀσίας, καὶ Εὐρώπης, καὶ Λυβίης, Θεῷ τε ἀγνώστῳ, καὶ ξένῳ."

---

18 Robinson, *Euthaliana*, 20.
19 Von Soden, *Schriften des Neuen Testaments*, 663; and Turner, "Patristic Commentaries," 527.
20 Von Soden, *Schriften des Neuen Testaments*, 663.
21 Dobschütz, "Euthaliusstudien," 145.
22 Vardanian, "Euthaliana," 39 (1925): 25 f.
23 Z 514; M 692.
24 Ἐπίγραμμα: 181 436 1875 2541. Πλοῦς: 81 88 181 436 (1067) 1875 2541.
25 See Z 514, n.1; M 692, n. 74, regarding different locations of the ἐπίγραμμα. In 88, the πλοῦς is located between parts of a long colophon, which appears as a unit in 015.

The second piece is a brief paragraph covering some of the details of Paul's sea voyage to Rome. It is headed Πλοῦς Παύλου τοῦ Ἀποστόλου ἐπὶ Ῥώμην.

These two pieces hardly have an integral place in the apparatus. Their attestation does not argue for much consideration; their lack of fixity in the tradition and their want of a place in the announced scheme of Euthalius all cast doubt on their authenticity. Primarily, then, their function may be to help group manuscripts associated with the Euthalian tradition.

Robinson notes, with respect to the first, that it is cited by Oecumenius on Acts, and he comments that the second is "peculiarly out of place."[26]

Πρὸς Ἐμαυτόν

In the manuscript used by Zacagni, at the end of the Catholic epistles and immediately before the colophon, which will be discussed later, there appears a short stichometrical summary of data in Acts and the Catholic epistles, both text and apparatus.[27] We have reserved the discussion of the whole matter of stichometry and its relationship to the Euthalian apparatus to an excursus,[28] but there is an enigmatic note in this summary, which we need to take up here. The note runs, "Καὶ τὸ πρὸς ἐμαυτὸν στίχοι κζ'." There is nothing in the material that Zacagni found in his manuscripts that corresponds to the summary item, and Zacagni did not have an explanation to propose.[29] Since 1698, however, others have suggested various alternatives, and finally, evidence for the existence of a text that carries this title and that fits the description has been uncovered.

Graux suggested that the mysterious phrase was the work of a very careful scribe who, in order to insure accuracy, accounted for that part of the writing that was the peculiar result of his own labours.[30] Von

---

26 Robinson, *Euthaliana*, 27.
27 Z 513; M 692A.
28 See pages 137–143 of this monograph.
29 Z 513; n. 3; M 692, n. 73. Westcott notes, "These difficulties seem to show that Euthalius did not compose the whole work, but in part transcribed it." (*General Survey*, 450, n. 2).
30 Charles Graux, "Nouvelles recherches sur la stichométrie," *RPh* New Series 2 (1878): 122.

Dobschütz calculated the lengths of several parts of the apparatus not included in the stichometric summaries in the list in which this note appears and was able to produce a total of twenty-seven στίχοι,[31] although
he was later prepared to rescind this proposal in the event that the implications of the Armenian evidence, to which he had access, and the
Greek evidence, of which he had heard, turned out to be correct.[32]
Robinson felt that it was clear in any case that the phrase could not
refer to the author of the prologues.[33]

   Conybeare noted a "prayer of Euthalius" in at least one Armenian
manuscript that he used,[34] and reference is made to it by Petermann
in an encyclopedia article.[35] Von Dobschütz provides a German translation of the Armenian version,[36] and von Soden has reproduced the text
of the Greek piece discovered by von der Goltz under the title πρὸς
ἐμαυτόν.[37] There is some variation in the two texts; Zahn finds one
line in the Greek text that he feels has been fundamentally misunder-
stood by the Armenian translator.[38] Zahn is also reminded, not only
by the title but also by the tone of the whole piece, of some works
of Gregory Nazianzus with the superscription πρὸς or εἰς ἑαυτόν.[39]
Both von Soden and Zahn[40] are confident that the author of this
piece is identical with the author of the prologues, Zahn noting the similarity of the rhythmic prose and the citation of a pagan piece of poetry
without naming the author. Zahn is, however, rather critical of the fan-
ciful uses to which von Soden puts this piece in his reconstruction of the
life of Euthalius.[41]

   Von Soden finds the paragraph containing the notice of the πρὸς
ἐμαυτὸν in four manuscripts, 181 623 1836 1898,[42] which Zahn describes as "eine Reihe von Handschriften des 10. und 11. Jahrhun-

31 Dobschütz, "Euthaliusfrage," 66, n. 1.
32 Dobschütz, "Euthaliusstudien," 115, n.1.
33 Robinson, *Euthaliana*, 35.
34 Conybeare, "Codex Pamphili," 245.
35 Julius Heinrich Petermann, "Armenien," *RE* 2:668.
36 Dobschütz, "Euthaliusstudien," 114 f., by Esnik Gjandschezian.
37 Soden, *Schriften des Neuen Testaments*, 646 f.
38 Zahn, "Neues und Altes," 315, n. 1.
39 *Ibid.*
40 Soden, *Schriften des Neuen Testaments*, 646; and Zahn, "Neues und Altes," 316,
    respectively.
41 Zahn, "Neues und Altes," 315, n. 1.
42 Soden, *Schriften des Neuen Testaments*, 646.

derts."[43] He believes that although the text of the prayer itself does not occur in them, the very existence of the note about it testifies to its antiquity and that the combination of this prayer with the textual labours of Euthalius is much older than the manuscripts.

Subscriptions

We have deferred to this point a discussion of some other supplementary notes and lists that Zacagni found in his manuscript(s). The colophon, which has played a larger part in the critical discussion, we will take up separately. Here we are concerned with subscriptions to the text of the letters and Acts and, secondly, materials associated with some of the quotation lists.

All of the letters have some sort of concluding note, stating the name of the letter just completed and a stichometric notation. The Pauline letters are also furnished with some additional information regarding the place from which the letter was sent and, frequently, the bearer. In our discussion of the *argumenta*, we noted that information they contain about the places of origin is, in several instances, in conflict with information contained in the subscriptions. In reference to the information in the subscriptions, Paley claims that six are false or impossible, either absolutely contradicted by the contents of the epistle (1 Corinthians, Galatians, 1 Timothy) or difficult to reconcile with them (1 and 2 Thessalonians, Titus).[44] Inconsistency was one of the criteria used to deny the *argumenta* to the original edition of the Euthalian apparatus, although we noted then that there was no evidence beyond proximity in the manuscripts that justified ascribing the subscriptions to Euthalius. This basis is, moreover, just as appropriate for the *argumenta*.

There are three tables that follow the short quotation list of the Pauline letters; since one of them is related to some of the information in the subscriptions, we will take it up next, even though it is the second of the three.

---

43 Zahn, "Neues und Altes," 315.
44 William Paley, *Horae Paulinae: Or, The Truth of the Scripture History of St. Paul Evinced* (New York: Robert Carter, 1849), 232 f., cited by Frederick Henry Ambrose Scrivener, *A Plain Introduction to the Criticism of the New Testament for the Use of Biblical Students* (3d ed., thoroughly revised, enlarged, and brought down to the present date; Cambridge: Deighton, Bell, 1883), 62 f.

This table is merely a list of the places from which the epistles were sent, summarizing the letters sent from each.[45] In addition to names of the cities or areas, it also includes, with a minor variant, lists of numbers: one a total and one for each letter indicating its canonical order. The locations are as follows: Corinth: Romans. Philippi: 1 and 2 Corinthians. Rome: Galatians, Ephesians, Philippians, Colossians, 2 Timothy, and Philemon "and Apphia, and Archippus the deacon of the Church in Colossae." Athens: 1 and 2 Thessalonians. Italy: Hebrews. Laodicea of Phrygia: 1 Timothy, "who was in Ephesus." Nicopolis of Macedonia: Titus, "who was in Crete."

This table agrees with the subscriptions in the points of origin with only a minor variation in the elaboration of a place name.

The first table following the short quotation list is a summary of the sources from which these quotations were purportedly taken, with the total number of quotations from each source and a grand total.[46] The list also attempts to indicate the number of times the same quotation has been used more than once, for example, for Proverbs, it states, "γ' καὶ ἄλλη μία ἐκ δευτέρου," which means that there are three quotations from Proverbs that have been used once and one that has been used twice. Notes indicating duplication are also made for Genesis, of which there are three, Leviticus, Isaiah, and Ezekiel; there is a quotation from Habakkuk, which is used three times.

There are a number of discrepancies that become apparent when the information in this list is compared to the actual tables. The grand total is given as 127 at several points in this list. The actual total, if the quotations are counted, is 128. The discrepancy comes at two points: The list has omitted any mention of the two quotations from III Kings; it has also cited Genesis as having thirteen quotations used once and three used twice, whereas the actual figure should have been ten quotations used once and three twice.

This longer paragraph is succeeded by a shorter one that has extracted the sources having quotations used more than once and has listed these separately. The shorter paragraph is introduced as follows: "Ὁμοῦ μαρτυρίαι ρκζ' καὶ ἐδισσολογήθεσαν ἐν διαφόροις ἐπιστολαὶ αἱ ὑποτεταγμέναι ια'."[47] There is a variant reading for the first figure show-

---

45   Z 546 f.; M 724C–725A.
46   Z 545 f.; M 724Af.
47   Z 546; M 724B.

ing 116.[48] Von Soden argues that this is the correct reading, inasmuch as the sum of 116 and 11 is 127.[49] This means that the problem of the numbers goes behind that corrected reading, for although the total listed as having been used only once is really 116, the number represented by the used-more-than-once paragraph is really twelve, since the quotation from Habakkuk is actually used three times.

In this list, so far as we can tell, the quotations having more than one source are all counted with the summary of the initial source.

The third table is a list of the persons involved in writing the fourteen letters of Paul.[50] These designations are in agreement with the first verse of each of the fourteen letters. There is a note at the end of the table indicating that there was one letter, Hebrews, which was written by Paul ἀνεπίγραφος and ἀνώνυμος. The only surprise in the list is that 2 Corinthians is listed as being from Paul and Silvanus. One would have expected that Timothy would have been named, not Silvanus; it is possible that this ascription arose through association with the names attached to 1 and 2 Thessalonians, but this reasoning is weak.

At the end of the long list of quotations for the Pauline letters, there is a table that purports to summarize the quotations that are used more than once in the Pauline letters.[51] On the face of it, there should be a co-relation between this table and the appropriate parts of the one following the short quotation list, even though the arrangement is somewhat different. The first one cited indicates the pattern that the others follow: "Ἐν τῇ πρὸς Ῥωμαίους ϛ', Γενεσέως α'. Ἐν τῇ πρὸς Γαλάτας α', Γενεσέως α'." In other words, the sixth quotation in Romans, which is the first one from Genesis, is identical with the first quotation in Galatians, which is also noted as the first from Genesis, although according to the cumulation by source in the longer list, this is the ninth quotation from Genesis. The criteria were not precise, inasmuch as the quotations are not always identical but are sometimes only parts of one or the other. There are eleven citations, including the triple one for Habakkuk. Among these, there are at least four that are erroneously put together, apart from the regular pattern of quoting the second source number the same as the first; this second characteristic may be a relic of an

48 623: Z 546, n. 4; M 723, n. 21.
49 Soden, *Schriften des Neuen Testaments*, 660.
50 Z 547 f.; M 725Af.
51 Z 568 f.; M 745Aff.

older arrangement, although it looks rather more like a conceit of the compiler.

1. Romans VIII and Hebrews XXVI are both cited as Genesis 4. Romans VIII, at 4:17, is Genesis 2, at 17:5; Hebrews XXVI, at 12:21, is Exodus 8, at 19:1 (so Zacagni; the citation must be Deut. 9:19). The co-ordinates are actually Romans XI, at 9:7, which is Genesis 4, at 21:12; this is also cited as Hebrews XXIII, at 11:18, which is Genesis 16.

2. Romans XX and Hebrews IX are both cited as Deuteronomy 4. Romans XX, at 9:33, is Isaiah 5, at 8:14; Hebrews IX, at 2:12, is Psalm 21, at Ps. 21:23. The co-ordinates are actually Romans XXXVIII, at 12:19, which is Deuteronomy 4, at 32:35; this is also cited as Hebrews XX, at 10:30, which is Deuteronomy 14.

3. Romans XXXI and 2 Corinthians VII are cited as Proverbs 1. Romans XXXI, at 11:3, is III Kings 1, at 19:10; 2 Corinthians VII, at 8:21, is Proverbs 3, at 3:4. The actual co-ordinate links the one cited in 2 Corinthians with Romans XXXVII, at 12:17, which is the same citation from Proverbs, except that it is numbered 1.

4. Romans XXXVI is cited as Isaiah 11; the quotation is supposedly repeated in 1 Corinthians I, which is cited as Isaiah 16 (*sic*, Zacagni only). The 1 Corinthians citation is incorrect, inasmuch as I, at 1:19, is Isaiah 15, at 29:14 (not 9:14). The actual co-ordinate is 1 Corinthians IV, at 2:16, which is Isaiah 16, like Isaiah 11, at 40:13.[52]

There are no such lists for Acts.

There is a table for the Catholic epistles,[53] which totals the quotations from each source like the first list following the short quotation list of the Pauline letters. The table for the Catholic epistles, however, follows the long list. There are no quotations that are used more than once, and there are no discrepancies discernable upon comparing the table with the two lists.

---

52 Zacagni (Z 569; M 746C) has "corrected" the problem by mis-translating the Greek, "ἐν τῇ πρὸς Κορινθίους πρώτῃ α′ Ἡσαΐου ις′" with "testimonium quartum in epistola I. ad Corinthios."

53 Z 485; M 676B.

8. Colophon

In a number of the Euthalian manuscripts, there is a colophon attesting the comparison of the text with an exemplar (or exemplars) found in the library of Caesarea. The text that we are citing is primarily that found in 015, based on Omont's transcription.[1] The annotations of the text show the variants in 88 and parallel passages from several points in other parts of the Euthalian apparatus, which happen to be largely from Acts and the Catholic epistles. In the section that follows the text and the annotations, we take up the theories that have been advanced regarding this colophon, including the discussions of the Armenian and Syriac traditions.

1 . . .
2 ἔγραψα καὶ ἐξεθέμην κατὰ δύναμιν στειχηρὸν
3 τόδε τὸ τεῦχος Παύλου τοῦ ἀποστόλου πρὸς
4 ἐγγραμμὸν καὶ εὐκατάλημπτον ἀνάγνωσιν τῶν
5 καθ' ἡμᾶς ἀδελφῶν, παρ' ὧν ἁπάντων τόλμης
6 συγνώνην αἰτῷ εὐχῇ τῇ ὑπὲρ ἐμῶν τὴν
7 συνπεριφορὰν κομιζόμενος·
8 ἀντεβλήθη δὲ ἡ βίβλος πρὸς τὸ ἐν καισαρία
9 ἀντίγραφον τῆς βιβλιοθήκης τοῦ ἁγίου Παμφίλου χειρὶ
10 γεγραμμένον· αὐτοῦ
11 προσφώνησις.
12 κορωνὶς εἰμὶ δογμάτων θείων διδάσκαλος·
13 ἐν τίνι με χρήσῃς· ἀντίβιβλον λαμβάνε οἱ
14 γὰρ ἀπόδοται κακοί.
15 ἀντίφρασις.
16 θησαυρὸν ἔχων σε πνευματικῶν ἀγαθῶν καὶ
17 πᾶσιν ἀνθρώποις ποθητόν· ἁρμονίαις τε καὶ
18 ποικίλαις γραμμαῖς κεκοσμημένον· νὴ τὴν
19 ἀλήθειαν· οὐ δώσω σε προχείρως τινί· οὐδ'
20 αὖ φθονέσω τῆς ὠφελείας· χρήσω δὲ τοῖς
21 φίλοις ἀξιόπιστον ἀντίβιβλον λαμβάνων.

---

1   Henri Auguste Omont, *Notice sur un très ancien manuscrit grec en onciales des épîtres de Saint Paul, conservé à la Bibliothèque Nationale*, in *Notices et Extraits des Manuscrits de la Bibliothèque Nationale* 33.1 (Paris: Imprimerie Nationale, 1889), 141–92.

Notes to Colophon

Line 1: This line is virtually obliterated in 015. Ehrhard[2] believes the line originally contained the name Εὐάγριος; Omont confirmed for him that this name could probably be traced in the erased material. Ehrhard further suggests that the line might have been completed with the phrase ὁ ἐν σκήτει or ὁ ἐν κελλίοις.[3] Robinson conjectures that the original first line included the name ΕΥΑΓΡΙΟC, rendering the last two letters as a ligature, then ΕΥΘΑΛΙΟC ΕΠΙCΚΟΠΟ overwritten, also with the final two letters as a ligature.[4] The probability of reading ἐπίσκοπος at the end of the line is also offered by von Gebhardt.[5]

Line 2: 88 reads Εὐάγριος ἔγραψα for ἔγραψα. 88 reads στιχηρὸν for στειχηρὸν.

Lines 2 ff.: The following parallels were originally cited by Ehrhard[6] and elaborated by Conybeare.[7] The numbers in parentheses in these and later parallels refer to pages in the editions of Zacagni and Migne: τὴν ἀποστολικὴν βίβλον στοιχηδὸν ἀναγνούς τε, καὶ γράψας (Z 404; M 629A). στιχηδὸν τὰς καθολικὰς . . . ἐπιστολὰς ἀναγνώσομαι (Z 477; M 668B). τὴν Παύλου βίβλον ἀνεγνωκώς (Z 405; M 629B). τὰς πᾶσας ἐπιστολὰς ἀναγνούς Παύλου τοῦ Ἀποστόλου . . . τοῦ ἀποστολικοῦ τεύχους (Z 548 f.; M 725Bf.).

Line 4: 88 reads ἀκατάληπτον for εὐκατάλημπτον. Parallel: πρὸς εὔσημον ἀνάγνωσιν (Z 410; M 633C).

Lines 5 f.: Parallels: συγγνώμην γε πλείστην αἰτῶν ἐπ᾿ ἀμφοῖν, τόλμης ὁμοῦ, καὶ προπετείας τῆς ἐμῆς, ἅπαντάς τε εἰκότως κοινῇ καθικετεύων ἀδελφούς τε, καὶ πατέρας (Z 405; M 629B). αἰτοῦντες συγγνώμην προπετείας ἡμεῖς (Z 428; M 652B).

2   Ehrhard, "Codex H," 397, 406. Cf. Robinson, *Euthaliana*, 5.
3   Ehrhard, "Codex H," 407.
4   Joseph Armitage Robinson, "The Armenian Version," in Edward Cuthbert Butler, *The Lausiac History of Palladius: a Critical Discussion Together with Notes on Early Egyptian Monachism* (TS 6.1; Cambridge: Cambridge University Press, 1898), 106, n. 1.
5   Cited by von Dobschütz ("Euthaliusfrage," 60) and von Soden (*Schriften des Neuen Testaments*, 681).
6   Ehrhard, "Codex H," 389 f.
7   Conybeare, "Codex Pamphili," 246 f.

Line 6: 88 reads συγγνώμην for συνγνώμην. 88 reads ὑμῶν for ἐμῶν. Von Dobschütz[8] believes this is the best evidence for the dependence of 88 on 015, unless it is also an error.

Lines 6 f.: Parallels: εὐχῇ, τῇ ὑπὲρ ἡμῶν, τὴν συμπεριφορὰν κομιζόμενοι (Z 428; M 652B). εὐχῇ τῇ ὑπὲρ ἡμῶν ἡμᾶς τῆς πειθοῦς διηνεκῶς ἀμειβόμενος (Z 477; M 668B).

Line 7: 88 reads συμπεριφορὰν for συνπεριφορὰν.

Line 8: 88 reads καισαρεία for καισαρία.

Lines 8–10: Parallel: Ἀντεβλήθη δὲ τῶν Πράξεων, καὶ Καθωλικῶν ἐπιστολῶν τὸ βιβλίον πρὸς τὰ ἀκριβῆ ἀντίγραφα τῆς ἐν Καισαρείᾳ βιβλιοθήκης Εὐσεβίου τοῦ Παμφίλου (Z 513; M 692Af.).

Line 10: αὐτοῦ is omitted by 88 and by Omont's transcription of 015.[9] Von Dobschütz refers to Montfaucon (Coislin), who shows the last letter of αὐτοῦ barely legible.[10] Von Dobschütz argues, against von Soden,[11] that the line, including the αὐτοῦ, is connected with the preceding material.[12] Conybeare, who prints the text of 015 "as it stands in Tischendorf's copy in his edition of the N.T. of 1849," includes the αὐτοῦ.[13] Zuntz shows the αὐτοῦ in his notes on 015 and 88, citing[14] Omont and Ehrhard. The manuscript evidence is, thus, erratically cited.

Conybeare's translation of the Armenian and Zuntz' Syriac both support reading αὐτοῦ.[15] Devreesse argues, "Mais l'υ n'est autre que celui de la seconde lettre du premier mot du colophon dont le dessin s'est imprimé dans la feuille de parchemin."[16]

---

8 Dobschütz, "Euthaliusfrage," 60.

9 Omont, *Notice sur un très ancien manuscrit grec*, 189. Also von Dobschütz ("Euthaliusfrage," 59, n. 1) referring both to 88 and to 015. See also Johann Albert Fabricius, *Bibliotheca graeca* (ed. by Gottlieb Christoph Harles; vol. 5; Hamburg: C. E. Bohn, 1796), 789.

10 Dobschütz, "Euthaliusfrage," p. 50, citing Montfaucon. The reference is to Henry Charles du Cambout, duc de Coislin, *Bibliotheca Coisliniana, olim Segueriana* (Paris: L. Guerin & C. Robustel, 1715), 260 ff., in which the first line of 14ᵛ of 015 is transcribed γεγραμμένον αὐτοῦ.

11 Soden, *Schriften des Neuen Testaments*, 680 f.

12 Ernst von Dobschütz, "The Notices Prefixed to Codex 773 of the Gospels," *HTR* 18 (1925): 284, n. 6. Zahn supports von Dobschütz here ("Neues und Altes," 322) .

13 Conybeare, "Codex Pamphili," 244, n. 1.

14 Zuntz, *Ancestry*, 15, n. 7.

15 Conybeare, "Codex Pamphili," 243, n.1; and Zuntz, *Ancestry*, 13, 23, respectively.

16 Robert Devreesse, *Introduction à l'étude des manuscrits grecs* (Paris: Imprimerie Nationale, 1954), 163, n. 5.

Line 11: 88 inserts the πλοῦς between lines 10 and 11.

Line 12: 88 reads ορωνὶς, omitting the preliminary initial. Robinson conjectures the omission of θείων.[17]

Line 13: 88 reads χρήσεις for χρήσης.

Line 14: Robinson conjectures the insertion of λαβόντες βιβλί following γὰρ.[18] Cf. Conybeare's rendering of the Armenian, ". . . for those who (? add 'have to') restore (i. e., books) are evil."[19]

Line 15: 88 omits this title. 773 reads ἀντιφώνησις.

Lines 17 f.: 773 omits ἁρμονίαις τε καὶ ποικίλαις.

Line 19: 773 omits σε.

Line 20: 88 reads φθονάσω for φθονέσω. Ehrhard[20] transcribes Omont αὐφθονέσω against von Dobschütz[21] and Robinson.[22] Von Dobschütz notes some verbal parallels between words in this line and the prologue to Acts (Z 404, lines 13, 17; M 629A).[23]

The fragmentary text of 015 breaks off following τῆς. The remainder of the colophon is provided from 88. Cf. Omont[24] and von Dobschütz.[25]

The more extensive form of the text, as we have it in 015 and 88, exists also in several Armenian manuscripts that Conybeare has studied, principally B. M. Add 19,730 (*ca.* 1270) as well as a codex of the whole Bible (1220) at S. Lazzaro and another belonging to Lord Zouche.[26] In the Armenian codices and in 88, the colophon comes at the end of Philemon; in 015, it follows Titus. The parallel cited for lines 8 ff. occurs in 181 at the conclusion of the Catholic epistles, as a subscription. This subscription also occurs in a number of other Greek manuscripts, 623 635 1836 1898, i. e., 1875.[27] In Cambridge Add. 1700 (1170 A.D.), a

---

17 Robinson, *Euthaliana*, 4.
18 *Ibid.*
19 Conybeare, "Codex Pamphili," 243.
20 Erhard, "Codex H," 388.
21 Dobschütz, "Euthaliusfrage," 59, n. 2.
22 Robinson, *Euthaliana*, 3.
23 Dobschütz, "Euthaliusfrage," 59, n. 2.
24 Omont, *Notice sur un très ancien manuscrit grec*, 189.
25 Dobschütz, "Euthaliusfrage," 60.
26 Conybeare, "Codex Pamphili," 242 f.
27 Soden, *Schriften des Neuen Testaments*, 681. Cf. Hans Lietzmann, *Einführung in die Textgeschichte der Paulusbriefe: An die Römer erklärt* (HNT 8; 3d ed.; Tübingen: Mohr [Siebeck], 1928), 13, cited by Harold S. Murphy, "The Text of Romans and 1 Corinthians in Minuscule 93 and the Text of Pamphilus," *HTR* 52 (1959): 121, n. 18.

Syriac manuscript, this same part of the colophon is imbedded in a more extensive colophon attached to the Pauline epistles.[28]

In addition to these instances, there is a remarkable parallel to the Armenian text of lines 2–4, which Robinson discovered in a manuscript dealing with Evagrius; the colophon connects the life of Evagrius with his works.[29] Finally, von Dobschütz found in 773, a manuscript of the Gospels, an extended introduction to the text that begins with the curious dialogue at the end of our text, lines 11–21.[30]

Shortly following the publication by Omont of the text of 015, Ehrhard wrote an article on the relationship between 015 and 88 and the identity of the author of the so-called Euthalian material.[31] Although Montfaucon had previously noted a parallel between part of the colophon in 015 and parts of the Euthalian apparatus,[32] Ehrhard was the first to collect systematically the parallels in the Euthalian material to phrases in the colophon. Ehrhard is persuaded by these parallels that the colophon is the work of Euthalius, or Evagrius, which Ehrhard believes is the name of the author.[33] Ehrhard reviews several judgments of the date of 015, which place it in the fifth century or the sixth.[34] He argues on other grounds that the original edition of the Euthalian apparatus appeared in 396; he does not believe these theories necessarily contradict the possibility that 015 was produced by the author of the prologues, or was at least one of the first copies of the original. He claims that a paleological argument cannot be raised against dating 015 near 396.[35] 88, he argues, does not go directly back to 015, as several orthographical variants, together with the insertion of the πλοῦς Παύλου and the omission of the phrase ἀντίφρασις, show.[36]

In a subsequent article, von Dobschütz attacks Erhard's theory of the production of the colophon.[37] Von Dobschütz believes that 015 is not the original edition and that the colophon was compiled from Euthalian

28 Zuntz, *Ancestry*, 13 f.
29 Robinson, "Armenian Version," 104 f.
30 Dobschütz, "Notices Prefixed to Codex 773," 280–84.
31 Ehrhard, "Codex H."
32 Coislin, *Bibliotheca Coisliniana*, 261. He refers to Pamphilus as the author of the Euthalian material that appears in Coisliniana XXV, i. e., 307.
33 See Ehrhard, "Codex H," 389 f., 397, and elsewhere.
34 *Ibid.*, 395 f.
35 *Ibid.*, 407, 409.
36 *Ibid.*, 389.
37 Dobschütz, "Euthaliusfrage."

phrases in parts of the apparatus. He is concerned with transcriptional errors of Ehrhard and the problems of ascribing itacisms to one who speaks of collation with the *Musterexemplar*. Moreover, he does not accept Ehrhard's treatment of the possible date of 015, preferring the standard sixth or second half of the fifth century as early limits.[38] In terms of 88, von Dobschütz agrees that the name Evagrius must have been in the *Vorlage* of 88 and that the signs in 015 point to Evagrius, not Euthalius. He does not believe, however, that 88 is an independent witness; if 015 is not directly the source of 88, it does lie in its background, and the subscription has been borrowed from it.[39]

Peter Corssen scrutinized the points of comparison between the colophon in 015 and the Euthalian apparatus; he notes that the verbal parallels occur primarily at three points in the Euthalian edition of Acts.[40] Corssen argues that it is quite unlikely that an editor or scribe would compose a subscription to the Pauline material from three disparate places in a prologue to Acts and the subscription to the collection.

He concludes that nothing speaks against the Euthalian origin of the subscription and much speaks for it.[41] 015, then, borrowed the subscription from Euthalius; the claim that 015 was compared to a manuscript of Pamphilus has no special significance for 015.[42]

Robinson, beforehand, took issue with this interpretation of the colophon. He recognized the similarities between parts of the Euthalian apparatus and the colophon.[43] In arguing that these parallels were due to the work of an editor, he had the predisposition of the strong case for a similar process in the *Martyrium*. Moreover, he offers the following observations:

1. The colophon is written in the singular, a characteristic of pieces whose authenticity Robinson has already rejected.
2. In addition to the parallels that Erhard produced, Robinson found these:
   a. Τὸ ἐξεθέμην in line 2, ἐκθέμενος ὀλιγοστὴν ἀνακεφαλαίωσιν (Z 410; M 633C) and ἐκτιθέμεθα γοῦν αὐτὴν (sc. κεφαλαίων ἔκθεσιν)

---

38   *Ibid.*, 50.
39   *Ibid.*, 60.
40   Peter Corssen, Review of Eduard von der Goltz, *Eine textkritische Arbeit des zehnten bezw. sechsten Jahrhunderts*, GGA 161 (1899): 671.
41   *Ibid.*, 672, in which he is supported by Conybeare ("Date of Euthalius," 49).
42   Corssen, Review, 676 f.
43   Robinson, *Euthaliana*, 70 f.

καθ' ἱστορίαν Λουκᾶ κ.τ.λ. (Z 428; M 652B). Robinson claims that Euthalius does not use ἐκτίθημι "in speaking of his edition as a whole," but in a different sense.[44]

   b. Το στειχηρὸν in line 2, he argues that there is a confusion here between στιχηρῶς and στιχηδόν, "the latter being the word used by Euthalius."[45]

   c. Robinson urges that the textual problem with ἐμῶν in line 6 is the result of the necessary alteration in the number of κομιζόμε-νοι to bring it into conformity with the colophon. Robinson suggests that the original editor or more likely the scribe of 015 altered ἡμῶν in the parallel to ἐμῶν. Von Dobschütz had already described ἐμῶν as an impossible reading, arguing that the ὑμῶν in 88 is either an emendation (if it is dependent upon 015) or a scribal error for ἡμῶν in its *Vorlage*, which indeed may be the case with the reading in 015.[46]

Given the association with the name Evagrius that this colophon has in 88 and the dating of the three paragraph version of the *Martyrium* at 396, Robinson is inclined to attribute this editorial work to Evagrius Ponticus.

    Corssen's assertion that the claim of the colophon has no special significance for the text of the manuscript points up another question, namely, the relationship between the text of a manuscript and the claims made for it by, for example, a colophon of the sort found in 015; secondly, one may ask about the relationship between the texts of two manuscripts with colophons making identical claims. Harold S. Murphy has published in two articles the results of his consideration of these questions in the instance of our materials.[47] His conclusions are as follows:

1. The two codices do not have the same text.[48]
2. The nature of the variants is such that it is impossible to think that the texts have been corrected against the same master manuscript.[49]

---

44 *Ibid.*, 70.
45 *Ibid.*
46 Dobschütz, "Euthaliusfrage," 60.
47 Harold S. Murphy, "On the Text of Codices H and 93," *JBL* 78 (1959): 228–37; the other article is "The Text of Romans and 1 Corinthians in Minuscule 93 and the Text of Pamphilus," previously cited.
48 Murphy, "Codices H and 93," 235.
49 *Ibid.*

3. To answer the question of which, if either, of these manuscripts may
   have been corrected against an exemplar of Pamphilus, Murphy
   takes 1739, Eusebius in Romans, and Eusebius in 1 Corinthians as
   possible representatives of the text such an exemplar may have
   had. He finds the resemblance of 88 to these texts is low. 015, on
   the other hand, which has a colophon like 88, apparently has a
   text like Eusebius.[50]

Conybeare observes that the full colophon appears in several Armenian
manuscripts.[51] He argues that they can hardly be peculiar to any one Armenian copy and must, therefore, have stood in the Greek copy from
which the Armenian version was translated. He is persuaded by his
own comparison of parallels between the language of 015 and parts of
the Euthalian apparatus that the colophon was written by Euthalius,
or at least that the author of the colophon was the author of the prologues.[52] In terms of text, he believes that the Armenian text is a
more accurate representation of the original text than that of 015.[53]

   Günther Zuntz focusses his attention, insofar as the colophon is concerned, on the colophon to the Pauline epistles appearing in the Syriac
manuscript Cambridge Add. 1700 (1170 A.D.).[54] The relevant parallel,
to lines 8–10, is a relatively small part of the whole Syriac colophon;
however, this parallel, together with the several lines that follow in
the Syriac version, constitutes an important part of Zuntz' thesis regarding the background of the Syriac version of the New Testament.

   On the basis of his manuscript, Zuntz offers a reconstruction of the
subscription in the Greek manuscript from which the Philoxenian version was made:[55]

Ἀντεβλήθη πρὸς τὸ ἀντίγραφον τὸ ἐν Καισαρείᾳ τῆς Παλαιστίνης· τῆς
βιβλιοθήκης τοῦ ἁγίου Παμφίλου· χειρὶ γεγραμμένον αὐτοῦ· (*quae erant*
[i.e., ὅπερ ἦσαν?]) ἐπιστολαὶ δεκατέσσαρες· ὧν εἰσὶν πάντων ὁμοῦ· ἀναγνώσεις λα'· κεφάλαια ρμζ'· μαρτυρίαι ρκζ'· στίχοι τετρακισχίλιοι ꝛλϛ'.

A crucial element in the link that Zuntz wishes to establish between the
early forms of the Syriac version and Caesarea is the theory that the last
three lines of the reconstructed subscription are quoted from Pamphilus'

50 Murphy "Romans and 1 Corinthians," 131.
51 Conybeare, "Codex Pamphili," 243.
52 *Ibid.*, 246 f.; also Conybeare, "Date of Euthalius," 49.
53 Conybeare, "Codex Pamphili," 259.
54 Zuntz, *Ancestry*, 13 f.
55 *Ibid.*, 77.

autograph and are not "an independent extract from the properly 'Euthalian' tables."[56] Without passing under review all of the evidence that Zuntz gathers, we are able to report that his general conclusions regarding the form of the materials, which provided the basis for the original edition of the Euthalian apparatus, seem logically sound. It is necessary, however, to modify somewhat Zuntz' comprehensive statement:[57]

> An identical subscription, modelled on various passages from the "Euthalian" prologues and testifying to collation with Pamphilus' autograph, recurs under the Greek "Euthalian" MSS. H and 88 as well as under the Armenian "Euthalius" codices and in turn the Philoxenian colophon. It is naive to ascribe this coincidence to the caprice of an obscure scribe miraculously perpetuated in manuscripts not directly interdependent. This subscription was an integral part of the original equipment of this ἔκδοσις.

The subscriptions to which Zuntz refers are not, of course, identical. None of the others has the added note considered so crucial to Zuntz' case. While all of the manuscripts cited either contain or are wholly parallel to the first part of the reconstruction offered by Zuntz, 015, 88, and the Armenian manuscripts have considerable matter preceding and succeeding this part. Thus, it is not so clear as it seemed just what form the colophon had in its earliest edition.

One could argue, as von Dobschütz does on the basis of the presence in a Gospel manuscript, 773, of the concluding dialogue also found in 015 and 88, that the dialogue was taken from a Gospel manuscript, where it better fits, into the ancestor of the group of Euthalian manuscripts represented by 015 and 88, characterized by the name Evagrius instead of Euthalius.[58] Zuntz, however, disagrees with this supposition[59] and appears to think that this concluding dialogue was at least part of the Euthalian ἐκδόσεις.

It is possible to bring together some of these interpretations of the colophon without producing an incompatible arrangement. The work of an editor, while it would be unacceptable to Corssen, does not conflict with the concerns of Zuntz, for the part of the colophon connecting the work with Caesarea, lines 8–10, is the very part that is common to all of the recensions of the subscription. Further, we have learned from Murphy not to place great stress upon the witness of a colophon

---

56   *Ibid.*, 78. See also 16, n. (c).
57   *Ibid.*, 87.
58   Dobschütz, "Notices Prefixed to Codex 773," 284.
59   Zuntz, *Ancestry*, 101, n. 5.

in evaluating the probable worth and/or provenance of a text to which it may be attached.

This makes any firm conclusions difficult. *A priori*, we are inclined to agree with the doubts of Corssen as to the probability of any editor functioning in the fashion described, yet the conclusions of Robinson regarding the background of the *Martyrim* suggest a precedent. Whether the facts are sufficiently unlike in the second instance, or even whether Robinson's case is sustained in the first, is not certain. Further, we are attracted by Zuntz' general theory regarding the composition of the exemplar upon which Euthalius based his work. We are not, however, so clearly persuaded that his argument regarding the original form and source of the colophon is conclusive or that, as such, it is an integral part of his general reconstruction or the history of the Euthalian apparatus.

Part Three: Versions

9. Armenian

The principal secondary sources dealing with the evidence of the Armenian tradition that are pertinent to the Euthalian apparatus are two articles by F. C. Conybeare,[1] parts of *Euthaliana* by J. Armitage Robinson, a critical introductory note by the same scholar in an edition of Palladius' *Lausiac History*,[2] and a series of articles by Aristaces Vardanian.[3]

The manuscript sources of Conybeare and Robinson were the following: B. M. Add. 19,730 (dated *ca.* 1270), a codex containing the entire Bible at S. Lazzaro (dated 1220), the text belonging to Lord Zouche, and the text behind the edition of Zohrab (1805).[4] Vardanian used a collection of manuscripts at the Venetian library where he worked.

Conybeare and Robinson devoted themselves, for the most part, to whole parts of the apparatus and the Armenian New Testament text. Although the work of Vardanian reviews that of the other two, it is really a much more detailed investigation of the Armenian text of the apparatus.

Given the fact that parts of the Euthalian apparatus appear in Armenian texts of the New Testament, we have to ask whether there is any information in these texts or in other Armenian sources that suggests something other than what we have in the Greek tradition or whether there is additional support for some parts of the Greek tradition. Conybeare found in the British Museum codex, in addition to a peculiarly arranged order of the New Testament, the three Euthalian prologues, something he calls the "Voyage of Paul," which must be the πλοῦς, a list of the apostles, and a colophon very similar to the one found in 015 and 88.[5] The *Martyrium* appears in the printed text of the Armenian

---

1   Conybeare, "Codex Pamphili" and "Date of Euthalius."
2   Robinson, "Armenian Version."
3   Vardanian, "Euthaliana."
4   Robinson, *Euthaliana*, 8, and Conybeare, "Codex Pamphili," 242 ff.
5   Conybeare, "Codex Pamphili," 242 f.

New Testament, and Conybeare also confirms its text in the codex of Lord Zouche and an ancient fragment.[6]

On the basis of his analysis of the relationship of the colophon in the Armenian codices, 015, and Euthalius, i. e., 181, as well as an examination of the possible relationships between these two sets of evidence and other witnesses that Bousset describes collectively as the Codex of Pamphilus, Conybeare concludes that there is a close connection between 015, the Armenian tradition, and the text of Pamphilus; moreover, the Armenian is probably the best witness.[7] Robinson is rather critical of the approach taken by Conybeare.[8] He notes that it is difficult to decide which of the different shapes that the apparatus assumes in the Armenian tradition should be taken as closer to the original; he also points out that there is no assurance that a colophon was taken from the same manuscript as the text. Robinson embarks upon a much more detailed investigation of the Armenian text of the Gospels and epistles and, more particularly, 015. We are not going to review that evidence here more than to note that Robinson finally concludes that Conybeare's evidence was "wholly insufficient to support his position."[9]

Although this leaves the discussion of the texts unclear, there is other evidence that Robinson does not directly contest. Conybeare notes that the material in the first part of the *Martyrium* translated "secundum Syro-Macedones, quae apud Aegyptios dicitur quinta mensis Epiphi" as well as the stichometric note and the last paragraph are missing from the Armenian tradition,[10] which led him to conjecture that the first edition of the *Martyrium* did not contain these additions. In his first essay, he believes that Euthalius, who might have been as young as twenty in 396, could have made the addition himself.[11]

In his first essay, he proposes that the Armenian translation of the Euthalian apparatus was made early in the fifth century.[12] In the second

---

6 *Ibid.*, 249, n. 1.
7 *Ibid.*, 255–59 and other places. Cf. Bousset, *Textkritische*; and Ernst von Dobschütz, review of Wilhelm Bousset, *Textkritische*, LCD 45 (1894): 913.
8 Robinson, *Euthaliana*, pp. 74 ff.
9 *Ibid.*, p. 98. Robinson's theory about the relationship of the Armenian to the Syriac version was attacked by Frédéric Macler, *Le Texte arménien de l'Evangile d'après Matthieu et Marc* (AMGBE 28; Paris: Imprimerie Nationale, 1919).
10 Conybeare, "Codex Pamphili, 249.
11 *Ibid.*, 250 f. By the end of the second essay ("Date of Euthalius," 52) he argues for a suspension of judgment regarding the date.
12 Conybeare, "Codex Pamphili," 250.

essay, with a view to specifying the date further, he has examined the language more thoroughly; moreover, he has carefully considered the inferences that may be drawn from the Armenian dating in the *Martyrium*. "In translating dates fixed in the Julian calendar the Armenians were wont to add the name of the month which in their vague calendar answered at the time of the translation to the Julian month mentioned."[13] He concludes, on the basis of the co-ordination of the calendar possibilities, that the *Martyrium* was translated into Armenian between 388 and 508; he believes that 448 was the most likely year.[14]

Conybeare, in addition to these internal arguments, also brings evidence from non-Biblical sources, which are basically three: (a) material from the book of the Caesars,[15] (b) an historical chronicle, which Conybeare attributes to Ananias of Shirak,[16] and (c) a passage from a commentary on Acts by "a certain presbyter Matthew in A.D. 1411."[17]

The book of the Caesars, undated by Conybeare, contains what he believes may be independent information about the Euthalian tradition. He thinks that the following four "facts" are added: (a) Euthalius undertook the two parts of his work for different people. (b) The work on the Paulines was undertaken for Theophilus. (c) Athanasius, for whom the work on Acts and the Catholic epistles was done, was a royal ecclesiastic. (d) Euthalius' motive for developing the lists of quotations was to refute those who rejected the Old Testament.[18] Robinson, in contrast, believes that this material is "obviously based on the Prologues and on the *Martyrium*,"[19] although only the first "fact" may really be deduced from the prologues.

The chronicle that Conybeare cites, supported by independent evidence, provides essentially the same information as the book of Caesars. This chronicle, however, may be dated before 700 A.D., which means that there was an Armenian version of the apparatus at that time that must have been translated earlier.

---

13 Conybeare, "Date of Euthalius," 50.
14 *Ibid.*
15 Conybeare, "Codex Pamphili," 251.
16 Conybeare, "Date of Euthalius," 45 f.
17 *Ibid.*, 47 ff.
18 Conybeare, "Codex Pamphili," 252.
19 Robinson, *Euthaliana*, 101, n. 1. Cf. the opinion of von Dobschütz ("Euthaliusstudien," 113) that the material going beyond that in the prologues and the *Martyrium* appears to be a "freie Phantasie eines armenischen Haereseologen."

The material in the third source brings Conybeare to the following conclusions:

1. The information is not obtained from the prologues, but it agrees with and explains them.
2. This source is independent of the chronicle; moreover, it contradicts it, placing Euthalius under Alexander, who died a few months following Nicea.
3. Matthew, the presbyter, knows that the "honored father" of the Pauline prologue is this Alexander.
4. Matthew says that Athanasius of the prologue to Acts was a monk of the Thebaid. "If we allow for the tendency to ascribe everything to the great leader of orthodoxy, we must admit Matthew here displays very special knowledge, and appears to be very reliable."[20]
5. "He knows that the Athanasius in question was the one who drew up or corrected the creed, which from time immemorial has been in use in the Armenian church, and is not identical with the Nicene."[21]

The fifth observation rather weakens the strength of the fourth; there are other chronological difficulties that Conybeare faces, and we will discuss these and his proposed solutions in the chapter on dating, authorship, and provenance. Conybeare has considerable confidence in the validity of the information contained in this fifteenth century source.[22]

Vardanian has made a very extensive survey of the Armenian evidence and the secondary literature related to it as well as that more broadly based. Although he sometimes makes use of internal probability in his suggestions, the most regularly used criterion for constructing his picture of the original edition of the Euthalian apparatus is his evaluation of the linguistic peculiarities of the period in which he believes the apparatus was translated.[23] On the basis of what is or is not linguistically appropriate to the fifth century period of Armenian literary activity, he rules pieces, or parts, authentic or inauthentic. He concludes that Euthalius constructed the prologue to the Pauline epistles in 396 and shortly thereafter, the material for Acts and the Catholic epistles. Also

---

20 Conybeare, "Date of Euthalius," 48.
21 *Ibid.*
22 *Ibid.*, 49, 52.
23 Vardanian, "Euthaliana," 38 (1924): 407 ff.

included were several smaller pieces.[24] Vardanian believes with Conybeare that this material was translated in 448, but he does not believe
that the interval was sufficient to permit any interpolation or revision
to have occurred. Therefore, those parts of the apparatus that reflect
the nuances of a mid-fifth century translation are all parts of the authentic original edition.[25]

On this basis, Vardanian qualifies the prologues. The *Martyrium* was
translated at the same time as the prologues.[26] He notes that Robinson's
argument centering on the interpretation of κατ' αὐτὸν is demolished by
the fact that the Armenian translates this phrase "his."[27] This translation
does not, of course, affect Robinson's argument at all.

Vardanian also admits the "lection" list for the Pauline material, the
paragraph following with the stichometric notations, both quotation lists
with accompanying προγράμματα, and the chapter lists. In the section
on Acts and the Catholic epistles, he does not find the "lection" lists for
either section, nor does he find either sort of quotation list, nor any
προγράμματα.[28] We already noted von Soden's bewilderment at not
finding any reference to the "lection" list in the prologue to the Catholic epistles; however, we are not prepared to push Vardanian's theory
as the most probable solution. Although the prologue to Acts fails to
mention the quotation list(s), there are some indications in the prologue
to the Catholic epistles. Vardanian suggests that these should be taken to
refer to very short summaries that occur after the heading of each of the
Catholic epistles, which provide very much the same information as that
contained in the lists of "lections." Vardanian suggests that in the Greek
tradition, the "lection" lists, προγράμματα, and the quotation lists were
composed in conscious imitation of the genuine Euthalian work on the
Pauline epistles. We have noted in the descriptive discussions the great
similarity or identity of the προγράμματα. He rejects Zahn's theory that
some of the quotations in the Pauline list were later interpolations.[29]

In the case of the fashion in which the numbering of the subdivisions of the chapter lists was carried out, Vardanian claims that all the
relevant Armenian manuscripts follow the pattern laid out in 015 for

---

24 *Ibid.*, 39 (1925): 1 f.
25 *Ibid.*, 1–4.
26 *Ibid.*, 7 f.
27 *Ibid.* He cites the Syriac as also supporting this translation (cf. von Dobschütz,
    "Euthaliusstudien," 134).
28 Vardanian, "Euthaliana," 39 (1925): 11 f.
29 *Ibid.*, 19 f.

most, although not all, of the Pauline letters. Vardanian is not able to provide a rational explanation for the divergence that occurs from this pattern.[30]

With regard to some of the other items that are included by Zacagni in his edition of the Euthalian apparatus, Vardanian observes that although the *argumenta* are included in his manuscripts, as they are in virtually all of the Greek manuscripts, linguistically they are not connected with the original translations of the Euthalian material and are, hence, not from the original edition. Only the last part of the *argumentum* to Hebrews, as it is reported in Zacagni's edition, shows the linguistic characteristics that are associated with the period in which the Euthalian apparatus was translated.[31]

Vardanian pronounces authentic the colophon, which he finds in his Armenian manuscripts,[32] as well as the ἀποδημίαι and the πλοῦς.[33] Moreover, he finds that the two tables following the short quotation list, which designate the cities from which the letters were written and the authors of the letters, as well as the table of contents, i. e., the τάδε ἔνεστιν, are all linguistically characteristic of the appropriate period and therefore, are part of the original edition,[34] as is the prayer of Euthalius.[35]

Vardanian finds that the thirty-six chapter list for Acts is missing from his Armenian codices.[36] Moreover, he does not feel that the Διὰ τί is authentic.[37]

Vardanian's arguments are more detailed than this summary exposition suggests. In addition to the lengthy preliminary discussions, he provides a critical edition of the apparatus in Armenian. Although there is no evidence in the Greek tradition for the radical reduction of the contents of the original edition, in terms of eliminating the "lection" lists and quotation lists with their προγράμματα, other of his suggestions have internal merit as well as some support in the Greek tradition. In the latter instance, his final picture of the *Martyrium* is in line with good witnesses among Greek manuscripts. His argument for the omis-

---

30 *Ibid.*, 103 f.
31 *Ibid.*, 107 f.
32 *Ibid.*, 111 f.
33 *Ibid.*, 113 f.
34 *Ibid.*, 25 f.
35 *Ibid.*, 115 ff.
36 *Ibid.*, 105 f.
37 *Ibid.*, 105 f.

sion of the etymological pun on Paul's name has support. His use of linguistic criteria to eliminate the *argumenta*, although they appear in the
Armenian manuscripts, supports evidence available elsewhere. Moreover, he argues that statements in the prologue to Acts justify his interpretation of the absence of major pieces for Acts and the Catholic epistles, namely, "διεπεμψάμην ἐν βραχεῖ τὰ ἕκαστά σοι, καὶ καθ᾽ ἀκολουθίαν
ἐκθέμενος ὀλιγοστὴν ἀνακεφαλαίωσιν."[38]

It needs to be recalled that the Greek tradition itself, in terms of the
manuscripts available, dates almost entirely from a manuscript, or a family, that included the *argumenta*, unanimously agreed to be late. Many of
Vardanian's suggestions, then, in spite of lack of corroborative evidence
in the present Greek tradition, must be given serious consideration. We
believe that the conclusions drawn by Conybeare from the supplementary Armenian witnesses are helpful, insofar as they confirm an early tradition of the Euthalian apparatus, although we are rather skeptical of the
reconstruction that Conybeare attempts in full reliance on this material.
We have made previous note of Harris' discoveries of parallels between
the Euthalian prologues and a couple of Armenian historians of an early
period. Harris was very dubious, though, that Lazarus of Pharbi, for example, would have imitated Euthalius, preferring to believe that both
were dependent upon some now unknown Greek Christian historical
writer. On the other hand, his reluctance to credit Euthalius with significance in the eyes of these Armenian historians is not supported by
the fact that Euthalius was early translated into Armenian, in a period
of classical literature, associated with the Bible. It seems possible,
then, that the prologues may have had some literary appeal.

---

38 Z 410; M 633C, cited by Vardanian, "Euthaliana," 39 (1925): 19 f.

10. Syriac

As in the case of the Armenian material, we are here going to present the critical results of investigations. The problems associated with the development of the Syriac New Testament are varied and complex,[1] and we have no intention of attempting to review the discussion of the relationship of the Peshitta, Philoxenian, and Harclean versions. We have no standing to offer substantive criticisms of these studies and feel that our primary responsibility is to get conclusions from work with these versions related to the Euthalian apparatus before the scholarly world in a summary fashion. The main work here is an extended article by Ernst von Dobschütz and a book, together with several articles, by Günther Zuntz.[2] There is a critical note by Bertrand Hemmerdinger that deals with a very limited part of the apparatus and is dependent, in terms of much of the evidence, upon the article by von Dobschütz.[3]

Zuntz, it happens, is primarily interested in dealing with the relational problems we noted, and discussion of the Euthalian apparatus is useful to him primarily for its illumination of the development of the Syriac text. For the most part, his theory about the origin of the Euthalian apparatus is based upon inferences and evidence in the Greek tradition. Zuntz concludes that the Philoxenian was a revision of the Peshitta on the basis of a Euthalian exemplar in 508.[4] He believes that this exemplar was a copy of a master manuscript made at the library of Caesarea and that a century later in 616 Thomas of Harkel used another copy in his revision of the Philoxenian.

---

1   See Bruce Manning Metzger, *The Text of the New Testament: Its Transmission, Corruption, and Restoration* (2d ed.; New York; Oxford: Oxford University Press, 1968), 68−71.

2   Dobschütz, "Euthaliusstudien," especially 115−54; and Zuntz, *Ancestry*; also "Etudes Harkléennes," *RB* 57 (1950): 550−82; and "Die Subscriptionen der Syra Harclensis," *ZDMG* New Series 26 (1951): 174−96. This subject comes up, of course, in other of Zuntz' writings.

3   Hemmerdinger, "Euthaliana."

4   Zuntz, *Ancestry*, 113.

Von Dobschütz spends a large part of his article discussing the different parts of the Euthalian apparatus that he finds in two Syriac manuscripts, B. M. Add 7157 (768 A.D.) and Oxford New College 333 (eleventh century). He designates these two manuscripts L and O respectively.[5] Von Dobschütz submitted these texts to very close scrutiny; he concludes that the two manuscripts reflect three different witnesses to the Euthalian tradition. He outlines these conclusions in a chart, which is reproduced below:[6]

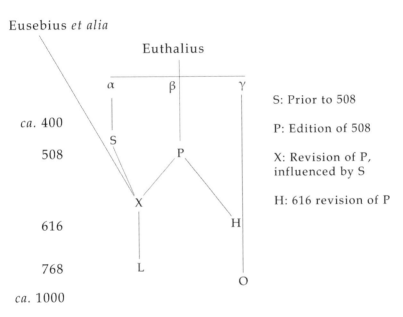

In addition to suggestions about parts of the apparatus, which we will discuss below, his summary conclusion is that these manuscripts give us almost conclusive evidence that in 508 the Euthalian apparatus for the Pauline letters was translated by Polycarp for Philoxenos (P) and that a revision was made by Thomas of Harkel (H) on the basis of other Greek manuscripts.[7] Von Dobschütz found no trace of any part of the apparatus for Acts or the Catholic epistles.

We may here summarize some of the suggestions that von Dobschütz offers regarding the probable form of the early tradition of the

5   Dobschütz, "Euthaliusstudien," 116.
6   *Ibid.*, 144 f.
7   *Ibid.*, 153.

apparatus as well as some observations about variants of the tradition in
Syriac.

In L, there is an abbreviated summary of the prologue to the Pauline
letters. Originally, he thought that this might be an early form that Euthalius enlarged, but examination convinced him that it was a later revision, composed of scraps and phrases, much like the colophon.[8] Instead of the whole prologue, L contains a revision that has displaced
the entire section dealing with the summary of the letters and the
brief statement of the purpose of Euthalius. Many of the smaller pieces
of the apparatus appear.[9] In O, the prologue is intact, and most other
parts are present, including the προγράμματα, both quotation lists,
chapter lists, "lection" lists, the τάδε ἔνεστιν, the pieces about the places
of origin and the co-authors of the letters, and one of the two pieces
dealing with the quotations used twice.[10] The *argumenta* are lacking, except for the long paragraph at the end of the *argumentum* for Hebrews, as
it is printed by Zacagni.[11] There are no stichometric notes, although in L
there are notes regarding *Petgamē*, which seem to have a function similar
to that of stichometric notes, although not the same as argued by Harris.[12] The Διὰ τί is omitted from O.[13]

Von Dobschütz makes a number of novel suggestions on the basis of
his analysis of these Syriac witnesses. He thinks that the original form of
the apparatus in the Syriac may have had all the chapter lists together.[14]
He argues that the language of the prologue is no barrier to this suggestion, and it may have been only misunderstanding and/or practical considerations that led to the distribution of the chapter lists among the various letters as is already found in 015. Zuntz thinks that this observation
by von Dobschütz regarding the interpretation of the language of the
prologue is correct, as well as his interpretation of the language of the
heading of the chapter list of Romans, which appears to be something
that would come at the beginning of a list of all the chapter lists, not just
one. Zuntz, however, thinks that this formation of chapter lists, gathered in a single collection at the front of a codex, was only what Eutha-

---

8   *Ibid.*, 122 f.
9   *Ibid.*, 123–25, 127.
10 *Ibid.*, 129 f.
11 See page 69, n. 4 of this monograph for a discussion.
12 See von Dobschütz' critique of Harris' (*Stichometry* [1893], 65–68) equation of
    Petgamē and stichometry ("Euthaliusstudien," 118 f.).
13 Dobschütz, "Euthaliusstudien," 130.
14 *Ibid.*, 149.

lius found in the exemplar in Caesarea and that Euthalius himself distributed the lists among the letters.[15]

Von Dobschütz thinks also that the original form of the quotation
lists has been reversed in the present Greek tradition. He believes that
the short quotation list functioned as a sort of summary of the longer
one. He notes that the problem, observed elsewhere,[16] of the impossibly
large stichometric figure for the short table in Acts may be an indication
of this, in that it may be interpreted as considering the two tables as a
single unit, for stichometric purposes.[17]

15 Zuntz, *Ancestry*, 82 f.
16 Charles Graux, "Nouvelles recherches sur la stichométrie," *RPh* New Series 2 (1878): 120, n. 59.
17 Dobschütz, "Euthaliusstudien," 150.

11. Minor Versions

Gothic

This discussion reviews an article and a pamphlet.[1] The author of the article, Marchand, is in turn, dependent upon three other articles, two by Braun and one by Kauffmann.[2] Both of our resources deal with an analysis of three Gothic manuscripts: Ambrosianus A, Ambrosianus B, and Carolinus. Marchand claims that the first two must be dated around the sixth century.[3]

Our resources concentrate upon divisions in these manuscripts that are analogous to those ascribed to Euthalius: colometric divisions[4] or continuous script marked with points and spaces.[5] There are also marginal notes indicating, in Ambrosianus B, a fourfold division of the text. Here Marchand relies upon Braun who finds forty-four sections marked *laiktjo*,[6] sixty-eight (or seventy-nine) noted with a numerical sign, ninety-thee with a "division sign of the first order," and 170 with a "division sign of the second order." Marchand finds considerable agreement with the "lections" of Euthalius. Since there are only thirty-one "lections" in Euthalius' Pauline letters, it is difficult to understand what Marchand can mean when he says that there is agreement in twen-

---

1   James Woodrow Marchand, "The Gothic Evidence for 'Euthalian Matter,'" *HTR* 49 (1956): 159–67; and Karl Marold, *Stichometrie und Leseabschnitte in den gotischen Episteltexten* (Königsberg: Hartung, 1890).
2   Wilhelm Braun, "Die Lese- und Einteilungszeichen in den gotischen Handschriften der Ambrosiana in Mailand," *ZDPh*, 30 (1898): 433–48; "Ein satzphonetisches Gesetz des Gotischen mit vorwiegenden Rücksicht auf die Codices Ambrosiani," *GRM* 5 (1913): 367–91; and Friedrich Kauffmann, "Beiträge zur Quellenkritik der gotischen Bibelübersetzung. 7. Der Codex Carolinus," *ZDPh* 43 (1913): 401–28.
3   Marchand, "Gothic Evidence," 160.
4   Ambrosianus A: Rom. 6:23–1 Cor. 5:4; and Carolinus, so Marchand, "Gothic Evidence," 161, 163.
5   Ambrosianus A (the remainder), Ambrosianus B, so Marchand, "Gothic Evidence," 161 f.
6   Braun, "Lese- und Einteilungszeichen," 435 ff., cited by Marchand, "Gothic Evidence," 162, n. 14. Marold, however, finds twenty-five (*Stichometrie und Leseabschnitte*, 15).

ty-six instances and differences of only a few verses in the remaining eighteen.[7]

Marchand finds a similar degree of agreement in the places marked by a numerical sign;[8] he is uncertain what may be the relationship of the last two divisions. Marold also concludes that the numbers in the margin of Ambrosianus B clearly signify the Euthalian divisions, the minor variations being scribal errors.[9] He further argues that the marginal signs, probably equivalent to Marchand's "division signs," have nothing to do with Euthalius.

Marchand claims that the exemplar on which Ambrosianus A and B were based, "which must be placed in the fifth century, had a division into cola, along with the Euthalian *lectiones* and *capita*."[10]

Marchand concludes by bringing in some evidence related to the early development of the Gothic Bible.[11] He believes that it is likely that the colometric arrangements go back to Ulfilas himself and are derived from the Euthalian materials. Thus, he decides, the evidence may suggest that "we must place Euthalius well into the 4th century, . . . probably in the first half of the fourth century."

Latin and Georgian

Secondary literature on the remaining versional evidence of the apparatus is very occasional. We can only collect and describe it with no attempt at a critical evaluation.

For the Latin material, we have already noted the discussions of the relationship between the chapter list of Acts and the divisions of Acts in Fuldensis, seventy-four, and Amiatinus, seventy.[12] Robinson views as

---

7   Marchand, "Gothic Evidence," 162. There are no extant Gothic manuscript texts for Acts, the Catholic epistles, Hebrews, and the Apocalypse – so Arthur Vööbus, *Early Versions of the New Testament; Manuscript Studies* (ETSE 6; Stockholm: [Estonian Theological Society in Exile], 1954), 304. Marold, however, also concludes that these *laiktjo* are Euthalian in origin, with some re-division into smaller parts (*Stichometrie und Leseabschnitte*, 15).

8   Marchand, "Gothic Evidence," 162. Marold (*Stichometrie und Leseabschnitte*, 13) finds several marginal notes in Carolinus that agree with the chapters and subdivisions.

9   Marold, *Stichometrie und Leseabschnitte*, 15.

10 Marchand, "Gothic Evidence," 162.

11 *Ibid.*, 166 f.

12 See page 54 of this monograph.

significant the fact that in three places where there is no corroboration by Sinaiticus and Vaticanus of the Euthalian division, it is found in Amiatinus and Fuldensis.[13] Moreover, in three places of displacement, Amiatinus and Fuldensis side with Euthalius. "These facts are confirmatory of the view that the system found in Euthalius is the ultimate source."[14]

Von Dobschütz cites a study by Riggenbach that showed that the chapter table in Fuldensis and Cod. Vat. Reg. 9 for Hebrews is a translation of the Euthalian chapter list; the common *Vorlage* lacked chapters thirteen through twenty-three.[15] Von Dobschütz had hoped that Berger's work[16] would show additional traces of the Euthalian chapter lists. This hope was not fulfilled, and Berger further demonstrates that certain stichometrical notations, which according to von Dobschütz were falsely ascribed to Euthalius, were taken over directly from a group of Vulgate manuscripts.[17]

Zuntz brings our attention to the possibility of the existence of the Euthalian apparatus in the Georgian version.[18] He cites an article by Theodor Kluge[19] who reports his examination of a number of Georgian manuscripts of the Apostolos. He notes that two of them originate in the same year, 399, and "dieses Jahr befindet sich ausführlich am Ende der Paulusvita,"[20] which sounds as though he is looking at the *Martyrium*.

---

13 Robinson, *Euthaliana*, 43.
14 *Ibid.*
15 Eduard Riggenbach, "Die Kapitelverzeichnisse zum Römer- und zum Hebräerbrief im Codex Fuldensis der Vulgata," *NJDTh* 3 (1894): 350–63, especially, 360–63, cited in Dobschütz, "Euthaliusstudien," 111, n. 1.
16 Samuel Berger, *Histoire de la Vulgate pendant les premiers siècles du Moyen Age* (Paris: Hachette, 1893).
17 Dobschütz, "Euthaliusstudien," 111.
18 Zuntz, *Ancestry*, 120, n. 8.
19 Theodor Kluge, "Die georgischen Übersetzungen des Neuen Testamentes," *ZNW* 12 (1911): 344–50.
20 *Ibid.*, p. 349. See also Kirsopp Lake, *The Text of the New Testament* (rev. Silva New; Oxford Church Text Books; 6th ed.; London: Rivingtons, 1928), 60.

Part Four

12. Dating, Authorship, and Provenance

The questions of who wrote which parts of this material, when, and where, have occupied much of the secondary literature. There are pieces of data within or associated with the apparatus in the manuscripts that need to be taken into consideration in trying to deal with these questions, and it will be well to get these clearly in mind before examining the various ways they have been put together or interpreted to produce the different answers that are offered for the questions.

First, we may consider the headings of the prologues. In the text edited by Zacagni, the heading for the Pauline letters is as follows: "Εὐθαλίου ἐπισκόπου Σούλκης πρόλογος προτασσόμενος τῶν δεκατεσσάρων ἐπιστολῶν Παύλου τοῦ ἁγίου Ἀποστόλου."[1] Von Soden, who describes many variant forms of this heading,[2] concludes that the original must have been "πρόλογος Εὐθαλίου διακόνου προτασσόμενος τῆς βιβλοῦ τῶν ἐπιστολῶν Παύλου τοῦ ἀποστόλου."[3] Vardanian, on the basis of the evidence in the Armenian tradition, argues that the original ran "πρόλογος Παύλου τοῦ ἀποστόλου προτασσόμενος εἰς τὴν κεφαλὴν τῆς βίβλου."[4] Von Dobschütz isolated three major variant identifications of Euthalius, with one sub-variant.[5] He found that the prologue appears most frequently in a completely anonymous form. He also found that mention was made of a Εὐθάλιος διάκονος, Εὐθάλιος ἐπίσκοπος σούλκης, Εὐθάλιος ὁ σούλκης ἐπίσκοπος.

Zacagni edits the heading of the prologue to Acts as follows: "Εὐθαλίου ἐπίσκοπ Σούλκης ἔκθεσις κεφαλαίων τῶν πράξεων σταλεῖσα πρὸς Ἀθανάσιον Ἐπίσκοπον Ἀλεξανδρείας."[6] Von Soden again discusses variants in the tradition and is uncertain of the original form.[7] Frequently the title is merely πρόλογος τῶν πράξεων.[8] Zacagni edits the title of the

---

1   Z 515; M 693 f.
2   Soden, *Schriften des Neuen Testaments*, 649 f.
3   *Ibid.*, 649.
4   Vardanian, "Euthaliana," 39 (1925): 3 f.
5   Dobschütz, "Euthaliusfrage," 61.
6   Z 403; M 627 f.
7   Soden, *Schriften des Neuen Testaments*, 667.
8   Z 475; M 665 f.

prologue to the Catholic epistles in a very similar fashion, substituting τῶν καθολικῶν ἕπτα ἐπιστολῶν for τῶν πράξεων. Von Soden suggests πρόλογος τῶν καθολικῶν or merely πρόλογος.[9]

The titles, then, if their witness is accepted at face value, offer three pieces of information. They speak of a Euthalius who was once a deacon and now a bishop, of a place named Sulca. They also speak of an Athanasius who was bishop of Alexandria. The only Euthalius identified as a deacon (or archdeacon) appears at the Council of Chalcedon in 451.[10] From the beginning, critics have been at a loss as to the possible identity of the city in question. The best possibility seems to be Sulca in Sardinia, but that poses peculiar geographical problems. Zacagni thinks that Pselcha, which he identifies as "urbs Syeni Thebaidis," might have been intended.[11]

A colleague of von Soden discovered in a manuscript of one of the monasteries on Athos a confession of faith with the following title: "Εὐθαλίου ἐπισκόπου Σούλκης ὁμολογία περὶ τῆς ὀρθοδόξου πίστεως."[12] On the basis of internal evidence, primarily the theological concerns evidenced and the historically identifiable persons mentioned, von Soden dates this confession in the second half of the seventh century.[13] Zahn, who subjected von Soden's analysis to very critical scrutiny, is prepared to accept this dating of the confession, although he argues that most of the conclusions that von Soden draws from this document are not warranted.[14]

The most obvious Athanasius who was a bishop of Alexandria is the saint, who lived from 295 to 373.[15] There is, however, at least one other possibility that must be considered, namely, another Athanasius, who became bishop of this city in 490; he was also called Celetes.[16] The name Athanasius also occurs in the text of the prologue to Acts, where he is addressed as a brother.[17]

---

9 Soden, *Schriften des Neuen Testaments*, 673.
10 Mansi, 6.1096, as cited by Ehrhard, "Codex H," 386.
11 Zacagni, *Collectanea*, lxiv.
12 Soden, *Schriften des Neuen Testaments*, 638. He identifies the manuscript as Athos Lawra 149 and prints the text on pages 638–41.
13 *Ibid.*, 643.
14 Zahn, "Neues und Altes," 305–14.
15 Altaner, *Patrology*, 312.
16 Zacagni, *Collectanea*, lxiv.
17 Z 409; M 633C.

In the text of the prologue to the Pauline epistles, Euthalius acknowledges his reliance upon Eusebius, making specific mention of the *Chronicles* and the *Ecclesiastical History*.[18] Eusebius himself lived from *ca.* 263 to 339.[19] The first of the sources cited was probably published around 303; in the case of the second, the last supplement was probably published "soon after 324"[20] although the first part could have been published as early as 303 or 312.[21] We have noted previously that Eusebius is given a sort of title in the prologue to the Pauline epistles, the Chronicler,[22] and it is possible to speak, as Harris does,[23] of a certain deference paid to Eusebius on account of the way he is cited, together with the fact that it is his work that is used to document the period of the last years of Paul's life.[24] We are not aware of any parallels to this characterization in this early period; hence, any estimate of the minimum time required for Eusebius' reputation to have reached this point must take into account several factors, such as location and theological orientation, most of which must be evaluated in something of a subjective fashion.

The *Martyrium* carries, in its fullest form, two dates that could be used to locate the production of these materials: 396 and 458.[25]

The quotation list for Acts lists, as a source, the *Apostolic Constitutions*.[26] The ascription in question could not have been made to any other than the final recension of the *Apostolic Constitutions*,[27] which could not have appeared before 380.[28]

Euthalius describes himself in the prologue to Acts as "νέος ἀμαθής" and claims "ἔναγχος τοίνυν . . . τὴν Παύλου βίβλον ἀνεγνωκώς, αὐτίκα

---

18   Z 529; M 708B and Z 531; M 709B, respectively.

19   Altaner, *Patrology*, 263–71; Johannes Quasten, *The Golden Age of Greek Patristic Literature from the Council of Nicea to the Council of Chalcedon* (vol. 3 of *Patrology*; Utrecht: Spectrum, 1960), 309–45.

20   Altaner, *Patrology*, 264 f.

21   Quasten, *Golden Age*, 315.

22   Z 534; M 713A. See page 17 of this monograph for the earlier discussion.

23   Harris, "Euthalius and Eusebius," 83.

24   Z 534; M 713A.

25   Z 536 f.; M 713B-716A. We are not considering, for the moment, some variants on these dates in the Greek and other traditions.

26   Z 415, 420; M 640A, 644D.

27   See *Didascalia et Constitutiones Apostolorum*, 4.3.

28   Altaner, *Patrology*, 57 ff. Cf. Otto Bardenhewer, *Geschichte der altkirchlichen Literatur* (vol. 4; 2d rev. ed.; Freiburg im Breisgau: Herder, 1924), 263 f.; and Schwartz, "Unzeitgemässe Beobachtungen," 178.

δῆτα, καὶ τήνδε τὴν τῶν ἀποστολικῶν πράξεων, ἅμα τῇ τῶν καθολικῶν ἐπιστολῶν ἑβδομάδα πονέσας."[29]

We would like to know, of course, the identity of the mysterious Πατὴρ τιμιώτατος of the Pauline prologue[30] and the unnamed fathers and teachers to whom Euthalius attributes τὸν τρόπον καὶ τὸν τύπον of his work on the chapters of Acts.[31] We know of at least one manuscript that attributes a list of chapters of Acts, identical with the longer one edited by Zacagni under the preface noted, to Eusebius τοῦ Παμφίλου.[32] Moreover, we know of at least four manuscripts that attribute the same list to Pamphilus himself.[33]

In the colophon at the end of Titus in 015, the first line is mostly illegible; it is claimed, on the basis of close scrutiny[34] or ultraviolet light,[35] that the name Evagrius may be in the first line. Moreover, in the similar colophon in 88, the name Evagrius is clear, and this name is attached to another part of the Euthalian apparatus in 915. Two men by the name of Evagrius have been suggested as prominent possibilities: Evagrius of Pontus, who lived from 346 to 399,[36] and Evagrius of Antioch, who was made bishop of that city in 388 or 389 and lived at least to 392.[37]

The combinations that various critics have made of these various pieces of data and the conclusions drawn are about as numerous as the critics themselves. Some have attempted to co-ordinate and interpret the pieces of information in such a way as to develop the thesis that required distortion or extraordinary interpretation of the fewest pieces. Others, despairing this route and/or believing that there were substantial grounds for seeking another solution, have proposed pseudonymous production or other theories that eliminate the need to co-ordinate all of the pieces of the puzzle in the same picture. Naturally,

---

29 Z 404, 405; M 629A, 629B.
30 Z 515; M 693A.
31 Z 428; M 652B.
32 808, so Devreesse, *Manuscrits grecs*, 162, n. 3.
33 307 453 610 1678, according to von Soden, *Schriften des Neuen Testaments*, 683, cited by Zuntz, *Ancestry*, 87, n. 1. Cf. Coislin, *Bibliotheca Coisliniana*, 78, in particular regard to 307.
34 Ehrhard, "Codex H," 397.
35 Bertrand Hemmerdinger, "L'Auteur de l'édition 'Euthalienne,'" in *Acten des XI. Internationalen Byzantinistenkongresses, München 1958* (ed. by Franz Dölger and Hans-Georg Beck; Munich: C. H. Beck, 1960), 227.
36 Altaner, *Patrology*, 306; cf. Quasten, *Golden Age*, 169–76.
37 John Gibson Cazenove, "Evagrius (5)," *DCB* 2:419.

this alternative course is justified only when there appears to be no way in which all of the pieces of data may be brought into the same focus.

Instead of developing several idealized theories to cover the material available and then lining up the secondary literature behind one or more parts, we are going to describe the positions taken by several critics, which will substantially accomplish the same purpose.

Zacagni, in keeping with the inclusive tendency manifest in his collection of the data in the manuscripts containing the apparatus, adopts the broadest possible approach to the material. He believes that Euthalius was first a deacon, whose presence was noted at the Council of Chalcedon in 451.[38] Euthalius produced the work on the Pauline letters in 458 as indicated by the second date in the *Martyrium*. The earlier date in this piece was due to the father to whom Euthalius is indebted; the father is not Eusebius or Ammonius.[39] The phrases in the prologue and the preface to the chapter list for Acts that suggest that Euthalius was, at the time he wrote the material on Acts and the Catholic epistles, still a young man are to be taken figuratively.[40] One reason for this interpretation is that Zacagni takes the dedication to Athanasius, a bishop of Alexandria, seriously. Since Athanasius the Great has died before this, it is necessary to posit the construction of the sections on Acts and the Catholic epistles no earlier than 490, when another Athanasius, also named Celetes, became bishop of Alexandria.[41] Euthalius' own bishopric is not in Sardinia, the only place where a town named Sulca has been found, but in Egypt; Zacagni speculates that hiding behind the Greek may be Pselcha.[42]

Most of the premises of Zacagni's thesis have been attacked at one time or another in the history of the discussion. We have already discussed Robinson's argument that the entire *Martyrium* is a development subsequent rather than prior to the writing of the prologue to the Pauline letters.[43] Before his detailed argument, others had observed that the last paragraph, in view of the textual evidence and its own construction, was a manifest addition that was thoughtlessly transmitted.[44] Ehrhard concludes that a mutation of Pselcha to Sulca is paleographically inde-

38 Zacagni, *Collectanea*, lxii.
39 *Ibid.*, lviiif.
40 *Ibid.*, lxiif.
41 *Ibid.*, lxiv.
42 *Ibid.*
43 See pages 61 f. in this monograph for this discussion.
44 Erhard, "Codex H," 408 f. See Robinson, *Euthaliana*, 5.

fensible.[45] Ehrhard and many others following him have argued that
whatever the theoretical need, the vocabulary of the prologue to Acts
will not sustain the thirty year gap that Zacagni requires between the
two sections of the apparatus.[46] Von Dobschütz suggests that the problem — which of the two Alexandrian bishops named Athanasius is intended in the headings — disappears if one accepts his interpretation,
namely, that the specific identification of Athanasius mentioned as a
brother in the text of the prologue to Acts is a later development,
and an improper one.[47]

Conybeare, in his first article dealing with the Euthalian material,
inclines to the earlier date in the *Martyrium* as the one for which Euthalius was responsible.[48] On the basis of evidence in the Armenian sources
related to the apparatus, he believes the prologue to the Pauline material
was addressed to a Theophilus of Alexandria.[49] Accepting a thesis developed by J. Rendel Harris, that the prologue to Acts was originally addressed to a Meletius, whose name was later erased and an orthodox
Athanasius inserted, Conybeare suggests that the final paragraph might
have been interpolated in the *Martyrium* to avoid an implausible chronological situation to develop, inasmuch as the obvious Athanasius died
before 396.[50] He subscribes to the interpretation that places the development of the two parts of the apparatus close in time.[51] Possibly, if Euthalius were a very young man in 396, he himself might have made the
alterations, which occurred in 458.[52]

In a second article, which followed publication of the essays by
Robinson and von Soden, Conybeare is persuaded by Robinson that
the *Martyrium* was not written by Euthalius. He has made additional investigations into Armenian materials and on this basis proposes some
substantial revisions in his original thesis. The Armenian version of
the apparatus itself, he believes, was translated in the fifth century, probably in 448.[53] Relying on extra-apparatus Armenian witnesses, he wishes

---

45   Ehrhard, "Codex H," 402.
46   *Ibid.*, 400. Cf. Gregory, *Textkritik*, 873, n. 1.
47   Dobschütz, "Euthaliusfrage," 65.
48   Conybeare, "Codex Pamphili," 241.
49   *Ibid.*
50   *Ibid.*, 250.
51   *Ibid.*
52   *Ibid.*, 250 f.
53   Conybeare, "Date of Euthalius," 50, 52.

to place the development of the apparatus between 320 and 326.[54] The work was done in Egypt under Alexander. Athanasius was a fellow monk, not the great bishop. In order to fit all of this activity in with the known publication dates of the works of Eusebius, Conybeare posits a visit by Euthalius to Caesarea, where he saw the *Ecclesiastical History* just completed.[55] Such a visit would also explain the colophon in 015, which Conybeare in the earlier essay attributed to Euthalius, although it would now no longer be possible to suggest, as he did at that time, that 015 might, itself, be from the hand of Euthalius.[56]

The essay by Robinson on the Euthalian apparatus, in which he presents a persuasive argument for the dependence of the *Martyrium* on the prologue, raises serious questions for previous discussions of the problem of dating. We have seen the effect of this essay, for example, in the before and after articles of Conybeare. Robinson's arguments have been taken very seriously in all subsequent attempts to deal with the questions of Euthalius except for that of von Soden, who goes his own way. On the basis of his thesis concerning the dependence of the *Martyrium*[57] Robinson believes that the work on the prologues must be placed between 323 and 396.[58] Given this period, there is no reason not to think that the Athanasius mentioned is the one most well-known.[59] The work was probably done in the neighborhood of Alexandria, although Robinson is not inclined to put much weight on this.[60] The connection with Caesarea, then, was established at a later stage.[61]

Robinson is impressed by the mystery of some pieces of the data and considers this characteristic as a sign of authenticity. He observes, for example, that Euthalius' name, as well as that of his see, could not be deduced from the contents of the prologues, although possibly his designation as bishop, assuming the knowledge that the prologue to Acts was addressed to a bishop.[62]

---

54 *Ibid.*, 48, 52.
55 *Ibid.*, 49.
56 Conybeare, "Codex Pamphili," 248.
57 Robinson, *Euthaliana*, 28–30.
58 *Ibid.*, 30 f.
59 *Ibid.*, 31.
60 *Ibid.*, 43.
61 *Ibid.*, 35.
62 *Ibid.*, 100.

The colophon came from a later editorial reviser who, if the manuscript evidence be given full credence, may have been Evagrius, possibly
Evagrius of Pontus, who may also have been the one who constructed
and added the first parts of the *Martyrium* as well as the colophon.[63]

The work of von Soden on the Euthalian apparatus, at critical points
in his discussion of dating and provenance, is decisively influenced by a
co-worker's discovery, in a manuscript on Mt. Athos, of a confession
written by Euthalius, Bishop of Sulca. Von Soden identified this
Sulca as the locality in Sardinia and was able, on the basis of evidence
in the confession, to date the work in the second half of the seventh
century.[64] Having committed himself to this location in this period,
von Soden must bend many other factors to fit this interpretation.
We have reviewed some of these in discussing different parts of the apparatus. He reconstructs the career of Euthalius as follows: Euthalius was
originally a deacon in a church in the Orient, the province of Syria, perhaps Antioch.[65] The local patriarch at that time was named Athanasius.
Between the writing of the Pauline material and that on the Catholic
epistles and Acts, Euthalius suffered defeat in some dogmatic struggle
and was transferred to Sardinia. There, he did the work on the second
section; this work was not really for the Greek speaking islands of the
West but for his original province.[66] Von Soden, then, although for different reasons, argues that the temporal expressions suggesting relatively
little time between the two sections must not be pressed.[67] There is a
little more on his side in this argument inasmuch as we, too, noted
the different temper in the prologues of the second section. If Vardanian's argument that the second section originally did not contain either of
the two types of quotation lists or the "lection" lists were sustained, then
more is to be given to von Soden. We believe, however, that there are
more credible theories that take into consideration the discovery of the
bishop's confession.

Von Soden also supposes that the *Martyrium* was taken over by Euthalius in the shorter, 396, form, and that the Egyptian dating was unknown to him.[68] The unnamed father to whom Euthalius owed at least

63 *Ibid.*, 71.
64 Soden, *Schriften des Neuen Testaments*, 643.
65 *Ibid.*, 648, 680.
66 *Ibid.*, 680.
67 *Ibid.*, 644.
68 *Ibid.*, 658.

the chapter lists in the Pauline letters could have been Pamphilus, on whose name the expression φιλόχριστος would have been a wordplay.[69]

Although von Soden's interpretation has received some support, even recent,[70] it has, in general, been heavily and, we believe, mortally attacked. Zuntz reflects this conclusion when he states in a 1953 article that the view of von Soden "no longer requires refutation."[71] Conybeare initiated the substantive criticism of von Soden in his second article on the Euthalian apparatus, noted above, where he brings together his further researches on the Armenian materials with the work of Robinson and von Soden.[72] He argues that the study by Robinson is not sufficiently considered by von Soden. In addition to being persuaded by Robinson's analysis of the *Martyrium*, which contradicts von Soden's interpretation, Conybeare does not believe that the variant occurrences of the Euthalian material in eighth to tenth century manuscripts are compatible with a date of 670, particularly in view of the variety of texts involved.[73] He notes that von Soden believes that Euthalius used the form of the *Martyrium* that did not have the Egyptian dating or final paragraph. He argues that whichever form Euthalius may have used, if one assumes priority of the *Martyrium*, then "the uniform conjunction of his prologue with the rival form becomes a miracle."[74] Conybeare suggests that a more credible interpretation of all of the evidence is that Euthalius, whose name was associated with the apparatus before the era of the confession,[75] became identified with the bishop of Sulca following the publication of the confession in 670. The prologues, he finishes, existed in Armenian at least as early as 685.[76]

Zahn also published shortly after Conybeare a long article critical of von Soden's conclusions.[77] Although Zahn recognizes the genuineness of the confession, more or less as outlined by von Soden, he argues that the genuineness of the confession in no way makes self-evident

---

69 Soden, *Schriften des Neuen Testaments*, 665 f.; cf. 671.
70 Wilhem Bousset, Review of Hermann von Soden, *Die Schriften des neuen Testaments in ihrer ältesten erreichbaren Textgestalt*, *TLZ* 22 (1903): 324–30; Turner, "Patristic Commentaries"; and Devreesse, *Manuscrits grecs,* 164 ff.
71 Günther Zuntz, "Euthalius = Euzoius?" *VC* 7 (1953): 19, n. 21.
72 Conybeare, "Date of Euthalius," 40 ff.
73 *Ibid.*, 42 f.
74 *Ibid.*, 44.
75 *Ibid.*, 45.
76 *Ibid.*
77 Zahn, "Neues und Altes," 305–30, 375–90.

the identity of its author with the author of the prologues.[78] He suggests
that anyone who wishes to embrace the characterization of Euthalius as
bishop of Sulca on the basis of the evidence of the titles in the prologues
must also accept the witness of the same sources that the Athanasius
mentioned was Athanasius the Great.[79] He is generally critical of von
Soden's interpretation of what Zahn takes to be the clear sense of the
texts. Von Soden, he claims, vainly tries to weaken the force of the
phrases that suggest a close temporal connection between the two sections of the work in order to gain time to arrange a fictitious "Stück
Lebensgeschichte des Euthalius."[80] He is further critical of von Soden's
handling of Euthalius' description of what he has done with the text.
Since we already have in 015 a colometrically arranged text, it is necessary for von Soden to deal with Euthalius' apparent claim to originality
here. Von Soden's interpretation is so tortured that Zahn describes it as a
clear contradiction.[81] Zahn concludes that the work of von Soden so vi-
olates the sense of the texts and what is known of textual history that
one must assume that he has never deigned to look at the work of
Graux, Blass, Robinson, and others in regard to sense lines and stichometry.[82]

Ehrhard is impressed with the association of the name Evagrius with
parts of the Euthalian apparatus. He surmises that the most likely Evagrius was Evagrius of Pontus.[83] This conclusion is based on a number
of factors. First, he believes that the name Evagrius is discernable
through the erasure in 015.[84] This manuscript, he feels, is either the autograph or one of the first copies of Euthalius' work.[85] Evagrius is not
merely the name of a scribe or copyist, given the way the name appears
in the colophon. On the other hand, Ehrhard is unable to find, on the
basis of a thorough analysis, that any one of the historically attested bear-
ers of the name Euthalius really matches the criteria required for the author of the prologues and the colophon.[86] The paucity of manuscripts in
which Euthalius is actually named, together with the factors just re-

---

78 *Ibid.*, 311.
79 *Ibid.*, 313.
80 *Ibid.*, 318.
81 *Ibid.*, 380.
82 *Ibid.*, 381.
83 Ehrhard, "Codex H," 403 ff.
84 *Ibid.*, 397.
85 *Ibid.*, 410.
86 *Ibid.*, 401 ff.

viewed, leads Ehrhard to conclude that some *Evagrius* must have been the original author.[87] The shift in some witnesses from Evagrius to Euthalius may have been intentional or accidental.[88]

Ehrhard feels that the last paragraph in the *Martyrium* is chronologically inappropriate for Evagrius of Pontus, who died in 399.[89] Since Evagrius, in these times, must have been in his fifties, the phrases picturing the author as a young man may not be taken literally.[90] Ehrhard locates the production of this work in Egypt with a trip to Caesarea thrown in to justify the colophon.[91] The unidentified father of Euthalius' reference is not, against Mill, Swete, and Gregory, to be identified with Theodore of Mopsuestia, but rather we have to do with "einen aegyptischen Kirchenschriftsteller."[92] Ehrhard is not, however, able to detect any striking linguistic similarities between the work of Euthalius, so-called, and that of Evagrius of Pontus.[93]

Von Dobschütz criticizes the conclusions of Ehrhard although he agrees with a number of Erhard's preliminary observations. He acknowledges that the name Evagrius was in the *Vorlage* of 88 rather than being the product of its scribe.[94] Moreover, signs in 015 also point to Evagrius, not Euthalius. Von Dobschütz does not believe, however, that Ehrhard offers a persuasive explanation for the transformation of Evagrius to Euthalius. The very uncertainty of the name speaks for its genuineness.[95] Von Dobschütz devises an alternative interpretation of the colophons in 015 and 88: Evagrius was the scribe who composed the colophon in its original form from Euthalian phrases;[96] he points out, in support of this, that the name Evagrius, in these instances, appears in a subscription while the name Euthalius always appears in a superscription.

In this first article, von Dobschütz thinks that Euthalius was responsible for the final paragraph in the *Martyrium*, dating the work on the Pauline letters in 458/9, shortly followed by the work on the second

---

87 *Ibid.*, 398, 403 ff.
88 *Ibid.*, 406.
89 *Ibid.*, 407 ff.
90 *Ibid.*, 409
91 *Ibid.*, 407.
92 *Ibid.*, 411.
93 *Ibid.*, 409.
94 Dobschütz, "Euthaliusfrage," 60.
95 *Ibid.*, 62.
96 *Ibid.*, 65 f.

section.[97] The Egyptian insertions in the first part of the *Martyrium* may be due to Euthalius, although the *Martyrium* was originally composed in Syria, possibly by the unnamed father, who may have been Theodore of Mopsuestia.[98] In a later article, published in 1898, he retracts his endorsement of this date and his criticism of Ehrhard's attack on this late date.[99]

In his extensive article critical of von Soden's position, Zahn offers a number of his own observations on the ways in which the several pieces of data could be fitted together. He argues, against Ehrhard and von Dobschütz, that the name of Evagrius in 68 and 637 is clearly a later insertion. If, he observes, the author of the colophon had intended to indicate that he here introduces something new over against the original editor, he would have written ἐγὼ Εὐάγριος.[100] Evagrius, then, is a later scribe; if he were the original author, then it would be impossible to explain the rise of the Euthalius tradition. Zahn suggests that Evagrius of Antioch is a better supposition than Evagrius of Pontus.[101] The name Euthalius for the unknown author, as well as the titles, could have been a conjecture, but a false one. This explanation, Zahn feels, is not only possible, but it is the "allein Wahrscheinliche."[102] Although Robinson had considered it possible that Evagrius was the redactor of the 396 edition, Zahn regards this as unlikely, arguing that neither Evagrius nor Euthalius would have identified himself as the author by putting his name at the head of the paragraph following the "lection" list.[103]

Zahn reviews some evidence that he finds in a commentary that is possibly by Bishop Hilarius of Arles (*ca.* 428–55).[104] He finds references in this commentary to an unnamed Greek bishop who used the Catholic and Pauline epistles in a particular order. Zahn conjectures, on the basis of some of the remarks made about this unnamed Greek bishop, that he was probably Euthalius. He feels that this is evidence that by 450 an anonymous edition of the Euthalian material was widespread.

---

97 *Ibid.*, 68.
98 *Ibid.*, 66 ff.; cf. Dobschütz, "Euthaliusstudien," 153.
99 Dobschütz, "Euthaliusstudien," 137, n. 1.
100 Zahn, "Neues und Altes," 321.
101 *Ibid.*, 324.
102 *Ibid.*, 317.
103 *Ibid.*, 326 f.
104 *Ibid.*, 327 ff.

He summarizes his conclusions:[105] Euthalius was responsible for both the prayer and the prologues. The unnamed father in the prologue to the Pauline epistles may have been Pamphilus, based on the evidence of the chapter list heading in 307. In Greek Syria, Euthalius produced this material between 330 and 390; Zahn believes that it is important not to draw chronological conclusions from the presence of references to the *Apostolic Constitutions* in the quotation lists, arguing that it is an interpolation.[106] The Athanasius mentioned in the text of the prologue to Acts is not Athanasius the Great, who was not a fellow countryman. Possibly, Zahn suggests, he may be the bishop of Anagastus by that name (*ca.* 325), who was a student of Lucian, or the bishop of Scythopolis (*ca.* 370–80). In the light of the warmth with which Eusebius is cited and defended, Zahn thinks that Euthalius should be sought among the semi-Arian circle to which both of the two bishops with the name Athanasius belonged.

Very early, as the secondary literature goes, J. Rendel Harris was intrigued with the possibility that some cryptic wordplays in parts of the apparatus reveal the true identity of some of the persons related to this material. In an essay written before the work of J. Armitage Robinson, he accepts Zacagni's chronological interpretation of the *Martyrium* and some of the conclusions that Zacagni draws from it, namely, that Euthalius was an Alexandrian deacon in 458 and subsequently bishop of Sulca, "supposed by some persons to be a city in Upper Egypt."[107] Harris focusses his attention on the rhetorical discussion of μελέτη in the heart of the prologue of Acts and concludes that this is the "key-word to the understanding of the passage."[108] Harris argues, on the basis of his analysis that we have reviewed previously,[109] that the person to whom this prologue was dedicated was named Meletius; the writer was named Euthalius, who played with his own name as well as that of Meletius. At a later time, the name Meletius was erased and the name Athanasius was inserted.[110]

Now, Harris asks, which Meletius could it have been? The presumed reason for the erasure was that the Meletius who was in question

---

105 *Ibid.*, 377, n. 2; 388 ff.
106 *Ibid.*, 388, n.1.
107 Harris, *Stichometry*, 35.
108 *Ibid.*, 80.
109 See pages 19 f. of this monograph.
110 Harris, *Stichometry*, 82.

fell under an ecclesiastical cloud. "There never was a Meletius, worth mentioning," Harris asserts, "who was not a schismatic."[111] He considers three in particular:

1. The author of the Meletian schism, he decides, is too early.
2. Meletius of Antioch, who died in 381, is also too early for the 396 date. Robinson in reviewing this work of Harris, notes that Harris could, given Robinson's interpretation of the dates of the *Martyrium*, take this Meletius, although Robinson does not believe that a case has been made out for deletion to begin with.[112] Harris, in an essay written subsequent to these remarks of Robinson, says that he may have been too hasty in his decision to dismiss this Meletius as a possibility.[113]
3. Meletius of Mopsuestia, who was a disciple and successor to Theodore of Mopsuestia, seems to Harris to be all right.[114] Harris then suggests that Theodore of Mopsuestia may have been the unnamed author of the chapter list mentioned in the Pauline prologue.[115] Furthermore, Nestorius may have been the father to whom the Pauline work was sent, the πατὴρ τιμιώτατος.[116]

Euthalius did his work in Caesarea, following the witness of the colophons in Zacagni's edition and in 015.[117] He takes note of the attribution in 307 of the chapter list for Acts to Pamphilus. He suggests that Euthalius got it from this source if the list is really due to Pamphilus;

111 *Ibid.*, 83.
112 Robinson, *Euthaliana*, 34.
113 Harris, "Euthalius and Eusebius," 63. He points out that Meletius was one of the names played upon by Eusebius (73, 75). On account of Euthalius' treatment of Eusebius, Harris (83) dates the prologue subsequent to 340.
114 Harris, *Stichometry*, 85.
115 *Ibid.* Cf. Mill (cited here by Harris as page lxxxvi in the Oxford edition of Mill's prolegomenon to the New Testament) and *Theodori Episcopi Mopsuesteni in epistolas B. Pauli commentarii: The Latin Version with the Greek Fragments* (with an introduction, notes, and indices by Henry Barclay Swete; vol. 1; Cambridge: Cambridge University Press, 1880), lxi, arguing that Theodore of Mopsuestia is the "father" on the basis of congruence of chapter divisions. Moreover, Theodore shares with Euthalius the theory that Paul had not seen the Ephesians at the time Ephesians was written.
116 Harris, *Stichometry*, 86 f.
117 *Ibid.*, 87 f.

if not, it shows that "Euthalius was believed to have had literary relations with that father."[118]

We have already made note of the long review by Günther Zuntz of the development of the Euthalian corpus.[119] In his early work, *The Ancestry of the Harklean New Testament*, he is more directly concerned with the original composition and development of these materials. Fundamentally, he argues that Euthalius' primary work is not at all original but consists to a large extent in transcription and rearrangement of the work that he found already available in texts in the library at Caesarea. The Christ-loving father, it is clear, must have been Pamphilus.[120] Although Zuntz first thought that the Athanasius mentioned might be the Great,[121] he later shifts from this middle-of-the-road position and suggests that the semi-Arian orientation of Caesarea makes this improbable.[122] He then claims that "no Athanasius and no Euthalius can be pointed out who could reasonably be identified with the editor and promoter of this Caesarean work of scholarship."[123] Having come to this conclusion, he thinks it is not inappropriate to suggest that the work may have been issued pseudonymously, either upon a whim or from a desire to circulate the work without the danger of dogmatic prejudice.[124] As a clue to the identity of possible real authors, he notes Euthalius' interest in the "true" meaning of names.[125] Zuntz believes that the author may have been Euzoius and that the one to whom the prologue to Acts is dedicated was Acacius. Acacius of Caesarea was the "disciple and successor to Eusebius as bishop."[126] Euzoius was a bishop there from 376 to 379.[127] Zuntz notes that the "labored" play on the notion of immortality ("ἀθανασία") at the beginning of the prologue to Acts is available for speculation; moreover, he continues, in the same context, the rare word εὐθαλές appears. This word reappears at the end of the same

---

118 *Ibid.*, 88.
119 See page 102 of this monograph.
120 Zuntz, "Subscriptionen der Syra Harclensis," 180; cf. Zuntz, "Etudes Harkléennes," 553.
121 Zuntz, "Etudes Harkléennes," 554.
122 Zuntz, "Subscriptionen der Syra Harclensis," 181.
123 Zuntz, "Euthalius = Euzoius?" 20.
124 *Ibid.*, 21.
125 *Ibid.*, 20, n. 26.
126 Altaner, *Patrology*, 271.
127 Zuntz, "Euthalius = Euzoius?" 21; and Zuntz, "Subscriptionen der Syra Harclensis," 180.

prologue and at the beginning of the prologue to the Pauline letters as well.[128] He sees that the first letters of each of the two pairs are the same, more in one of them, and that the endings are similar. He also notes that "he who 'lives well' may be said to 'flourish well' and he who is 'without evil' may trust in immortality."[129] Finally, Zuntz claims that the literary activities of these two, together with their concern for the library at Caesarea, fit well with the characteristics that may be inferred from the sorts of motives that led the author of the Euthalian materials to their publication.

Bertrand Hemmerdinger picks up a suggestion made much earlier by Zahn connecting this material with Evagrius of Antioch.[130] Hemmerdinger places the construction of this material prior to 396 on the basis of Robinson's demonstration of the dependence of the *Martyrium*.[131] Much of Hemmerdinger's argument centers around an interpretation of material found in 015 and, particularly, 88. He takes note of Ehrhard's evaluation of this material, especially the appearance of the name Evagrius in both of these manuscripts.[132] In 88, in addition to considerable Euthalian material, there is also a second prologue to Acts. Von Dobschütz has previously provided a translation of this prologue and, in a careful analysis, concludes that the author of this other prologue was Theodore of Mopsuestia.[133] Hemmerdinger rejects this interpretation of the other prologue and argues, primarily on the basis of parallels that he sees in style, that both prologues are from the same author.[134] He notes that Evagrius of Antioch was responsible for a translation of the life of Athanasius into Latin, according to Jerome.[135] The two men named Eusebius in the other prologue are not necessarily both bishops, as von Dobschütz had thought; the second one may have been St. Eusebius of Vercelli (*ca.* 362), and the former was the better known Eusebius of Caesarea whose chapter list, according to 808, Evagrius reproduced.[136] The enmity between Athanasius the Great and Eu-

---

128 Zuntz, "Euthalius = Euzoius?" 21, n. 27.
129 *Ibid.*, 21.
130 Zahn, "Neues und Altes," 324.
131 Hemmerdinger, "Auteur," 227.
132 *Ibid.*
133 Dobschütz, "Hitherto Unpublished Prologue," 386.
134 Hemmerdinger, "Auteur," 229 f.
135 *Ibid.*, 228.
136 *Ibid.*, 230 f.

sebius was the reason that the name of the latter was not mentioned in the prologue to Acts.

On the basis of information in the second prologue in 88, Hemmerdinger argues that the *terminus post quem* for the work on the material in Acts is 340; therefore, both prologues were probably written between 340 and 350; on the other hand, there are also signs in the second prologue that the period marked by the death of Eusebius of Caesarea appears to have been considerably prior to the contemporary period, in which case, the time when the so-called Euthalian material was produced would have to be posterior to 350.[137]

In response to this thesis, we have already noted arguments that dissociated the name of Evagrius from any original work on the Euthalian material.[138] Zuntz summarizes these positions in asserting that the name Evagrius "is nowhere found in connection with the 'Euthalian' prologues. In [015] it is (or, rather, it was – *ante rasuram*) prefixed to the colophon, and this colophon – more precisely, its first part – is a cento made up of 'Euthalian' phrases and that not by 'Euthalius.'"[139] In regard to the appearance of the name in 88 and 637, Zuntz asserts that Evagrius is an "intrusion in the earlier, and anonymous, 'Euthalian' form of the summary."[140]

---

137 *Ibid.*, 230 f.
138 See, e. g., page 122 of this monograph.
139 Zuntz, "Euthalius = Euzoius?" 17.
140 *Ibid.*, 18.

Conclusions

Our original purpose was to collect and consolidate the results of previous, diverse scholarly studies of the Euthalian materials and to provide some stimulus to further investigations. We believe that these ends have been attained: the first through a critical review of books and articles that deal in whole or in part with this question; the second through translation of the prologue to the Pauline epistles and the summary census of a large number of manuscripts relevant to this study.

We did not begin this monograph with the expectation of settling any particular questions associated with the origin and history of this material; we do think, however, that the arguments in one or two areas are conclusive, that the support for some others is increased, and that the improbability of still others is more likely.

In the instance of the prologues, particularly the prologue to the Pauline epistles, the direction indicated for further consideration is a careful analysis of the distinctive features of the narrative in terms of possible connections with more widely known figures or schools in the patristic period. We have noted some of the obvious textual developments of the Pauline prologue. The need for a critical edition of this prologue, indeed, the entire apparatus, remains as great as it was when Robinson made the same observation in 1905.[1]

The "lection" lists are still something of an enigma. We are, however, inclined to accept as the one dealing most comprehensively with the data, the theory proposed by Zuntz, namely, that the system that we find in the tables was not developed by Euthalius nor, against Robinson, was it a later development. Rather, it represents material that Euthalius found in his *Vorlage* and incorporated in his own edition.

The quotation lists represent an area that attracted much of our attention, both in reflection on problems and in collection of information from the manuscript tradition. We believe that the hypothesis that we presented regarding the pattern of development of these lists has merit. Moreover, we think that the longer quotation lists, although in our theory they are a secondary development, should be an unusual

---

1   Joseph Armitage Robinson, "Recent Work on Euthalius," *JTS* 6 (1904–5): 90.

source of evidence for the history of the text of the New Testament. These lists reflect a text that has not always been harmonized with the text of the New Testament with which it is associated in a particular manuscript. It is likely, therefore, that variants found in the lists represent a tradition that is older than the associated text of the New Testament.

Euthalius himself acknowledges his indebtedness to a predecessor for the chapter lists associated with the Pauline epistles. Robinson urges, on the basis of style and vocabulary, that all the chapter lists were from the same hand, and Zuntz' theory, that the chapter lists constituted a sort of preface to an entire text, which Euthalius merely distributed among the letters and Acts, deals decisively with the variety of data.

We believe, on the basis of both internal and external warrants embraced by a persuasive theory, that these parts constituted the "first edition" of the Euthalian apparatus. There are some additional pieces, which we have reviewed, with regard to which the evidence is inconclusive; these include the *Martyrium*, the so-called prayer of Euthalius, and the colophon(s).

The *Martyrium* is clearly a secondary construction, which is dependent upon the prologue. It is not so clear, however, that the construction was the work of another than the author of the prologues. Those parts of Robinson's arguments that suggest a distinction between the two have been seriously eroded by Harris' demonstration both of the substantial dependence of the author of the prologues upon Eusebian material and of the congruence among Eusebius, the prologues, and the *Martyrium* where contrast had been argued. It is difficult to know how to evaluate the observation that the *Martyrium* was not announced in the prologue. It could hardly be conclusive of itself and only has weight when taken together with other arguments, which we do not believe can be sufficiently marshalled in this case. Inclusion in the earliest edition has been claimed on the evidence from the Armenian version. Although we are not in a position to evaluate this argument first hand, it does not seem to us possible to push the linguistic evidence beyond the claim that the *Martyrium* must have been present already at the time of the first Armenian translation.

The prayer of Euthalius is available as a text only in the Armenian tradition and in one Greek manuscript, although there are allusions to it in another part of the Greek tradition. We have not studied it carefully ourselves but merely reported that others argue that there is stylistic evidence that the author of the prayer is the same as the author of the prologues.

It would appear that the colophon, in the expanded form found in 015 and 88, exhibits characteristics of eclectic production similar to the *Martyrium*. It would be natural, then, to link them to the same period of activity, whether simultaneous with or following the production of the prologues.

No great steps, we believe, have been taken in the area of dating and authorship; Caesarea, however, appears a stronger and Egypt a weaker candidate as the original location of the work. The *terminus post quem* has remained the end of the first quarter of the fourth century. The *terminus ante quem* has been a matter of considerable disagreement. The evidence that is presently available to us, while it is not conclusive, does point in a certain direction. Taken at face value, the *Martyrium* fixes the upper limit at 396; the form of the citation of the *Apostolic Constitutions* in the quotation lists fixes the lower limit at 380. The configuration of other data, e. g., the evidence of the versions – particularly the Armenian – and the internal evidence of the prologue to the Pauline epistles, albeit subjectively evaluated, tends to support or at least does not rule out production within the above dates.

When the question of the identity of the author is brought into the picture, we do not feel that there is warrant for specific conclusions. It is true that some suggestions are rather clearly excluded, e. g., von Soden's candidate, the seventh century bishop of Sulca. On the other hand, other candidates, e. g., Rendel Harris' Meletius and Zuntz' Euzoius, are supported by ingenious, attractive arguments. On the whole, however, these attractive possibilities require, in each case, the resolution of one or more subjective arguments: If dogmatic considerations or literary convention may be assumed to be a factor, then the probability of the use of a pseudonym is higher. If the apparatus were produced in the library of Caesarea, then the high estimate of Eusebius at an early stage is more plausible. There are sufficient variables that we do not feel that the evidence available to date permits a wholly satisfactory solution to the question of the identity of the author.

It was also our intention in this monograph to outline what directions further study of this question should take. We have indicated a couple of these in the discussion of the prologues and the quotation lists. The summary of the investigation of the manuscript tradition indicates those manuscripts that should receive further scrutiny. We have not attempted any classification of the manuscripts according to the nature of the New Testament text contained, nor have we made any effort to group manuscripts according to the configuration of the apparatus that is contained. These moves, however, are obviously the next ones to be made. The examination of the manuscripts that we were able to make did not occasion any serious revision of theories based on smaller samples of the tradition. We did turn up evidence of modifications to the apparatus not hitherto known. We did find, in some instances, that there is other evidence for what appeared to be a unique feature of one manuscript; we have not, however, made a determination that these additional witnesses constitute a significant testimony. While the method by which the preliminary selection of manuscripts was made dictated that a substantial number of the manuscripts would contain the spurious *argumenta*, it was nevertheless significant that fewer than five minuscule manuscripts were encountered that were without the *argumenta*; we have noted earlier the implication that this piece of evidence, if substantiated by an exhaustive examination of the entire manuscript tradition of the New Testament, has for the age of the tradition in the bulk of the manuscripts containing the apparatus.

Of the versions, the Armenian and the Syriac offer the most attractive potential for further investigation. We have reviewed the divergent theories with respect to the original makeup of the apparatus that Vardanian developed on the basis of the Armenian manuscripts that he used. Vardanian has edited a critical edition of the apparatus in Armenian, and this work must be included in any comprehensive edition that is contemplated. Moreover, there is other secondary literature in Armenian that was not accessible to us, of which account will need to be taken. Von Dobschütz has, in his work concentrated upon only two Syriac manuscripts, indicated something of the complexity of the tradition to which that version provides access.

In the review of our discussion of the quotation lists, we touched briefly upon the evidence that may be available in them for the New Testament text of the passages cited. We know enough at this point to be wary of any simplistic assumption that there is a one-to-one relationship between the text that is associated with the apparatus in a particular manuscript and the text that was connected with the apparatus in its original edition. Clearly, there has to be some relationship, but we know that it is not possible to speak of a Euthalian text as though it is represented by the text of a particular manuscript that we are now able to identify. There are, however, clues to parts of the text with which Euthalius worked.

J. Rendel Harris noticed that the citation in the quotation list reported for Galatians XI, at 6:15, attributed to the Apocryphon of
Moses, supports the reading of P⁴⁶ B 1739 and a few other texts. Harris
observes, "I suppose we may assume the genuineness of these quotations, for either Euthalius verified them himself or . . . he referred to
some earlier writer, a supposition which by no means detracts from
the value of the quotations."[2]

In Romans XXV, which is at 10:15, Robinson found that the citation in the quotation list supports the omission of τῶν εὐαγγελιζομένων
εἰρήνην with ℵ* A B C 81 630 1739 and others, including Origen in
both Greek and Latin texts.[3] It is notable, for example, that this is against
the text in 88 and 181, both of which contain most parts of the apparatus.[4]

In his summary of Colossians in the prologue to the Pauline epistles,
Euthalius includes the following remark: "Εἶναι γὰρ οὐ καθαρὰν θρη-
σκείαν ἀλλ' ἀφειδίαν σώματος."[5] Von Dobschütz argues from this language that Euthalius did not read at Col. 2:23 "καὶ ἀφειδίᾳ σώματος"
but, with B, Origen's translation, the Pseudo-Augustinian *Speculum*,

---

2   Harris, *Stichometry*, 54. The citation appears at Z 561; M 737C.
3   Robinson, *Euthaliana*, 103. The citation appears at Z 553; M 729C.
4   This example also indicates a deficiency in the apparatus of *The Greek New Tes-
     tament*, Kurt Aland et al., eds. (New York: American Bible Society, 1966 [im-
     print varies]). The editors refer to earlier printed editions of the Greek New
     Testament for most of the evidence cited for the Church Fathers (xxx), and
     we presume that the source for the citations of Euthalius was Constantin von
     Tischendorf, ed., *Novum Testamentum Graece* (Editio octava critica maior; 2
     vols.; Leipzig: J. C. Hinrichs, 1872). The explanation for the possible support
     of the same figure for divergent readings is, however, inaccurate in the instance
     of the citation of Euthalius on both sides of the variation here discussed. Ti-
     schendorf's apparatus (*ad loc.*) shows Euthal⁵⁵³ supporting the omission and Eu-
     thal^cod supporting the longer reading. The latter citation does not really repre-
     sent a text of Euthalius any more than does the New Testament text of 88 or
     181, for it is merely the siglum used by Tischendorf to indicate the reading of
     the upper writing of the palimpsest codex P^apr. See Caspar René Gregory, *Pro-
     legomena* (vol. 3 of Tischendorf, *Novum Testamentum Graece*), 417, 1188. Also
     see William Henry Paine Hatch, *The Principal Uncial Manuscripts of the New Tes-
     tament* (Chicago: University of Chicago Press, 1939), page facing Plate LI, n.2.
     The distinction between the New Testament text of a manuscript that contains
     the apparatus and the reading of Euthalius inferred from the apparatus itself has
     been dissolved by the apparatus of the edition of the Greek New Testament
     under discussion.
5   Z 525; M 704B.

and other Latin witnesses, that he read "ἀφειδίᾳ σώματος" as a predicate nominative to ἐστιν.[6]

We have not made any attempt to search out other instances in which a text standing behind the apparatus may be inferred with greater or less accuracy. We believe, however, that the suggestions made by these three scholars constitute an invitation to a very profitable line of investigation. Obviously, such an investigation is heavily dependent upon a prior or, failing that, a concurrent establishment of a critical text.

Finally, we would like to call attention to the potential merit of a detailed analysis of the apparatus, with particular attention to the prologues and the chapter lists, in the light of patristic exegesis. We have noted some of the instances in the annotations to the Pauline prologue where Euthalius offers an unusual or notable observation, exegesis, or other piece of information. The question of the identity of the author is likely to be nearer a compelling solution when he is located in a discernable theological milieu with greater precision than is now the case.

---

6   Dobschütz, "Euthaliusstudien," 110.

Excursus

Stichometry

Stichometry and the history of the discussion of this area provide materials easily adequate for another dissertation. We do not propose to offer a comprehensive discussion of the problems related to the interpretation of stichometry and colometry. There is, however, a rather important aspect of the Euthalian apparatus that raises questions related to this area, and therefore we feel that some clarification is necessary.

First of all, we should see what it is in the apparatus that gives rise to the questions. There are two stretches in the prologue to Acts:

πρῶτον δὴ οὖν ἔγωγε ἀποστολικὴν βίβλον στοιχιδὸν ἀναγνούς τε, καὶ γράψας, πρώην διεπεμψάμην πρός τινα τῶν ἐν Χριστῷ πατέρων ἡμῶν, μετρίως πεποιημένην ἐμοί, οἷά τις πῶλος ἀβαδής, ἢ νέος ἀμαθὴς ἐρήμην ὁδόν, καὶ ἀτριβῆ ἰέναι προστεταγμένος. οὐδένα γάρ που τῶν, ὅσοι τὸν θεῖον ἐπρεσβεύσαντο λόγον, εἰς δεῦρο διέγνων περὶ τοῦτο τῆς γραφῆς ταύτης εἰς σπουδὴν πεποιημένον το σχῆμα.[1]

ἔναγχος ἐμοί γε τήν τε τῶν πράξεων βίβλον ἅμα, καὶ καθολικῶν ἐπιστολῶν ἀναγνῶναί τε κατὰ προσῳδίαν, καὶ πῶς ἀνακεφαλαιώσθασθαι, καὶ διελεῖν τούτων ἑκάστης τὸν νοῦν λεπτομερῶς, προσέταξας, ἀδελφὲ Ἀθανάσιε προσφιλέστατε, καὶ τοῦτο ἀόκνως ἐγώ, καὶ προθύμως πεποιηκώς, στοιχηδόν τε συνθεὶς τούτων τὸ ὕφος, κατὰ τὴν ἐμαυτοῦ συμμετρίαν, πρὸς εὔσημον ἀνάγνωσιν, διεπεμψάμην ἐν βραχεῖ τὰ ἕκαστά σοι.[2]

Each of the tables of ἀναγνώσεις is followed by a brief summary paragaph. These are very similar and have been cited in full on page 24 of this monograph.

There is a table in the edition of Zacagni at the conclusion of the text of Jude that summarizes stichometrical data for the texts of Acts and the Catholic epistles, the prefaces to these two parts, and a fifth part labeled "τὸ πρὸς ἐμαυτόν." This is followed by a concluding sentence, "Ἀντεβλήθη δὲ τῶν Πράξεων καὶ καθολικῶν ἐπιστολῶν τὸ βιβλίον

---

1   Z 404; M 629Af.
2   Z 409 f.; M 633Bf. Cf. the statement cited on page 5 of this monograph from the Catholic epistles (Z 477; M 668).

πρὸς τὰ ἀκριβῆ ἀντίγραφα τῆς ἐν Καισαρείᾳ βιβλιοθήκης Εὐσεβίου τοῦ
Παμφίλου."[3]

In addition to these statements, many parts of the apparatus are provided with stichometrical sums at the conclusions;[4] moreover, the Vatican text that was the primary source for Zacagni, 181, has marginal notations in the text denoting every fiftieth stichometrical measure. There
have been serious questions raised in the secondary literature about the
appropriateness of attributing some of these parts to Euthalius, but bearing this in mind, let us see what sorts of claims are being made in these
several pieces and what precisely is being described. Euthalius does not
explicitly state what it is to write στοιχηδόν; he does not say how what
he has done is πρὸς εὔσημον ἀνάγνωσιν. He does claim that he is making a contribution that has no precedent. Robinson notes, "We see that
Euthalius felt that he was there [in the Pauline epistles] breaking new
ground in one important particular. He was contributing to an intelligent reading of the sacred text by distributing it into short sentences."[5]
Euthalius' vocabulary at these points, together with the implications of
the figures associated with the apparatus, suggests that this aspect of his
work was somehow connected with quantitative measurements. The
mere accumulation of this data is not very decisive; thus, it is appropriate to ask about the evidence that may be available in the patristic period
that could clarify the alternatives.

---

3   Z 513; M 692A.
4   For the stichometrical data available in Zacagni, see his own edition or the re-
    prints. This information is summarized by Harris (*Stichometry*, 37–48) and
    Graux ("Nouvelles recherches sur la stichométrie," 104–12). Stichometrical
    data not found in Zacagni's edition or subsequent studies are as follows:
    Catholic Epistles: Prologue: λζ′ in 88 (489) 1828 1845 1846 1875
                        3 John: γ′ in 88
                                    ϛ′ in 452 623 1244 1352 1828 1845 (1846)
                                    1933
    Pauline Epistles: πρόγραμμα to Long Quotation List: (θ′ *vid.* 81)
        Chapter Lists: 1 Cor.:   κβ′ in 88 915
                                   κϛ′ in 81 466 637 699 1244 1352 1735 1845
                                   1995
                         Titus: ϛ′ in 93
                                   η′ in 015 325 458 517 1105 1719 1735 1744
                                   1845 1854 1874
                         Philemon: γ′ in 325 452 517 637 917 1735 1845
                                   1854 1874
5   Robinson, *Euthaliana*, 13.

We may note first that "Origen reckons the second and third epistles of John to be less than a hundred verses, and the first epistle to contain a very few."[6] Eustathius of Antioch (died *ca.* 337) claimed that there were 135 στίχοι in the section John 8:59–10:31.[7] Moreover, there is also evidence that Origen was responsible for an arrangement of at least parts of the Old Testament that must have resembled the modern method of writing poetry: "All these [versions of the Psalms] he brought together, dividing them into clauses [πρὸς κῶλον] and placing them one over against the other."[8] Jerome also stated, in his preface to Isaiah:

> Nemo cum prophetas versibus viderit esse descriptos metro eos aestimet apud Hebraeos ligari, et aliquid simile habere de Psalmis vel operibus Salomonis; sed quod in Demosthene et Tullio solet fieri, ut per cola scribantur et commata, qui utique prosa et non versibus conscripserunt: nos quoque utilitati legentium providentes, interpretationem novam, novo scribendi genere distinximus.[9]

Finally, Hesychius of Jerusalem (fifth or sixth century[10]) made some prefatory remarks to his work on the minor prophets:

> Ἔστι μὲν ἀρχαῖον τοῦτο τοῖς θεοφόροις τὸ σπούδασμα, στιχηδὸν ὡς τὰ πολλά, πρὸς τὴν τῶν μελετωμένων σαφήνειαν, τὰς προφητείας ἐκτίθεσθαι. Οὕτω τοιγαροῦν ὄψει μὲν τὸν Δαυὶδ κιθαρίζοντα, τὸν Παροιμιαστὴν δὲ τὰς παραβολάς, καὶ τὸν Ἐκκλισιαστὴν τὰς προφητείας ἐκθέμενον. Οὕτω συγγραφεῖσαν τὴν ἐπὶ τῷ Ἰὼβ βίβλον· οὕτω μερισθέντα τοῖς στίχοις τὰ τῶν ᾀσμάτων Ἄσματα· πλὴν ἀλλὰ καὶ τὴν ἀποστολικὴν βίβλον οὕτω τινὶ συγγραφεῖσαν εὑρών, οὐ μάτην ἐν ταῖς δυόδεκα βίβλοις τῶν προφητῶν καὶ αὐτὸς ἠκολούθησα· ἀλλ' ἐπειδὴ πολλὰ μὲν τῶν ἀσαφῶν ἡ τῶν στίχων σαφηνίζει διαίρεσις, διδάσκει δὲ καὶ τῶν στιγμῶν τῶν ἀπόρων ποῦ δεῖ τάττειν τὰς πλείονας, ὥστε καὶ τὸν ἰδιώτην καὶ τὸν ἄγαν ἐπιστήμονα τρυγῆσαί τι πάντως ἢ μικρὸν ἢ μέγα τοῦ πονήματος χρήσιμον.[11]

---

6 Harris, *Stichometry*, 35.
7 In *De engastrimytho adversum Origenem*, cited by Roland Schütz, "Die Bedeutung der Kolometrie für das Neue Testament," *ZNW* 21 (1922): 169, n. 2. Cf. Harris, *Stichometry*, 35.
8 Eusebius, *Hist. eccl.*, 6.16.4, taken from the translation by J.E.L. Oulton (LCL; London: William Heinemann, 1932).
9 *PL* 28, col. 285, cited by Harris, *Stichometry*, 22 f. There is an English rendition in James Rendel Harris, "Stichometry," *NSHE* 11:93.
10 Died "about A.D. 438" (Robinson, *Euthaliana*, 36), "most probably . . . after 450" (Quasten, *Golden Age*, 489). Dated in the sixth century by Harris, *Stichometry*, 32. Cf. Ernst von Dobschütz, "Euthalius," *NSHE* 4:215.
11 *PG* 93:1340 f., quoted by Harris, *Stichometry*, 32 f. Cf. Robinson, *Euthaliana*, 36.

There is, moreover, a manuscript that is generally dated in the sixth century, 015, in which the letters of Paul are written in large uncial, in lines
of varying length, much like modern poetry. Among other things, this
manuscript contains the Euthalian chapter lists, stichometric notation at
the conclusion of some of the pieces, and a colophon at the conclusion
of the subscription to Titus that contains elements identical with those
in the concluding sentence of the stichometrical paragraph cited by Zacagni at the conclusion of Jude (see p. 137 above), as well as other indications of a connection with Euthalian activity.[12] The colophon is
studied at greater length at another point in this monograph (pp. 83–
92).

Put very briefly, these data, taken together with other relatively
contemporary materials, lead to the conclusion that we have to do
here with two different sorts of scribal activity. To one form is given
the name stichometry, to the other, colometry. There is general agreement now that these two forms are quite distinct and were employed for
different, although not necessarily incompatible, purposes. The literature here is substantial, and we do not propose to review it.[13]

We believe that it is reasonably settled that stichometry is a form of
quantitative measurement of prose writing. Harris, we believe, has sat-
isfactorily demonstrated that the στίχος[14] was a sixteen syllable or thirty-
six letter line of writing. The probable purposes of this counting of lines
of prose works have been summarized by R. Schütz as follows:[15] (a) to
show the length of the book, (b) to provide a standard for payment of
the scribe and pricing the book, (c) to guard against later interpolations,
and (d) to permit, through the marginal notation of the στίχοι by fifties,
general location of citations.

---

12 See Omont, *Notice sur un très ancien manuscrit grec*; Kirsopp Lake, ed., *Facsimiles of
    the Athos Fragments of Codex H of the Pauline Epistles* (Oxford: Clarendon Press,
    1905); and Robinson, *Euthaliana*, 50–65, including his notes on Omont's tran-
    scription, 66 ff.
13 See the writings of Graux, "Nouvelles recherches sur la stichométrie;" Frie-
    drich Wilhelm Blass, "Zur Frage über Stichometrie der Alten," *RhMus* N. F.
    24 (1869): 524–32; also by Blass, "Stichometrie und Colometrie," *RMP*
    New Series 34 (1879): 214–36; Harris, *Stichometry*; and Schütz, "Bedeutung
    der Kolometrie." There is extensive literature cited in these materials.
14 See also B. Botte, "Manuscrits grecs du Nouveau Testament," *DBSup* 5:
    col. 823.
15 Schütz, "Bedeutung der Kolometrie," 164 ff.

The purpose of colometric writing was, on the other hand, to permit the easier and more intelligible public reading of the text.[16] This was accomplished by dividing the lines according to the sense of the text.

There are some additional conclusions that may be helpful. Stichometry, as an aspect of the book art, must have preceded colometry.[17] Origen was apparently familiar with some form of both of these practices, although colometry was limited, so far as the report goes, to the poetical books of the LXX.[18] There were probably attempts to write colometrically in such a fashion that the number of κῶλα were approximately equivalent to the number of στίχοι known for the particular book.[19] Since a κῶλον may run several lines, containing, thus, several κόμματα, many of the purposes of stichometric writing are still defeated. In any case, the motivation behind and the production of these two patterns of book manufacture are absolutely distinct.[20]

Where does this leave us in our examination of the work of Euthalius? Harris has demonstrated that the stichometrical notations at the conclusions of different parts of the Euthalian apparatus and text reflect measurement in the classic stichometric sense: sixteen syllable lines thirty-six letters in length.[21] On the other hand, it is hard to interpret the different ways in which Euthalius describes what he is about in any other than pointing to colometric writing of the text. It is fairly clear that Euthalius' assertions about being the first in the field, unless they are discounted as statements of fact, put some limits to the discussion. How, then, are the various pieces of the data to be put together in a way that provides a rational explanation for the largest number of facts with the least strained interpretations?

Von Soden has dated Euthalius very late, in the second half of the seventh century.[22] He believes that Euthalius felt his own most important contribution to be the arrangement of these parts of the New Tes-

---

16 See von Dobschütz, "Euthalius," 215; and Zahn, "Euthaliana," 594.
17 Harris, *Stichometry*, 21, 31.
18 Theodor Birt, *Das antike Buchwesen in seinem Verhältniss zur Litteratur: Mit Beiträgen zur Textgeschichte des Theokrit, Catull, Properz und anderer Autoren* (Berlin: Wilhelm Hertz, 1882), 180.
19 Harris, "Stichometry," 93.
20 Among others, see Birt, *Antike Buchwesen*, 180, and C. Wachsmuth, "Stichometrisches und Bibliothekarisches," *RMP* New Series 34 (1879): 51.
21 Harris, "Stichometry," 93 f.
22 Soden, *Schriften des Neuen Testaments*, 643.

tament for "Lektionsgebrauch."²³ Von Soden describes Euthalius' pro-
cedure as a stichometric evaluation of the different parts, a marginal
marking of the lections, and a division of the text into sense lines,
this latter step being accomplished through (red?) points in the text it-
self.²⁴ Since we have evidence for both stichometric and colometric
work on those parts of the New Testament with which Euthalius
worked much earlier than the seventh century, von Soden makes a distinction, in trying to reconcile these facts with Euthalius' claims of
uniqueness, between *writing* in στίχοι, i.e., colometrically, and *dividing*
στίχοι:

> "Wir besitzen nun in [015] einen Pls-Codex, der selbst älter ist als Eutha-
> lius, und der in Stichen abgesetzt geschrieben ist. Dass Euthalius das letztere
> auch gethan habe, behauptet er nicht, sondern nur, dass er ihn in Stichen
> geteilt habe."²⁵

The interpretation of von Soden bas been heavily attacked by Theodor
von Zahn.²⁶ Zahn suspects, correctly we believe, that von Soden has
come to conclusions, because of his fixation with a late date for Euthalius, that violate the clear meaning of the text. Euthalius, Zahn argues,
claims not to have sent a text marked with points or lines, but a text,
preceded by prologues and other matter, that he himself has written stichometrically. The mere translation of Euthalius' own words, he continues, is sufficient to demonstrate the contrary of what von Soden
takes to be self-evident.

Robinson lays primary emphasis upon an exegesis of statements in
the prologues. As we noted earlier, he interprets the various phrases
that Euthalius uses as follows: "He was contributing to an intelligent
reading of the sacred text by distributing it into short sentences."²⁷ Taking this purpose to be primary and exclusive for Euthalius, Robinson
moves to the formulation of a more general criterion, which he pro-
ceeds to use to discriminate between Euthalian and non-Euthalian originated parts of the present apparatus: "Now we have no ground for attributing to Euthalius any interest at all in stichometry proper; that is, in
the numeration of measured στίχοι, as opposed to what is conveniently

---

23 *Ibid.*, 659.
24 *Ibid.*, 659, 666.
25 *Ibid.*, 680.
26 Zahn, "Neues und Altes," 379 f.
27 Robinson, *Euthaliana*, 13.

called colometry, or the distribution of the text into sense lines."[28] Robinson later suggests that these stichometrical additions to the Euthalian material were made by a later editor, possibly Evagrius, whose name is connected with this sort of labor in a colophon in 88.[29]

The most recent attempt to resolve these complexities is that of Günther Zuntz.[30] Zuntz feels that it is quite clear that the terminology used by Euthalius in his prologues is not compatible with the calculations appearing at the conclusion of sections and notations by fifties announced in summary statements.[31] He argues, however, that these stichometrical calculations preceded rather than followed the work of Euthalius. Euthalius himself was rather unimaginative, and all the stichometrical equipment that we find in marginal notations in the text as well as the summaries of these calculations in the tables of ἀναγνώσεις, including the concluding paragraphs to those tables claiming stichometrical notations, all these things Euthalius has simply copied from the exemplar that he used at the library in Caesarea.[32] Euthalius has added his own prologues and set out the text of Pamphilus in a fashion that indicated the grammatical structure of the phrases in fragments.[33] Why, then, does Euthalius use terminology that is so likely to lead to confusion? Zuntz suggests that Euthalius anticipated that his readers were likely to associate a text, written in the fashion that his was, with the poetical books of the Old Testament. These books, according to Zuntz, were known to the Christian reader as "στιχήρεις βίβλοι."[34] Euthalius "completely adapts himself to the notions of his Christian readers. Hence he uses exclusively the term στίχος, little concerned about its inadequacy and the clash with its different, and correct, use in the sections that he copied from Pamphilus."[35]

---

28 *Ibid.*, 17. Note the way he uses this criterion on pages 27, 34.
29 *Ibid.*, 101 f. Cf. 6.
30 Zuntz, *Ancestry*, "Etudes Harkléennes," and other articles.
31 See Corssen, Review, 675 f., brought to our attention by Zuntz, *Ancestry*, 88, n. 1.
32 Zuntz, *Ancestry*, 84–88.
33 Zuntz, "Etudes Harkléennes," 554. Zuntz prefers not to use the expression "colometry" for prose texts (*Ancestry*, 96, n. 1).
34 Zuntz, *Ancestry*, 99.
35 *Ibid.*, 100.

Appendices

1. The Prologue of Euthalius, Bishop of Sulca, Prefixed to the Fourteen Letters of the Blessed Apostle Paul

Admiring your fond desire for learning and zeal, most reverend father, yielding both to respect and to persuasion, I have myself ventured, by some strait, indeed, a sleight of research, to compose this prologue to the study of Paul and, in fear of disobedience, have undertaken a work much greater than appropriate for us.[1] For I know what is said in Proverbs, "The disobedient son shall perish,"[2] but the obedient shall be far from this. But come now, give me your prayers, and like oars to guide me from here to the other side, stretch out your hands to God, just as that great Moses stretched out his hands before, that time when he came to the aid of Israel in encampment. [Please do this] in order that I may avoid the mounting stormy winds and, holding the course of my speech straight,[3] may bring for you the ship of [my] discussion into a calm harbor. Therefore, beginning the speech here, I shall narrate things as they really are.

Paul the Apostle was by race a Hebrew of the tribe of Benjamin, with respect to sect, a Pharisee, educated in the law of Moses by the faithful teacher Gamaliel; in addition to this [he] lived in the "eye of Cilicia," Tarsus,[4] persecuting and ravaging the Church of God. On this account, he was also present at the murder of Stephen the apostle and martyr and was, then, an associate of the killing, receiving to guard the clothes of all those who were stoning him in order that he might use the hands of all for the murder. He used to appear everywhere foremost among the rioters, being zealous to seize those who were the leading persons of the Church. Many and great were the things that happened to the Church on his account, and he omitted nothing in an extreme of madness; for in this he thought that he was acting piously and was accomplishing deeds of greatness, as he himself confesses in [his] letters and Luke states in his second book. Formerly, not only did he hate and turn away from the preaching of truth, in common with many of the Jews, but already he was arousing

Z 515
M 693A
Z 516
M 696A
Z 517
M 696B
Z 518

---

1 The marginal notations to the editions of Zacagni and Migne are, of course, only approximate. Some adjustment of tenses has been made in the interest of a consistent narrative.
2 Prov. 13:1b (LXX).
3 Reading λήγων for λέγων, with von Soden (*Schriften des Neuen Testaments*, 650).
4 See Ruge, "Tarsos," *PW* 4.2: cols. 2413 – 39, especially cols. 2430 f.

a wrath even greater than the whole nation. For as he saw that the kerygma shone abroad and the flourishing word of truth had a greater impact than the Jewish teaching, he was grieved at this and thought that the greatest things were being injured, their teaching being overthrown. He directed all [his] zeal and eagerness against the sheep of the Church to the end that he might either separate them from the   M 696C
true teaching or exact a penalty deserved for faith in Christ. Having obtained at that time from the priests and teachers letters to the Jews in Damascus, Paul rushed on, roaring, as if some stormy, turbulent thing, intending to engulf the disciples in Damascus and to throw them into the pit of perdition. Now because the Lord knew that [Paul] had acquired an unjust madness by what was at least a just   M 697A
intention,[5] he robbed him of his sight with a bright light, appearing in the midst of the journey, and [Paul] changed over so much that he who once had not failed to wish every terrible thing against the Church and had thought besides to destroy utterly all the disciples,   Z 519
now in a split second, this one came to consider [the Church] worthy of his own love and strongest devotion. For the enemy immediately became the suppliant of Jesus and at once, having cast aside the form of madness, he proceeded to the mission, and he confessed devotion to Christ and was sent to Ananias, a certain disciple in Damascus. And God, the examiner of truth, saw that the man had regained his sanity   M 697B
and had attained from an evil, a better disposition. The Lord said that he had been freed from punishment in no other way than this. So it was that he went to Ananias and was baptized, and he became a sharer of the secret mysteries, both a protector and a fellow combatant worthy of the kerygma. He was entrusted with the new preaching by God, and he held fast the newer basis of salvation.

The blessed Paul, therefore, when he had experienced this change, also changed his name and proved true to his other name as well – for Saul used to "shake" [ἐσάλευε] the whole church, but Paul "ceased" [πέπαυται] from further persecution and maltreatment of the disciples   Z 520
of Christ.[6] He was converted to a strong passion for piety so that he would strengthen the disciples of piety through writing, if at any time   M 697C
it happened that he was absent, in order that they might acquire for the future his teaching not only in deeds but also in words and that fortified by both, they might carry about an unmoveable bulwark of piety in the soul.

After some time, Paul again went forth to Jerusalem and saw Peter. On that occasion they also divided the whole world between

---

5   This is a remarkable rationalization of the stimulus for Paul's conversion.
6   This section is omitted in many manuscripts. For details, see Appendix Three, which describes the manuscript census. See page 14 of this monograph for the limits of the omission.

themselves. Paul, when he received the Gentile part – just as Peter was assigned to teach the Jewish people – circulated among many cities and many lands and filled almost all Illyrica with the teachings of devotion to Christ. In fact, he suffered and endured countless terrible things for faith in Christ, and he ran many and varied hazards for the Gospel, as he himself describes. All these he conquered, even though he had to struggle hard for the faith. For God then intended Paul, [that is] the secret plan of the Lord and his foreordination prevailed, that this one should live among men until he preached the Gospel to all the nations.

M 700A

Z 521

Late then in the hour, Paul again goes up to Jerusalem to visit the saints there and to aid the poor. Meanwhile, a certain discord had seized the city, and the populace was in considerable disturbance, Jews having stirred up the community. For they considered it a harsh and serious matter to be accused by the one who was formerly the mainstay and the accomplice of their madness, and they were hastening to kill him. But at once, the military tribune Lysias seized [Paul] and sent [him] with an auxiliary military force to Caesarea, to the governor. Therefore, they carried him off and led him to the ethnarch. Felix was his name. Realizing that the Jews had undertaken some kind of plot against him, Paul immediately, before the tribunal, appealed to Caesar and, for a time, was released from the trial, and the plot intended by the Jews against him came to nothing. Later he was sent to Rome by the leaders to Caesar, and there, having demonstrated the same struggles and toiled hard for the same prizes, he was finally deprived of life itself for the teachings of truth, judging that life with Christ was better than this mortal and perishable life. For a little later, the Caesar, Nero, as he desired to expel him from this life, freely gave him true and genuine life and made a citizen of heaven, the one whom he deprived of the earth.[7] So there the blessed Paul, "having fought the good fight,"[8] as he says himself, was decorated with the crown of the conquering martyrs of Christ. The Romans have enclosed his relics in beautiful and regal shrines and celebrate an annual day of remembrance for him, commemorating the feast of his martyrdom on the third day before the calends of July, on the fifth day of the month of Panemos.[9]

M 700B

Z 522

M 700C

M 701A

Z 523

---

7   Note the relatively brief period in Rome implied, with no release and second defense.

8   2 Tim. 4:7.

9   We have alluded above and below to the problem within the prologue itself to the last year(s) of Paul's life. See to this also August Otto Kunze (*Praecipua patrum ecclesiast. testimonia, quae ad mortem Pauli Apostoli spectant* [Göttingen: Vandenhoeck & Ruprecht, 1848], 32) cited by Friedrich Spitta, *Zur Geschichte und Litteratur des Urchristentums* (vol. 1 Göttingen: Vandenhoeck & Ruprecht, 1893), 93. Spitta (*Geschichte*, 93 f.) also notes that the references even at this point go beyond the witness of Acts and must be dependent upon extra-canonical reports of preaching and struggles.

Before this time blessed Paul the Apostle had already composed many exhortations to a virtuous life and introduced much advice concerning what men ought to do. Moreover, throughout the course of these fourteen letters, he described for men the whole way of life.[10] Thus, the letter to the Romans contains Christian catechetical instruction, based largely upon demonstration from natural reasoning; it is, therefore, placed first, on the grounds that it was written to those   M 701B who had the foundation for reverence of God.

Second after this is the [letter] to the Corinthians, men who   Z 524 already believed but were not behaving in a manner worthy of faith. Because of this he found serious fault with them, and when they had repented at his rebuke, he sent another [letter] with the same general content, through which he confirmed them in their amendment by promising and threatening his own coming.

After these, the [letter] to the Galatians is placed fourth. It was written against those who fell away into Judaism, to whom, after his arguments, he bids a kind of farewell, saying, "For the rest, let no one   M 701C trouble me, for I bear the marks of Christ in my body."[11]   M 704A

Fifth is placed the [letter] to the Ephesians, men who were faithful and had remained steadfast. In the prologue of the [letter] the mystery is explained in a way similar to Romans, and to both as to [those who were] well-known by report.[12] Now these [two letters], in contrast to the others, are starting points for catechumens and elementary treatises for faithful persons.

Sixth is placed the [letter] to the Philippians. [It was] written   Z 525 concerning an additional measure of growth to people who were both faithful and had already borne fruit. [Paul] bears witness to them that he had perceived the finest [fruits of their piety] while he was present, and he exhorts them while he is absent to add to [them] still more. This epistle is to be contrasted with [those to] the Corinthians, for he says to them, "Become imitators of me,"[13] but to the   M 704B Philippians, "Become fellow imitators of me."[14] Yet he names them

---

10 Devreesse (*Manuscrits grecs*, 165, n. 3) argues that the following summary "se rapproche quelquefois mot pour mot d'anciens textes latins," referring to Donatien de Bruyne, *Préfaces de la Bible latine* (Namur: Auguste Godenne, 1920), 217 f.

11 Gal. 6:17.

12 This interpretation of Ephesians is also found in Theodore of Mopsuestia (Louis Pirot, *L'Œuvre exégétique de Théodore de Mopsueste 350 – 428 aprés J.C.* [SPIB; Rome: Sumptibus Pontificii Instituti Biblici, 1913], 289 f.).

13 1 Cor. 4:16; 11:1.

14 Phil. 3:17.

both a crown and a joy,[15] so much do they differ from the Corinthians.

Next is the [letter] to the Colossians, written to those not known in the flesh, but faithful and steadfast. He also commands them, while making progress, to guard against the deceits of philosophy and not to devote themselves to systems of the Jewish observances, on the grounds that this is not pure worship but merely bodily severity. He also commands them to discern the meaning of [his] letters. And he also writes them to enjoin upon Archippus an attentive exercise [of his ministry].

After [the epistles] mentioned, the two letters to the Thessalonians were probably written, the first of which contains a commendation of their ready obedience springing from continued growth, even as far as having had a trial of afflictions; he also compares them to those who had believed in Judea, saying [they] had suffered in the same manner as those had at the hand of their own countrymen. These he also names the crown of his boasting and joy, and he encourages [them] especially in [their] sufferings.

After this [letter], he writes another to the same people, which contains a testimony to their continued growth and to the endurance that they have in afflictions and a teaching concerning the consummation of this age and attention to conduct.

After these is the [letter] to the Hebrews of whom he said the aforementioned [i.e., the Thessalonians] were imitators. [Hebrews] contains a discussion of Jewish mysteries and the change from these to Christ, which had been announced beforehand by the prophets. Thereupon, the letters deal with individual growth of the people.

After these are placed the letters to Timothy. The first of these contains discussion of those matters upon which teachers should be intent, of order in the Church, and of how ruling and being governed ought to be done. The second, which was written to the same person, contains, as a sort of climax, an encomium of his ancestral faith, since it came to him from [his] grandmother and mother. Following this in the same [letter], he also accuses those who were with him in Asia, criticizing [them] as men of little faith; he testifies only in the case of Onesiphorus to a very great concern. And Timothy himself he exhorts to make himself a stranger to worldly matters, and he reminds and also bears witness for the sake of the kerygma. After he has delivered sufficient praise and foretold the rise of heretics and how one ought not be surprised, he sends news of his

M 704C
Z 526

M 705A

Z 527

M 705B

---

15   Phil. 4:1.

final journey from this world. Having exposed the character of many
[of the heretics], he commands [Timothy] to come to him quickly,
perhaps so that he might be able to see [him] at the end of his   Z 528
fulfilment, which he indicated by saying, "I am already poured out
and the time of my release has been set."[16]

The [letter] to Titus describes what sorts of persons clerics are and   M 705C
the order of the Church.

The letter to Philemon was written concerning a faithful servant
Onesimus who, though he was at first useless, turned back and was
deemed worthy of freedom, the Apostle interceding. Moreover, he
also became a martyr of Christ in the city of the Romans at the time
of Tertullus, who was holding the prefectoral authority at that time.
[Onesimus] submitted to the sentence of martyrdom through the
breaking of the legs.[17]

Thus, the [Pauline] corpus as a whole includes every aspect of   M 708A
behavior, [each] presented to foster an increase of growth. Let what
we have said about them so far suffice as a general summary. In what
follows, we shall introduce, concisely, with reference to each letter,
the exposition of the chapters, which was worked out by one of the
most clever fathers, a lover of Christ. Moreover, we have also   Z 729
systematically summarized the most precise divisions of the "lections"
and the acceptable list of the divine testimonies by reading through
the text. This [last] we shall set out, therefore, immediately after the
prologue.[18]

I have also thought it necessary to note briefly the chronology of   M 708B
the preaching of Paul, summarizing it on the basis of the
Chronological Canons [the Chronicles] of Eusebius of Pamphilus.
There, having taken the book in hand and having opened it, I find
that the passion of our savior happened in the eighteenth year of
Tiberius Caesar, and immediately afterwards the resurrection on the
third day, and the ascension of Christ back to heaven. I saw there that
after a few days the apostles were choosing for the diaconate one
appropriately named Stephen and those about him. Afterwards, I find
a very great disturbance of Jews—just as we said before—and Stephen   Z 530
striving there, and Paul, completely consenting to the murder. A little M 708C
later, [Paul] presented himself to the leaders of the Jews and obtained
letters to the Jews in Damascus against the disciples. In the middle of
the journey, the call came to him from God, when that year was
almost over. Then at the beginning of the nineteenth year of Tiberius M 709A

---

16   2 Tim. 4:6.
17   This is a notable contribution to the traditions of the early Church.
18   Cf. the interpretation of this paragraph offered by Zuntz (*Ancestry*, 78 – 85).

Caesar, the narrative says that Paul began to preach and travelled through the whole world preaching devotion to Christ until the thirteenth year of Claudius Caesar. Felix, before whom Paul defended himself when he was accused by the Jews and who shut the apostle up in the prison in Caesarea for two years, was the governor of Judea at that time.

Porcius Festus assumed the office after him and immediately began to examine the apostle so that by this he might lay up a great store of gratitude among the Jews. Blessed [Paul], then, since he supposed [he] would not be set free from the plot otherwise than by appealing to Caesar, stood at the tribunal, appealed to Caesar, and was sent to Rome, to Nero Caesar. With him were Aristarchus, whom he appropriately calls a fellow prisoner somewhere in the letters,[19] and Luke, who passed on the Acts of the Apostles in writing. There, in Rome, Paul was kept under guard for two more years, for Luke reports the events up to this point in the Acts of the Apostles. It was at that time he composed the book, and then he knew little of what was to follow; he did not even include [Paul's] martyrdom in the book, for Luke and Aristarchus went on, leaving [Paul] there.

Z 531

M 709B

Eusebius, however, since he took pains to provide an accurate account of the following period, has given us a narrative of [Paul's] martyrdom, as well, in the second book of his *Ecclesiastical History*. And he notes that Paul lived in freedom and preached the word of God without hindrance.[20] Thus, when Paul had defended himself before Nero, after he was released by Caesar, he was then sent back to the ministry of preaching, so the story goes, and he preached the Gospel for ten more years.[21] When Nero reached the height of

M 709C

Z 532

---

19 Col. 4:10. Cf. Eusebius, *Hist. eccl.*, 2.22.1.

20 Eusebius, *Hist. eccl.*, 2.22, has the parallels to this paragraph. Note, moreover, the tension between the intervals between Paul's two reported defenses in this section of the prologue, parallel to Eusebius, and the brief time elapsed in Rome, with no suggestion of a second defense, in the first part of this prologue. It is also noteworthy that neither Euthalius nor Eusebius specifies where Paul went between his first and second defenses.

21 Kunze (*Praecipua patrum*, 45, n. 1) notes that the edition of this material in Mill (*Novum Testamentum graecum*, 252 f.) has an addition to the text at this point. The text here is from 51, which is Mill's *Laud.* 2 (so Scrivener, *Plain Introduction*, 185). The text of the whole apparatus in this manuscript appears to have suffered considerably from dislocation and rearrangement. The addition is as follows: ἐν τούτοις τοῖς ἔτεσι λέγεται ἀποδημῆσαι εἴς τε Ἰσπανίαν τῆς Γαλλίας καὶ Ἰταλίας στείλασθαι τὸν τοῦ Χριστοῦ κήρυκα, καὶ κατασπεῖραι τὸν λόγον, καὶ πολλοὺς τῶν πατρίων ἀποσπάσαι θεῶν, καὶ τῇ ποίμνῃ τοῦ κυρίου ἐπισυνάψαι. ὅτι δὲ ἐν Ἰσπανίᾳ γέγονε κηρύσσων ὅδε Παῦλος, ἐν τῇ πρὸς Ῥωμαίους ἐπιστολῇ τοῦτο διαγορεύει, γράφων ὡδί. Νυνὶ δὲ μηκέτι τόπον ἔχων ἐν τοῖς κλίμασι τούτοις, ἐπιποθίαν δὲ ἔχων τοῦ ἐλθεῖν πρὸς ὑμᾶς ἀπὸ πολλῶν ἐτῶν, ὡς ἐὰν πορεύωμαι εἰς Ἰσπανίαν ἐλεύσομαι πρὸς ὑμας· ἐλπίζω γὰρ διαπορευόμενος θεάσασθαι ὑμᾶς. ἐπεὶ οὖν δὲ πρὸ τοῦ ἐν Ῥώμῃ γενέσθαι μελέτην εἶχεν εἰς Ἰσπανίαν κηρύξαι,

madness, first of all he destroyed Agrippina, his own mother, and then the sister of his father as well, and Octavia, his own wife and numberless others belonging to [his] family. Afterwards, he stirred up a general persecution of the Christians and thus was led [to bring] slaughter upon the apostles. For he summoned Paul and stood him once more before the tribunal. Luke was with him again. There, in the thirty-sixth year of the passion of the savior,[22] the thirteenth year of Nero, Paul came to suffer martyrdom, by decapitation with a sword.

M 712A

Moreover, [the period] from the nineteenth year of Tiberius Caesar, in which he began to preach the Gospel, until the twenty-second year is four years; the years of Gaius' [rule] are also four, and the years of Claudius' [rule] are a little less than fourteen. Nero succeeding him, killed the Apostle in the thirteenth year of his own office.

Z 533

Therefore, the same Apostle Paul is writing to Timothy concerning his first defense when he says, "At my first defense, no one took part for me; all deserted me. May it not be charged against them. But the Lord stood by me and gave me strength to proclaim the word fully, that all the Gentiles might hear it. So I was rescued from the lion's mouth."[23] By ["the lion"] he means Nero.[24] And it is in reference to the second, in which he is perfected in martyrdom before him, that he says, "Fulfil your noble ministry; for I am already

M 712B

εὐοδωθὲν αὐτῷ πρὸς τὴν πρώτην καταντῆσαι τῶν πόλεων, οὐκ ἠμέλησε τῶν προδεδογμένων. εἰ καὶ πάλιν ἀνακάμψας εἰς Ῥώμην, ἐν αὐτῇ τῶν μακρῶν ἀναπαύεται πόνων.

22 The dating of the martyrdom of Paul in the thirty-sixth year of the passion of Jesus coincides with one of the dates given in the *Martyrium*. The congruence of this date with the thirteenth year of Nero, also the year of the martyrdom of Peter, is attested by Eusebius' canons, so Lipsius (Richard Adelbert Lipsius, *Die apokryphen Apostel-geschichten und Apostellegenden: Ein Beitrag zur altchristlichen Literaturgeschichte* [vol. 2.1; Braunschweig: C. A. Schwetschke & Sohn {Wiegandt & Appelhans}, 1887], 25). There is a complex tangle of problems connected with this part of the early Church to which we are only able to allude here.

23 2 Tim. 4:16 f.

24 Kunze (*Praecipa patrum*, 45 f., n. 2) found the following addition to the text in Mill (*Novum Testamentum graecum*, 253), which is from 51: πρώτην ἀπολογίαν, τὴν ἐπὶ Νέρωνος πρώτην παράστασιν λέγει. παρέστη γὰρ ἤδη τῷ Νέρωνι καὶ διέφυγεν. ἐπειδὴ δὲ τὸν οἰνοχόον αὐτοῦ κατήχησε, τότε αὐτὸν ἀπέτεμεν. Ἄλλοι δὲ φασίν, ὅτι καὶ τὰς παλλακὰς αὐτοῦ κατήχησε. μαρτυρεῖ τῷ λόγῳ καὶ Ἰωάννης ὁ Χρυσοῦς τὴν γλῶτταν λέγων· ὅτι παλλακίδα τοῦ Νέρωνος σφόδρα ἐπέραστον τὸν περὶ πίστεως δέξασθαι λόγον ὁ Παῦλος ἔπειθεν, ὁμοῦ καὶ τῆς ἀκαθάρτου ἐκείνης συνουσίας ἀπαλλαγῆναι. ἐκεῖνος δὲ λυμεῶνα καὶ πλάνον τὸν Παῦλον ἀποκαλῶν, τὸ μὲν πρῶτον ἔδησε, τῇ εἱρκτῇ ἐγκλείσας. ὡς δὲ οὐκ ἔπειθε τῆς πρὸς τὴν κόρην ἀποσχέσθαι συμβουλῆς, τέλος ξίφει τὴν κεφαλὴν ἀπέτεμεν.

on the point of being sacrificed; the time of my departure has come."[25] A few [verses] later in the same letter he writes that Luke was again with him: "Luke who is with me greets you."[26] The whole time of Paul's preaching is, therefore, twenty-one years and another two years, which he spent in the prison in Caesarea, and in addition to these, another two years in Rome and the last ten years, so that all the years from his call to [his] consummation are thirty-five.

Z 534

Now, let no one find fault with my discussion and reject the events following Acts by saying that Luke did not mention them.[27] Any sensible man would ask such a person, "If, good friend, you do not accept the [events] that [happened] after Acts, give me," he would say, "the Luke who wrote the martyrdom of Paul." For if Luke had described the martyrdom for us and had limited Paul's life in Rome to these two years alone, we should have no need of any unnecessary labor over the times. But since he himself did not write about the martyrdom for us, for it happened much later than the period of the book, trust for the rest to Eusebius the Chronicler and accept the narrative with a reasonable spirit as a friend. For the disciples of Christ, in obedience and faith, by receiving the teachings and traditions of the fathers for edification, are established heirs of the kingdom of heaven.

M 712C

M 713A

Z 535

---

25   2 Tim. 4:5b f.

26   2 Tim. 4:11a. Zacagni notes here (Z 533, n. 15; M 712, n. 83) that there is some confusion between the phraseology here, which is "Λουκᾶς ἐστιν μόνος μετ' ἐμοῦ" and that in Col. 4:14, "ἀσπάζεται ὑμᾶς Λουκᾶς ὁ ἰατρος ὁ ἀγαπητὸς καὶ Δημᾶς."

27   Early on, it was suggested that this defensive tone of the prologue implies a polemic against description of a double defense and imprisonment in Rome. The material here, so Spitta (Geschichte, 93), is not derived so much from a self-supporting tradition as exegetical reflection, the motive of which lies on a foundation other than historical research.

2. Quotation List in Acts

We list below the double numeration system for the long quotation list in Acts. The manuscript witnesses are 915 919 1845; the following manuscripts have evidence of this system only in the margin of the text: 181 1875 (=1898). Minor variants have not been shown.

Consecutive	Source	Cumulative	Zacagni
α′	Ματθαίου Εὐαγγελιστοῦ	α′	I
β′	Ψαλμοῦ ξη′ καὶ ρη′	α′	II
γ′	Ἰωὴλ Προφήτου	α′	III
δ′	Ψαλμοῦ ιε′	β′	IV
ε′	Ψαλμοῦ ρλα′	γ′	V
ϛ′	Ψαλμοῦ ρθ′	δ′	VI
ζ′	Ἐξόδου	α′	VII
η′	Γενέσεως	α′	VIII
θ′	Ψαλμοῦ β′	ε′	IX
ι′	Γενέσεως	β′	X
ια′	Γενέσεως	γ′	XI
ιβ′	Ἐξόδου	β′	XII
ιγ′	Ἐξόδου	γ′	XIII
ιδ′	Ἐξόδου	δ′	XIV
ιε′	Ἐξόδου	ε′	XV
ιϛ′	Ἀμὼς Προφήτου	α′	XVI
ιζ′	Ψαλμοῦ ρλα′	ϛ′	XVII
ιη′	Ἀγγαίου Προφήτου	α′	XVIII
ιθ′	Ἠσαΐου Προφήτου	α′	XIX
κ′	Βασιλειῶν πρώτης	α′	XX
κα′	Ματθαίου Εὐαγγελιστοῦ	β′	XXI
κβ′	Ψαλμοῦ β′	ζ′	XXII
κγ′	Ἠσαΐου Προφήτου	β′	XXIII
κδ′	Ἀμβακοὺμ Προφήτου	α′	XXV
κε′	Ἠσαΐου Προφήτου	γ′	XXVI
κϛ′	Ἀμὼς Προφήτου	β′	XXVII
κζ′	Ἀράτου ἀστρονόμου καὶ Ὁμήρου ποιητοῦ	α′	XXVIII
κη′	Ἐκ τῶν διατάξεων	α′	XXIX
κθ′	Ἐξόδου	ϛ′	XXX
λ′	Ἠσαΐου Προφήτου	δ′	XXXI

3. Manuscript Survey

The survey on the following pages represents a condensation of notes taken during an examination of more than 400 manuscripts of the New Testament in the Institut für neutestamentliche Textforschung in Münster. Some manuscripts which were on our original list were not available. These include the following: 101 241 242 255 257 336 483 611 823 911 986 1040 1107 1108 1425 1433 1525 1759 1760 1766 1835 1865 1867 1960 2233. Information on some manuscripts was gathered from the notebooks of Gregory and the preliminary notes of Kurt Treu.

The abbreviations at the head of the columns represent the following:

P: Prologue to Acts
L: "Lection" List to Acts
S: Short Quotation List
L: Long Quotation List
A: *Argumentum* to Acts
a: ἀποδημίαι
I: Introduction to Chapters
4: 40 Chapter List
3: 36 Chapter List

P: Prologue to the Catholic Letters
L: "Lection" List to the Catholic Letters
S: Short Quotation List
L: Long Quotation List
A: *Argumenta*
L: Chapter Lists
e: ἐπίγραμμα
p: πλοῦς

P: Prologue to the Pauline Letters
p: Name Pun
M: *Martyrium*
E: Egyptian Paragraph
L: "Lection" List to the Pauline Letters
S: Short Quotation List
L: Long Quotation List

t: τάδε ἔνεστιν
d: διὰ τί
A: *Argumenta*
L: Chapter Lists

The columns are marked as follows: "x" represents a positive occurrence. "o" represents a positive omission. "p" represents a partial, incomplete, or variant occurrence. Occasionally, when only a minor part is missing, "p" is not used instead of "x." "?" represents uncertainty. "d" indicates that the part has been duplicated in the manuscript. In the column for the *Martyrium*, "E" indicates that it concludes with ἡμέρᾳ and "P" indicates that it concludes with παρουσίας.

Column groups — **Acts**: QL (P L S L A), ChL (a I 4 3); **Catholic Letters**: QL (P L S L A L), C (e p); **Pauline Letters**: QL (P p M E L S L t d A), C (L).

MS no.	P	L	S	L	A	a	I	4	3	P	L	S	L	A	L	e	p	P	p	M	E	L	S	L	t	d	A	L
018												x																
056												x															p	
1	x		x	x								x	x					x	x	E							x	p
2			x	x								x								P							x	
3				x								x															x	
5		x	x	x	x				x			x	x										x				x	x
6												x	p														x	
7																		x	o	P							x	
18												x															x	
33						x						x															x	
35												x															x	
36												x						p			E							
38												x															x	
42			x	x	x	x	?					x	x					x	o	d							x	x
51			x	x	x	x						x	x					p									x	x
61			x									p															x	
62												x	x					x	o	E							x	x
76				x	x							x	x														p	x
81																	x	x	o	E		x	x	x	x		o	x
82	x		x	x	x	x	x	x			p	x	p					x	o	E							p	x
88	x	x	x	x		x	x			x		x	x			x		x	o	E			x	p	x		x	x
90	x		x	x								p						x	o	E								
91									x			x	x					x	o	P							x	x
93	x		x	x								x	x								E				p		x	x
94			x	x								x						p			E						p	
97			x									x	p														p	p
102			x	x	x	x						x	x					x	o	E							x	x
110												p						x	o									
122			x									p															p	
131												x	x															x
133	x		x									x						x	x	E		x					x	x
141												x															x	
142			x	x								x																x
149												x																x
172												x						x	x								x	p
177												x	?														x	p
180				x																								
181	x	x	x	x	x	x	x	x	x	x	x	x	x	x	x	x	x	x	x	E	x	x	x	x	x	x	x	x
189												x	x														x	x
201												x															x	
203	x		x	x	x	x	x					x	x					x	o	P						x	p	p
204												x															x	
205				x								x															x	

MS no.	Acts									Catholic Letters								Pauline Letters										
	QL P	L	S	L	A	a	I	ChL 4	3	QL P	L	S	L	A	L	C e	p	QL P	p	M	E	L	S	L	t	d	C A	L
206				x	x					x								x									x	
209				x						x																	x	
216				x	x			x		x	x										E						x	x
218				x		x	x			x	x																x	?
221										x	x							x	o								x	x
223			x	x	x	x				x								p									x	
228				x		x	x											x	o	P							x	x
234			x	x	x	x				x	x							p									x	
250				x						x	x							x	x								x	x
254									?	x	x																x	x
302										x																	x	
307			x	x	x					x																	x	
308										x								x	o									
309																											p	
312										x	x																x	x
314										x	x							x	o								p	p
321										x																	p	p
325										x	x																x	x
326				x	x					x																	x	
327										x	x																x	x
328										x																	x	
330													x															x
337										x																	x	
339				x	x					x																	x	
356										x	x																	
363										x																	x	
367			x	x	x	x				x	x									P							x	x
378		x	x	x						x																	x	
384	x			x	x					p								x	o		E							
385										x																	x	
386										x																	x	
390				x						x								p									x	
393																											p	
394										x																	x	
400									x	x																	x	
404				x	x					x		p															x	x
421										x		p								P							x	x
424				x						x	x							x	x								x	x
425									x	x	x							p									x	x
429										x											E	?					x	
431										x																	x	x
432										x																	x	
436	x	x	x	x	x	x				x	x	x	x					x	x		E				p	p	x	x

MS no.	Acts									Catholic Letters								Pauline Letters										
	QL					ChL				QL					C			QL									C	
no.	P	L	S	L	A	a	I	4	3	P	L	S	L	A	L	e	p	P	p	M	E	L	S	L	t	d	A	L
440													x														p	
444													x														x	
450																		x	o		E							
451	x			x						x			x	x				d									x	x
452			x			x	x						x	x				x	o								x	x
453				x	x	x							x					p			E						x	x
454													x	x													x	x
456													x	p													x	x
457													x	p				p									x	p
458																											p	x
459			x	x	x	x							x	x							E						x	x
462	x	x	x	x	x	x				x			x	p				x	o		E						x	x
463		x											x	p				p			E						x	p
464		x								x			x	x				?									x	x
466										x			x	x				x	x				x	x	x	x	x	x
467							x	x		x			x	x				p									p	x
468		x											x	x				x	o								x	x
469													x														x	
479		x	x										x														x	
480													?														?	
489		x											x														x	
496		x	x										x	p													x	x
498	?			x									x					x	o								p	
506	x			x				p					x	x				x	o		P					x	x	x
517													p	p													x	x
522													x					?			E						x	
547													x					?									x	
567													p	p				p									p	p
592			x										x					p	x								p	
601										x			x	x				x	o		E						p	p
602																		x	o									
603	x	x	x	x	x	x							x	p				x	o		E							
604													x														x	
605	x												x	p							E			p			x	x
606													x	x				x	o								p	
614		x	x										x								P						x	
616													x					p	x								x	
617													x	p				x	o		P						x	
618													x														x	p
619	x	x	x	x	x	x	x	x		x	x	x	x	x			p	d	d				x	x	x	x	x	x
621	x	x				x	x	x		x			x	x							E					?	p	p
622													x	p														
623										x	x	x	x	x	x			x	x		E	x	x	x	x	x	x	x

| MS no. | Acts | | | | | | | | | Catholic Letters | | | | | | | | Pauline Letters | | | | | | | | | | |
| | QL | | | | | | | ChL | | QL | | | | | | C | | QL | | | | | | | | | C | |
	P	L	S	L	A	a	I	4	3	P	L	S	L	A	L	e	p	P	p	M	E	L	S	L	t	d	A	L
624														x	x												p	p
625	x		x	x	x	x				x				x	x			x	x	E							x	x
626														p	p													
627																		x	o	?	?							
628										x				x													x	
630														x													x	
632														x													x	p
633														x													x	
634														x													x	
635		x	x	x	x	x								x	x			x	o	E								
636		x	x											x	p												x	x
637																		x	o	P	x	x	x				x	x
638								x	x					x	x			x	x	E						x	x	x
639														x	x													
641														x				x	o								x	p
642									?					x	p												x	x
643														x	x													
644														p				p									p	
664														x													x	
665	x		x	x										x	x					E			p				x	x
680										x				x				x	o	E							x	
699														x	x			x	x	E							x	x
757														x													x	
794																									p		p	p
796														p													x	
801				x										x													x	
808	x			x				x	x					x	x												x	x
824														x													x	
901														x													p	
910																		x	o	E								
912			x	x										x				p									x	
913														x	x												x	x
915		x	x	x				x	x	x			p	x	x			x	o		x	x	x	x			x	x
917	x	x	x	x	x	x	x	x	x	x	x	x	x	x	x			x	x	E	x	x	x	x	x	x	x	x
919	x	?	?	?	x	x	x	x		x				x	x			x	x	E					x	?	x	x
927			x							x				x													x	
928														x													x	
935														p	p												p	
941								x																				
959														x													x	
996				x										x													x	
999														x													x	
1003														x													x	

Column groups: **Acts** — QL: P L S L A; ChL: a I 4 3 · **Catholic Letters** — QL: P L S L A; C: L e p · **Pauline Letters** — QL: P p M E L S L t d; C: A L

MS no.	P	L	S	L	A	a	I	4	3	P	L	S	L	A	L	e	p	P	p	M	E	L	S	L	t	d	A	L
1058													x														x	
1067													x	x		?		x	x		E			p			p	p
1069													x	x													x	x
1070													p	p													x	
1072													x														x	
1099																											x	p
1100													x														x	
1102		x	x	x	x								x	x				x	o		E						x	x
1103	x	x	p	x	x								x	x													x	x
1105			x	x									x	p													x	x
1161		x	x	x	x	x							x	x				x	o		E						x	x
1162	?	x	x	x	?	x	x	x		x	x	x	x	x	x			d		d	x	x	x	x	x	x	x	?
1175						x	?	?																				
1240		x	x			x							x	x													x	p
1241																												p
1243															x													p
1244	x	x	x	x	x	x	x	x					x	x				d					x	x	x	?	x	x
1247			x	x									x					p		P							x	
1248			x	x		x							x														x	
1249													x														x	
1250													x					x	o								x	
1251		x											x														x	
1270		x	x	x	x	x							x					p	o		E			p			p	
1292		x											x	x				x	o	P				?			x	x
1297		x	x	x	x								x					x	o		E						x	
1311		x		x	x								x	x										p				
1315		x	x		x								p	p													x	x
1352		x		x	x								x	x				x	o								x	x
1354																											x	
1360													?					x	x								p	p
1367			x	x									x														x	
1384			x	x									x														x	
1398																												p
1400													x														x	
1404		x											x														x	
1405		x	x	x	x								x	x				p									x	x
1409		x		x	x	x							x	x				p	o	P							x	x
1424																		x	o		E							
1448																		x	o	P							x	x
1456		x											p					p									x	
1482													x														x	
1501													x														x	
1503													x														x	

Column groupings:
- **Acts** — QL: P L S L A a I; ChL: 4 3
- **Catholic Letters** — QL: P L S L A L; C: e p
- **Pauline Letters** — QL: P p M E L S L t d; C: A L

MS no.	P	L	S	L	A	a	I	4	3	P	L	S	L	A	L	e	p	P	p	M	E	L	S	L	t	d	A	L
1521		x	x											x													x	
1523														p		p											p	p
1524		x	x		x									x		x											p	x
1548														x													x	
1573		x	x															p									p	
1594		x	x											x				p									x	
1597		x	x	x	x									x		x		x		o	E						x	x
1598		x	x	x	x			x						x				p		o	E						x	
1599		x	x											x													x	
1609														x				x	x								x	
1610														x		?					E						x	x
1611								x	x					x		x		x	x	?							x	x
1617		x												x													x	
1618		x												x													x	
1619														x													p	
1622														x		p											x	x
1626								x						x				x		o							x	x
1628														x													x	
1636														x													x	
1637		x												x													x	
1642		x	x											x													x	
1643		x	x	x	x									x		x					E						x	x
1649		x												x													x	
1656														x													p	
1668	x	x	x	x	x									x		x											x	p
1704														x													x	
1717														x													x	
1719														x		p					P						x	x
1720									x					p														x
1721																											x	
1723														x				p									x	
1724		x												p		p											x	
1725														x													x	
1726														x													x	
1728														x		p		x		o	E							
1729								x						x		x		x	x							x	x	x
1730														x		x		x	x								x	x
1731														x													x	
1732														x													x	
1733														x				p									x	
1734																		x		o	E							
1735	x							x	x					x		x		x		o							p	x
1736														p													x	

	Acts									Catholic Letters								Pauline Letters										
	QL					ChL				QL						C		QL									C	
MS no.	P	L	S	L	A	a	I	4	3	P	L	S	L	A	L	e	p	P	p	M	E	L	S	L	t	d	A	L
1737														x													x	
1738														x													x	p
1740														x													x	
1742			x	x										x													x	
1743							x	x						x	x												p	x
1744	?			x										x	x										p		p	p
1745														x													x	
1746														x													x	
1747				x										x	p												p	p
1748														x													x	
1749														x													x	
1750				x										x	p												x	p
1751				x	x									x	p						E			p			x	p
1752														x													x	
1753			x	x	x									x				p									x	
1754														x													x	
1755																											p	p
1756																											p	p
1761														x													x	
1763														x													x	
1767														x													x	
1768				x						x				x	x												x	p
1770																											x	p
1771																											p	
1795																											p	p
1827														x													x	
1828	x	x	x	x	x					x				x	x						E	x		p		x	x	x
1829										x				x	x													
1830														x	x						E						x	x
1831														x													x	
1836														p				x	x		E	x	x	x	x	x	x	x
1837				x										x													x	
1838														p				p			E						x	p
1840														p														
1841														x													x	
1843								x						x	x												x	x
1845	x	x	x	x	x	x	x	x		x	x	x	x	x	x			x	x		E	x	x	x	x	x	x	x
1846										x	x	x	x	p	p			x	?			x	x	x	x	x	p	p
1847		x	x	x	x					x				x	x			p			E						x	x
1848														p	p			x	o					p			x	x
1849	p	x												x	p						E						x	
1852										x				x	x									p			x	p
1854														x	x												x	x

Column groups — **Acts** [QL: P L S L A a I | ChL: 4 3], **Catholic Letters** [QL: P L S L A L | C: e p], **Pauline Letters** [QL: P p M E L S L t d | C: A L]

MS no.	P	L	S	L	A	a	I	4	3	P	L	S	L	A	L	e	p	P	p	M	E	L	S	L	t	d	A	L
1855										x																	x	
1856										x																	x	
1858										x																	x	
1859										x	p																	
1860			x					x		x	p																x	x
1861										x																	x	
1863			x	x	x	x				x				x				p									x	x
1870																		x	o	E								
1873								x	x	x				x													x	x
1874	x	x	x	x	x	x	x	x	x	x	x	x	x	x	x			x	x	E	x	x	x	x	x	x	x	x
1875	p	x	?					p	p	x	x	x	x	x	p	x	x	x	x	E	x	x	x	x	x	x	x	p
1876		x								x																	x	
1877		x	x							x								x	x	E	x						x	
1880								x		x				x				x	o	E							x	x
1886			x	x						x				x													x	x
1888										x				x				x	x								x	p
1889																											x	x
1890		x	x							p																	x	
1891		x	x	x	x	x				x				x			p	p									p	p
1892			x	x						x								x	o								x	
1893										p																	x	
1894		x								x								d		d							x	p
1895										x										E								
1896	x		x	x	x	x				p								p		E							x	x
1897										x																	p	
1903			x	x	x	x																						
1905																		x	o	P							x	
1906																				P							x	
1907																		x	o	P							x	p
1908																											x	
1912																											x	x
1914																		p	o								x	x
1916																											p	
1917																											x	
1920																		x	o	P			p				x	x
1921																		p		P							x	
1922																											p	p
1923																											x	
1924																		x	o	P							x	p
1927																											x	
1929																											p	
1932								x										p									x	
1933			x					x						x	x			d		P							x	x

MS no.	Acts QL: P	L	S	L	A	ChL: a	I	4	3	Cath QL: P	L	S	L	A	L	C: e	p	Paul QL: P	p	M	E	L	S	L	t	d	C: A	L
1934																		x	o	P							x	x
1941																											x	p
1951																											x	
1952						x												p	o	P							x	x
1954																											p	p
1956																		x	x								x	x
1959																		p					p				p	x
1970																		x	?	P							p	p
1972																		x	o	P							x	x
1975																											p	p
1980																											p	
1981																		x	?	P					x		p	
1982																											p	
1986																											x	
1994																											p	
1995																												p
1997																		x	o	P							x	
1998																		x	o	P							x	
2001																		x	o	P							p	
2004																		x	o	E							x	p
2009																											x	
2080												x															x	
2085						x	x					x						p									x	
2125												x		x				x	o	P							x	x
2131						x	x					x															x	
2143								x	x			x		x													x	x
2147												x															x	
2175																											p	
2180												p															p	p
2183						x												p		P							x	x
2189						x														P							x	p
2197												x						x	o				p				x	x
2221												x															x	
2242						x	x	x	x			x		x				x	x	P				p		x	p	p
2243	x					x	x	x	x											E								
2261												x															x	
2279						x	x	x				x						p									x	
2289												x															x	
2298								x	x			x		x													x	x
2401						x						x		p													x	
2441												p																
2464					x							x						p		E							p	
2466												x															x	

MS no.	Acts (QL)					Acts (ChL)				Catholic (QL)						Catholic (C)		Pauline (QL)									Pauline (C)	
	P	L	S	L	A	a	I	4	3	P	L	S	L	A	L	e	p	P	p	M	E	L	S	L	t	d	A	L
2484	x		x	x	x	x	x			x				p	x	p			x	o	E							p	x
2502				x	x	x	x																					p	p
2511																			p										
2516																			x	o								p	
2527												p	p															x	x
2541										x				x			x	x	x	o	E					p		x	x
2544												p																x	p

Bibliography

Selected Critical Books and Articles

(Additions to the original bibliography are shown with an asterisk.)

Allegro, John Marco. "Further Messianic References in Qumran Literature." *Journal of Biblical Literature* 75 (1956): 174–87.

Bardy, Gustave. "Euthalius." Pages 1215–18 in vol. 2 of *Dictionnaire de la Bible. Supplément.* 5 vols. Paris: Letouzey & Ané, 1895.

Berger, Samuel. *Histoire de la Vulgate pendant les premiers siècles du Moyen Age.* Paris: Hachette, 1893.

★Bianco, Maria Grazia. "Euthalius." Page 304 in vol. 1 of *Encyclopedia of the Early Church.* 2 vols. Edited by Angelo Di Bernardino. New York: Oxford University Press, 1992.

★Birdsall, J. N. "The Euthalian Material." Pages 362–3 in *From the Beginnings to Jerome.* Vol. 1 of *The Cambridge History of the Bible.* Edited by P. R. Ackroyd and C. F. Evans. 3 vols. Cambridge: Cambridge University Press, 1963–70.

★Birdsall, J. N.. "The Euthalian Material and Its Georgian Versions." *Oriens Christianus* 68 (1984): 170–95. Reprinted as pages 215–242 in J. Neville Birdsall, *Collected Papers in Greek and Georgian Textual Criticism.* Texts and Studies New Series 3. Piscataway, NJ: Gorgias Press, 2006.

Birt, Theodor. *Das antike Buchwesen in seinem Verhältniss zur Litteratur: Mit Beiträgen zur Textgeschichte des Theokrit, Catull, Properz und anderer Autoren.* Berlin: Wilhelm Hertz, 1882.

Blass, Friedrich Wilhelm. "Stichometrie und Kolometrie." *Rheinisches Museum für Philologie* New Series 34 (1879): 214–36.

Blass, Friedrich Wilhelm. "Zur Frage über die Stichometrie der Alten." *Rheinisches Museum für Philologie* New Series 24 (1869): 524–32.

Botte, B. "Manuscrits grecs du Nouveau Testament." Pages 819–35 in vol. 5 of *Dictionnaire de la Bible. Supplément.* 5 vols. Paris: Letouze & Ané, 1895.

Bousset, W. Review of Hermann von Soden, *Die Schriften des Neuen Testaments in ihrer ältesten erreichbaren Textgestalt. Theologische Literaturzeitung* 28 (1903): 324–30.

Bousset, W. *Textkritische Studien zum Neuen Testament.* Texte und Untersuchungen zur Geschichte der altchristlichen Literatur 11.4. Leipzig: J. C. Hinrichs, 1894.

Braun, Wilhelm. "Die Lese- und Einteilungszeichen in den gotischen Handschriften der Ambrosiana in Mailand." *Zeitschrift für deutsche Philologie* 30 (1898): 433–48.

Braun, W. "Ein satzphonetisches Gesetz des Gotischen mit vorwiegender Rücksicht auf die Codices Ambrosiani." *Germanisch-Romanische Monatschrift* 5 (1913): 367–91.

*Brinkmann, Hennig. "Der Prolog im Mittelalter als literarische Erscheinung: Bau und Aussage." *Wirkendes Wort* 14 (1964): 1–21.

*Brock, Sebastian P. "Hebrews 2: 9 B in Syriac Tradition." *Novum Testamentum* 27 (1983): 236–44.

*Brock, Sebastian P. "The Resolution of the Philoxenian/Harclean Problem." Pages 325–43 in *New Testament Textual Criticism: Its Significance for Exegesis: Essays in Honour of Bruce M. Metzger*. Edited by Eldon Jay Epp and Gordon D. Fee. Oxford: Oxford University Press, 1981.

*Brock, Sebastian P. "The Syriac Euthalian Material and the Philoxenian Version of the NT." *Zeitschrift für die neutestamentliche Wissenschaft* 70 (1979): 120–30.

*Burch, Vacher. "Two Notes on Euthalius of Sulci." *The Journal of Theological Studies* Old Series 17 (1916): 176–79.

Cazenove, John Gibson. "Evagrius (5)." Pages 419–21 in vol. 2 of *Dictionary of Christian Biography, Literature, Sects, and Doctrines*. Edited by William Smith and Henry Wace. 4 vols. Boston: Little Brown, 1877–87.

*Colwell, Ernest Cadman. Review of H. A. Sanders, *A Third-century Papyrus Codex of the Epistles of Paul*. *Classical Philology* 32 (1937): 385–87.

Conybeare, Frederick Cornwallis. "The Date of Euthalius." *Zeitschrift für die neutestamentliche Wissenschaft* 5 (1904): 39–52.

Conybeare, Frederick Cornwallis. "On the Codex Pamphili and the Date of Euthalius." *Journal of Philology* 23 (1895): 241–59.

Corssen, Peter. Review of Eduard von der Goltz, *Eine textkritische Arbeit des zehnten bezw. sechsten Jahrhunderts*. *Göttingische gelehrte Anzeigen* 161 (1899): 665–80.

*Crisp, Simon, "Scribal Marks and Logical Paragraphs: Discourse Segmentation Criteria in Manuscripts of the Pauline Corpus." Pages 77–87 in *Current Trends in Scripture Translation: Definitions and Identity*. Edited by Philip A. Noss. *UBS Bulletin* 198/199 (2005): 77–87.

*Dahl, Nils A., "The 'Euthalian Apparatus' and Affiliated 'Argumenta.'" Pages 231–75 in *Studies in Ephesians: Introductory Questions, Text- & Edition-critical Issues, Interpretation of Texts and Themes*. Edited by David Hellholm, Vemund Blomkvist, and Tord Fornberg. Wissenschaftliche Untersuchungen zum Neuen Testament 131. Tübingen: Mohr (Siebeck), 2000.

*Danelia, Korneli. "The Georgian Redaction of the Stichometry of Euthalius," (in Georgian) in *Dzveli kartuli enis k'atedris shromebi* [Works of the Department of Old Georgian Language] 20; Tbilisi: Tbilisi University Press, 1977, 53–150.

Devreesse, Robert. *Introduction à l'étude des manuscrits grecs*. Paris: Imprimerie Nationale, 1954.

Dobschütz, Ernst von. "Ein Beitrag zur Euthaliusfrage." *Zentralblatt für Bibliothekswesen* 10 (1893): 49–70.

Dobschütz, Ernst von. "Euthalius." Pages 215–16 in vol. 4 of *The New Schaff-Herzog Encyclopedia of Religious Knowledge*. Samuel Macauley Jackson, Editor-in-Chief. 13 vols. Grand Rapids, Mich.: Baker, 1949–50.

Dobschütz, Ernst von. "Euthaliusstudien." *Zeitschrift für Kirchengeschichte* 19 (1898): 107–54.

Dobschütz, Ernst von. "A Hitherto Unpublished Prologue to the Acts of the Apostles (Probably by Theodore of Mopsuestia)." *American Journal of Theology* 2 (1898): 353–87.

Dobschütz, Ernst von. "The Notices Prefixed to Codex 773 of the Gospels." *Harvard Theological Review* 18 (1925): 280–84.

★Dobschütz, Ernst von. Review of Wilhelm Bousset, *Textkritische Studien zum Neuen Testament*. *Literarisches Centralblatt für Deutschland* 45 (1894): 913.

Ehrhard, Albert. "Der Codex H ad epistulas Pauli und 'Euthalios diaconos.'" *Zentralblatt für Bibliothekswesen* 8 (1891): 385–411.

★Ehrman, Bart D., and Bruce Manning Metzger. *The Text of the New Testament. Its Transmission, Corruption, and Restoration*. 4th ed. New York: Oxford University Press, 2005.

★Finegan, Jack. "The Original Form of the Pauline Collection." *Harvard Theological Review* 49 (1956): 85–103.

★Fuhrer, Therese. "Euthalius." Pages 222–23 in *Dictionary of Early Christian Literature*. Edited by Siegmar Döpp and Wilhelm Geerlings. New York: Crossroad, 2000.

★Genette, Gérard. *Paratexts: Thresholds of Interpretation*. Translated by Jane E. Lewin. Literature, Culture, Theory 20. Cambridge: Cambridge University Press, 1997.

Graux, Charles. "Nouvelles recherches sur la stichométrie." *Revue de Philologie de Littératur et d'Histoire Anciennes* New Series 2 (1878): 97–143.

Gregory, Caspar René. *Prolegomena*. Vol. 3 of *Novum Testamentum Graece*. Edited by Constantin von Tischendorf. Editio octava critica maior. Leipzig: J. C. Hinrichs, 1894.

Gregory, Caspar René. *Textkritik des Neuen Testamentes*. 3 vols. Leipzig: J. C. Hinrichs, 1900–1909.

★Harnack, Adolf von. Review of *Excerpte aus dem Muratorischen Fragment (saec. XI. et XII.)*. *Theologische Literaturzeitung* 5 (1898): 131–34.

★Harris, James Rendel. "Credner and the Codex Bezae." *The Classical Review* 7 (1893): 237–43.

Harris, James Rendel. "Euthalius and Eusebius." Pages 60–83 in *Hermas in Arcadia and Other Essays*. Cambridge: Cambridge University Press, 1896.

★Harris, James Rendel. Review of F. H. A. Scrivener, *A Plain Introduction to the Criticism of the New Testament*. *American Journal of Philology* 5 (1884): 96–99.

★Harris, James Rendel. Review of *Novum Testamentum Graece ad antiquissimos testes*. Edited by C. R. Gregory and Ezrae Abbot. *American Journal of Philology* 6 (1885): 105–7.

★Harris, James Rendel. "Stichometry." *The American Journal of Philology* 4 (1883): 133–57, 309–31.

Harris, James Rendel. *Stichometry*. London: C. J. Clay & Sons, 1893.

Harris, James Rendel. "Stichometry." Pages 91–94 in vol. 11 of *The New Schaff-Herzog Encyclopedia of Religious Knowledge*. Samuel Macauley Jackson, Editor-in-Chief. 13 vols. Grand Rapids, Mich.: Baker, 1949–50.

★Hatch, William H. P. "The Position of Hebrews in the Canon of the New Testament." *Harvard Theological Review* 29 (1936): 133–51.

★Hellholm, David, and Vemund Blomkvist. "*Parainesis* as an Ancient Genre-designation: The Case of the 'Euthalian Apparatus' and the 'Affiliated Argumenta,'" Pages 467–519 (Bibliography, 535–78) in *Early Christian Paraenesis in Context*. Edited by Troels Engberg-Pedersen and James M. Starr. Beihefte zur Zeitschrift für die neutestamentliche Wissenshaft und die Kunde der älteren Kirche 125. Berlin; New York: Walter de Gruyter, 2004.

Hemmerdinger, Bertrand. "L'Auteur de l'édition 'Euthalienne.'" Pages 227–31 in *Acten des XI. Internationalen Byzantinistenkongresses, München 1958*. Edited by Franz Dölger and Hans-Georg Beck. Munich: C. H. Beck, 1960.

Hemmerdinger, Bertrand. "Euthaliana." *Journal of Theological Studies* New Series 11 (1960): 349–55.

★Hills, Edward F. "A New approach to the Old Egyptian Text." *Journal of Biblical Literature* 69 (1950): 345–62.

★Huffman, Norman. Review of Kenneth Willis Clark, *Eight American Praxapostoloi*. *Journal of Biblical Literature* 60 (1941): 342–43.

Hug, John Leonhard. *An Introduction to the Writings of the New Testament*. Translated by Daniel Guildford Wait. 2 vols. London: Printed for C. & J. Rivington by R. Gilbert, 1827.

Islinger, Michael. *Die Verdienste des Euthalius um den neutestamentlichen Bibeltext*. Stadtamhof: Joseph Mayr, 1867.

Jacquier, Eugène. *Le Nouveau Testament dans l'Eglise Chrétienne*. 2 vols. Paris: Victor Lecoffre, 1911–13.

Jülicher, Adolf. *Einleitung in das Neue Testament*. Revised with Erich Fascher. 7th ed. Tübingen: Mohr (Siebeck), 1931.

Jülicher, Adolf. *An Introduction to the New Testament*. Translated by Janet Penrose Ward, with a prefatory note by Mrs. Humphrey Ward. London: Smith, Elder, 1904.

Kauffmann, Friedrich. "Beiträge zur Quellenkritik der gotischen Bibelübersetzung. 7. Der Codex Carolinus." *Zeitschrift für deutsche Philologie* 43 (1911): 401–28.

Kluge, Theodor. "Die georgischen Übersetzungen des 'Neuen Testamentes.'" *Zeitschrift für die neutestamentliche Wissenschaft* 12 (1911): 344–50.

★Kluge, Theodor. "Über zwei altgeorgische neutestamentliche Handschriften," *Novum Testamentum* 1 (1956): 304–21.

Kunze, August Otto. *Praecipua patrum ecclesiast. testimonia quae ad mortem Pauli Apostoli spectant*. Göttingen: Vandenhoeck & Ruprecht, 1848.

★Lake, Kirsopp, and Silva Lake. "The Acts of the Apostles." *Journal of Biblical Literature* 53 (1934): 34–45.

★Lake, Kirsopp. Review of H. J. M. Milne and T. C. Skeat, *Scribes and Correctors of the Codex Siniaticus*. *Classical Philology* 37 (1942): 91–96.

⋆Lake, Kirsopp. "The Sinaitic and Vatican Manuscripts and the Copies Sent by Eusebius to Constantine." *Harvard Theological Review* 11 (1918): 32–35.

Lake, Kirsopp. *The Text of the New Testament*. Revised by Silva New. Oxford Church Text Books. 6th ed. London: Rivingtons, 1928.

⋆Lang, Friedrich Gustav. "Schreiben nach Mass: Zur Stichometrie in der antiken Literatur." *Novum Testamentum* 41 (1999): 40–57.

Langlois, Victor. *Collection des historiens anciens et modernes de l'Arménie*. 2 vols. Paris: Firmin Didot, 1867–69.

Lardner, Nathaniel. *The Credibility of the Gospel History*. 2 pts. in 13 vols. London: Printed for J. Chandler, 1727–55.

Lietzmann, Hans. *Einführung in die Textgeschichte der Paulusbriefe: An die Römer erklärt*. Handbuch zum Neuen Testament 8. 3d ed. Tübingen: Mohr (Siebeck), 1928.

Lipsius, Richard Adelbert. *Die apokryphen Apostelgeschichten und Apostellegenden: Ein Beitrag zur altchristlichen Literaturgeschichte*. 2 vols. Braunschweig: C. A. Schwetschke & Sohn (Wiegandt & Appelhans), 1883–87.

Macler, Frédéric. *Le Texte arménien de l'Evangile d'après Matthieu et Marc*. Annales du Musée Guimet. Bibliothèque d'Etudes 28. Paris: Imprimerie Nationale, 1919.

⋆Manson, T. W. Review of Günther Zuntz, *The Ancestry of the Harklean New Testament*. *The Classical Review* 60 (1946): 129–130.

⋆Manson, T. W., Review of James A. Kleist, *The Gospel of Saint Mark Presented in Greek Thought-Units and Sense-Lines with a Commentary*. *The Classical Review* 50 (1936): 149.

Marchand, James Woodrow. "The Gothic Evidence for 'Euthalian Matter.'" *Harvard Theological Review* 49 (1956): 159–67.

Marold, Karl. *Stichometrie und Leseabschnitte in den gotischen Episteltexten*. Königsberg: Hartung, 1890.

Martin, Jean Pierre Paulin. *Introduction à la Critique textuelle du Nouveau Testament. Partie théorique*. Paris: Au Secrétariat de l'Institut Catholique, [n.d.].

⋆Metzger, Bruce Manning. "History of Editing the Greek New Testament." *Proceedings of the American Philosophical Society* 131 (1987): 148–58.

⋆Metzger, Bruce Manning. *Manuscripts of the Greek Bible: An Introduction to Greek Palaeography*. New York: Oxford University Press, 1981.

⋆Metzger, Bruce Manning. Review of Hermann Josef Frede, *Altlateinische Paulus-Handschriften*. *Journal of Biblical Literature* 84 (1965): 335–36.

Metzger, Bruce Manning. *The Text of the New Testament: Its Transmission, Corruption, and Restoration*. 2d ed. New York: Oxford University Press, 1968.

Murphy, Harold S. "On the Text of Codices H and 93." *Journal of Biblical Literature* 78 (1959): 228–37.

Murphy, Harold S. "The Text of Romans and 1 Corinthians in Minuscule 93 and the Text of Pamphilus." *Harvard Theological Review* 52 (1959): 119–31.

⋆Nicklin, T. "Epimenides' *Minos*." *The Classical Review* 30 (1916): 33–37.

Oliver, Harold H. "'Helps for Readers' in Greek New Testament Manuscripts." ThM thesis, Princeton Theological Seminary, 1955.

Paley, William. *Horae Paulinae: Or, The Truth of the Scripture History of St. Paul Evinced*. New York: Robert Carter, 1849.

Petermann, Julius Heinrich. "Armenien." Pages 63–92 in vol. 2 of *Real-Ency-klopädie für protestantische Theologie und Kirche*. 2d ed. 24 vols. Leipzig: J. C. Hinrichs, 1894–1913.

Pirot, Louis. *L'Oeuvre exégétique de Théodore de Mopsueste 350–428 après J.-C.* Scripta Pontificii Instituti Biblici. Rome: Sumptibus Pontificii Instituti Biblici, 1913.

★Popkes, Wiard, "Paraenesis in the New Testament: An Exercise in Concep-tuality." Pages 13–46 in *Early Christian Paraenesis in Context*. Edited by Troels Engberg-Pedersen and James M. Starr. Beihefte zur Zeitschrift für die neutestamentliche Wissenshaft und die Kunde der älteren Kirche 125. Berlin; New York: Walter de Gruyter, 2004.

★Raible, Wolfgang. "Arten des Kommentierens – Arten der Sinnbildung – Arten des Verstehens: Spielarten der generischen Intertextualität." Pages 51–73 in *Text und Kommentar*. Edited by Jan Assmann and Burkhard Gla-digow. Beiträge zur Archäologie der literarisches Kommunikation 4. Mu-nich: W. Fink, 1995.

Rietschel, Georg. *Lehrbuch der Liturgik*. Revised by Paul Graff. 2d ed. 2 vols. in 1. Göttingen: Vandenhoeck & Ruprecht, 1951–52.

Riggenbach, Eduard. "Die Kapitelverzeichnisse zum Römer- und zum He-bräerbrief im Codex Fuldensis der Vulgata." *Neue Jahrbücher für deutsche Theologie* 3 (1894): 350–63.

Robinson, Joseph Armitage. "The Armenian Version." Pages 97–106 in Ed-ward Cuthbert Butler, *The Lausiac History of Palladius: a Critical Discussion Together with Notes on Early Egyptian Monachism*. Texts and Studies 6.1. Cambridge: Cambridge University Press, 1898.

Robinson, Joseph Armitage. *Euthaliana*. Texts and Studies 3.3. Cambridge: Cambridge University Press, 1895.

Robinson, Joseph Armitage. "Recent Work on Euthalius." *Journal of Theological Studies* 6 (1904–5): 87–90.

Ropes, James Hardy. *The Text of Acts*. Vol. 3 of *The Beginnings of Christianity*. Pt. 1. *The Acts of the Apostles*. Edited by Frederick John Foakes-Jackson and Kirsopp Lake. 5 vols. London: Macmillan, 1920–33.

Ruge, []. "Tarsos." Columns 2413–39 in vol. 4.2 of *Paulys Real-Encyclopädie der classischen Altertumswissenschaft*. 24 vols. Stuttgart: J. B. Metzler, 1894–1963.

★Rusten, Jeffrey. "Dicaearchus and the *Tales from Euripides*." *Greek Roman and Byzantine Studies* 23 (1982): 357–67.

Schmid, Otto. *Über verschiedene Eintheilungen der Heiligen Schrift: Inbesondere über die Capitel-Eintheilung Stephan Langtons im XIII. Jahrhunderte*. Graz: Leusch-ner & Lubensky, 1892.

Schütz, Roland. "Die Bedeutung der Kolometrie für das Neue Testament." *Zeitschrift für die neutestamentliche Wissenschaft* 21 (1922): 161–84.

Schütz, Roland. *Der parallele Bau des Satzglieder im Neuen Testament und seine Verwertung für die Textkritik und Exegese*. Forschungen zur Religion und Lit-eratur des Alten und Neuen Testaments, New Series 11. Göttingen: Van-denhoeck & Ruprecht, 1920.

Schwartz, E. "Unzeitgemässe Beobachtungen zu den Clementinen." *Zeitschrift für die neutestamentliche Wissenschaft* 31 (1932):151–99.

Scrivener, Frederick Henry Ambrose. *A Plain Introduction to the Criticism of the New Testament for the Use of Biblical Students.* 3d ed., thoroughly revised, enlarged, and brought down to the present date. Cambridge: Deighton Bell, 1883.

★Sievers, Joseph. "The Ancient Lists of Contents of Josephus' *Antiquities.*" Pages 271–92 in *Studies in Josephus and the Varieties of Ancient Judaism.* Edited by Shaye J. D. Cohen and Joseph J. Schwartz. Louis H. Feldman Jubilee Volume. Ancient Judaism and Early Christianity 67. Leiden; Boston: Brill, 2007.

Skehan, Patrick W. "The Period of the Biblical Texts from Khirbet Qumrân." *Catholic Biblical Quarterly* 19 (1957): 435–40.

Soden, Hermann von. *Die Schriften des Neuen Testaments in ihrer ältesten erreichbaren Textgestalt hergestellt auf Grund ihrer Textgeschichte.* 2 vols. in 4. Berlin: Alexander Duncker, 1902–13. Imprint varies.

Spitta, Friedrich. *Zur Geschichte und Litteratur des Urchristentums.* 3 vols. in 2. Göttingen: Vandenhoeck & Ruprecht, 1893–1907.

★Starr, James M., and Troels Engberg-Pedersen. "Introduction." Pages 8–9 [summarizing the essay of Hellholm and Blomkvist, *q.v.*] in *Early Christian Paraenesis in Context.* Edited by Troels Engberg-Pedersen and James M. Starr. Beihefte zur Zeitschrift für die neutestamentliche Wissenshaft und die Kunde der älteren Kirche 125. Berlin; New York: Walter de Gruyter, 2004.

★Tak, Johannes G. van der. *Euthalius the Deacon: Prologues and Abstracts in Greek and Church Slavic Translation.* Kirilo-Metodievski Studii 15. Sofia: Kirilo-Metodievski Nauchen Centar, 2003.

Tregelles, Samuel Prideaux. *An Introduction to the Textual Criticism of the New Testament.* Vol. 4 of *An Introduction to the Critical Study and Knowledge of the Holy Scriptures.* Edited by Thomas Hartwell Horne, Samuel Davidson, and Samuel Prideaux Tregelles. 10th ed., revised, corrected, and brought down to the present time. 4 vols. London: Longman, Brown, Green, Longmans & Roberts, 1856.

Turner, Cuthbert Hamilton. "Greek Patristic Commentaries on the Pauline Epistles." Pages 484–531 in vol. 5 (Supplement) of *A Dictionary of the Bible.* Edited by James Hastings. 5 vols. Edinburgh: Clark, 1898.

Vardanian, Aristaces. "Euthaliana." *Handes Amsorya: Monatschrift für armenische Philologie.* 38 (1924): 385–408, 481–98; 39 (1925): 1–26, 97–118, 203–26, 329–48, 423–34 513–30; 40 (1926): 1–15, 97–120, 193–208, 289–304, 417–36, 513–23; 41 (1927): 1–11, 97–107, 225–35, 353–66, 481–92, 545–58. This series of articles was later published in a single volume: *Euthalius Werke; Untersuchungen und Texte.* Edited by Aristaces Vardanian. Kritische Ausgabe der altarmenischen Schriftsteller und Übersetzungen 3.1. Vienna: Mechitharisten-Buchdruckerei, 1930.

Vööbus, Arthur. *Early Versions of the New Testament: Manuscript Studies.* Papers of the Estonian Theological Society in Exile 6. Stockholm: [Estonian Theological Society in Exile], 1954.

Wachsmuth, C. "Stichometrisches und Bibliothekarisches." *Rheinisches Museum für Philologie* New Series 34 (1879): 38–51.

Westcott, Brooke Foss. *A General Survey of the History of the Canon of the New Testament during the First Four Centuries.* Cambridge: Macmillan, 1855.

Zacagni, Lorenzo Alessandro. *Collectanea monumentorum veterum ecclesiae Graece.* Vol. 1. Rome: Typis Sacrae Congreg. de propag. fide, 1698.

Zahn, Theodor von. "Euthaliana." *Theologisches Literaturblatt* 16 (1895): 593–96, 601–3.

Zahn, Theodor von. "Der Exeget Ammonius und andere Ammonii." *Zeitschrift für Kirchengeschichte* 38 (1920): 1–22, 311–36.

Zahn, Theodor von. *Geschichte des Neutestamentlichen Kanons.* 4 pts. in 2 vols. Erlangen; Leipzig: A. Deichert, 1888–92. Imprint varies.

Zahn, Theodor von. "Neues und Altes über den Isagogiker Euthalius." *Neue kirchliche Zeitschrift* 15 (1904): 305–330, 375–90.

Zuntz, Günther. *The Ancestry of the Harklean New Testament.* The British Academy. Supplemental Papers 7. London. Published for the British Academy by Humphrey Milford, Oxford University Press, 1945.

Zuntz, Günther. "Etudes Harkléennes." *Revue Biblique* 57 (1950): 550–82.

Zuntz, Günther. "Euthalius = Euzoius?" *Vigiliae Christianae* 7 (1953): 16–22.

Zuntz, Günther. "Die Subscriptionen der Syra Harclensis." *Zeitschrift der deutschen Morgenländischen Gesellschaft* New Series 26 (1951): 174–96.

★Zuntz, Günther, "Wann wurde das Evangelium Marci geschrieben." Pages 44–71 (and plates) in *Markus-Philologie: Historische, literargeschichtliche und stilistische Untersuchungen zum zweiten Evangelium.* Edited by Hubert Cancik. Wissenschaftliche Untersuchungen zum Neuen Testament 33. Tübingen: Mohr (Siebeck), 1984.

★Zwaan, Johannes de. "Harklean Gleanings from Mingana's Catalogue." *Novum Testamentum* 2 (1958): 174–84.

Selected Texts and Reference Works

We include here texts of the Bible as well as patristic and medieval materials. Rather than following rigid schemes of classification, the main entry of many of these texts is by the editor. We have also included here texts in which our primary interest is actually centered on the introductory notes, for example, of the editor.

★Aland, Barbara, and Juckel, Andreas. *Das Neue Testament in syrischer Überlieferung.*
    1. Die grossen katholischen Briefe. Arbeiten zur neutestamentlichen Textforschung, 7. See especially "Das besondere Problem der Harklensis und ihrer Geschichte," pages 7–13, and "Die Handschriften der Harklensis," pages 32–37.
    2. Die paulinischen Briefe. Part 1. Arbeiten zur neutestamentlichen Textforschung 14; Part 2. Arbeiten zur neutestamentlichen Textforschung 23;

Part 3. Arbeiten zur neutestamentlichen Textforschung 32. Berlin; New York: Walter de Gruyter, 1986–1991.

Aland, Kurt. *Gesamtübersicht*. Vol. 1 of *Kurzgefasste Liste der griechischen Handscriften des Neuen Testament*. Arbeiten zur neutestamentlichen Textforschung 1. 1 vol. Berlin: Walter de Gruyter, 1963.

Aland, Kurt, et al., eds. *The Greek New Testament*. New York: American Bible Society, 1966. Imprint varies.

Altaner, Berthold. *Patrology*. Translated from the 5th German edition by Hilda C. Graef. New York: Herder & Herder, 1960.

Bardenhewer, Otto. *Geschichte der altkirchlichen Literatur*. 2d. rev. edition. 5 vols. Freiburg im Breisgau: Herder, 1913–32.

Brooke, Alan England, and Norman McLean, eds. *The Octateuch*. Vol. 1 of *The Old Testament in Greek According to the Text of Codex Vaticanus*. 2 vols. Cambridge: Cambridge University Press, 1917–40.

Bruyne, Donatien de. *Préfaces de la Bible latine*. Namur: Auguste Godenne, 1920.

Coislin, Henry Charles du Cambout, duc de. *Bibliotheca Coisliniana, olim Segueriana*. Paris: L. Guerin & C. Robustel, 1715.

Darlow, Thomas Herbert, and Horace Franklin Moule, comps. *Historical Catalogue of the Printed Editions of Holy Scipture in the Library of the British and Foreign Bible Society*. 2 vols. in 4. London: Bible House, 1903–11.

A Dictionary of Christian Biography, Literature, Sects, and Doctrines. Edited by William Smith . . . and Henry Wace. 4 vols. Boston: Little, Brown, 1877–87.

Dictionnaire de la Bible. Supplément. Edited by Louis Pirot et al. 7 vols. (continuing). Paris: Letouze & Ané, 1928-.

Didascalia et Constitutiones Apostolorum. Edited by Franz Xaver von Funk. 2 vols. in 1. Paderborn: F. Schoeningh, 1905.

Eusebius. *The Ecclesiastical History*. Books 1–5. [1926]. Translated by Kirsopp Lake. Books 6–10. [1932]. Translated by J. E. L. Oulton. LCL. London: William Heinemann,.

Field, Frederick, ed. *Prolegomena. Genesis-Esther*. Vol 1 of *Origenis Hexaplorum quae supersunt: Sive, veterum interpretum graecorum in totum Vetus Testamentum fragmenta*. 2 vols. Oxford: Clarendon Press, 1875.

Fabricius, Johann Albert. *Bibliotheca graeca*. Edited by Gottlieb Christoph Harles. 12 vols. Hamburg: C. E. Bohn, 1790–1809.

Gallandi, Andreas, ed. *Bibliotheca veterum patrum antiquorumque scriptorum ecclesiasticorum* . . .. 14 vols. Venice: Ex typographia Joannis Bapistae Albritii Hieron. fil., 1765–81.

Hastings, James, ed. *A Dictionary of the Bible*. 5 vols. New York: Scribner's, 1905–9.

Hatch, William Henry Paine. *The Principal Uncial Manuscripts of the New Testament*. Chicago: University of Chicago Press, 1939.

The Interpreter's Dictionary of the Bible. Edited by George Arthur Buttrick et al. 4 vols. New York; Nashville: Abingdon, 1962.

Hē kainē diathēkē: Novum Testamentum graecum. Edited by Johann Jakob Wettstein. 2 vols. Amsterdam: Ex officina Dommeriana, 1751–2.

Lake, Kirsopp, ed. *Facsimiles of the Athos Fragments of Codex H of the Pauline Epistles*. Oxford: Clarendon Press, 1905.

Lexikon für Theologie und Kirche. Edited by Josef Höfer and Karl Rahner. 2d revised ed. 11 vols. Freiburg: Herder, 1957–67.

Migne, Jacques Paul, ed. *Patrologiae Graece*. Vol. 85. Paris: [The Author], 1864.

Nestle, Erwin, and Kurt Aland, eds. *Novum Testamentum Graece*. 25th ed. Stuttgart: Würtembergische Bibelanstalt, [1963].

The New Schaff-Herzog Encyclopedia of Religious Knowledge. Edited by Samuel Macauley Jackson et al. 13 vols. New York; London: Funk & Wagnalls, 1908–14.

Novum Testamentum graecum. Edited by John Mill. Rotterdam: Caspar Fritsch & Michael Böhm, 1710.

Omont, Henri Auguste. *Notice sur un très ancien manuscrit grec en onciales des épîtres de Saint Paul conservé à la Bibliothèque Nationale*. Pages 141–92 of *Notices et Extraits des Manuscrits de la Bibliothèque Nationale* 33.1. Paris: Imprimerie Nationale, 1889.

Pamphilus. "An Exposition of the Chapters of the Acts of the Apostles." Pages 166–68 in vol. 6 of *The Ante-Nicene Fathers*. 10 vols. Buffalo: Christian Literature, 1886.

Pauly, August Friedrich von. *Paulys Real-encyclopädie der classischen Altertumswissenschaft*. New edition. Edited by Georg Wissowa. 24 vols. in 27. Stuttgart: J. B. Metzler, 1894–1963.

Quasten, Johannes. *The Golden Age of Greek Patristic Literature from the Council of Nicea to the Council of Chalcedon*. Vol. 3 of *Patrology*. Utrecht: Spectrum, 1960.

Rahlfs, Alfred, ed. *Septuaginta*. Stuttgart: Würtembergische Bibelanstalt, [1935].

Theodorus. *Theodori Episcopi Mopsuesteni in epistolas B. Pauli Commentari: The Latin Version with the Greek Fragments*. With an introduction, notes, and indices by Henry Barclay Swete. 2 vols. Cambridge: The University Press, 1880–82.

Tischendorf, Constantin von, ed. *Novum Testamentum Graece*. Editio octava critica maior. 2 vols. Leipzig: J. C. Hinrichs, 1872.

Treu, Kurt. *Die griechischen Handschriften des Neuen Testaments in der UdSSR: Eine systematische Auswertung der Texthandschriften in Leningrad, Moskau, Kiev, Odessa, Tbilisi, und Erevan*. Texte und Untersuchungen zur Geschichte der altchristlichen Literatur 5th Series 36. Berlin: Akademie, 1966.

Indices

There are three selective indices: Person, Place, and Subject; Manuscript; and Scripture. The index of manuscripts includes only notable witnesses, and the index of passages from the Scripture reflects only texts attractive for further research.

Bold page references are to the major discussion or representation of the subject.

Person, Place, and Subject

Manuscript Index

Scripture Index